Marxism
and the
Great French Revolution

**Paul McGarr, Alex Callinicos
and John Rees**

INTERNATIONAL
SOCIALISM ★

Quarterly Journal of the Socialist Workers Party

Marxism and the Great French Revolution
by Paul McGarr, Alex Callinicos and John Rees
Published June 1989
International Socialism, PO Box 82, London E3.
Copyright © International Socialism
Issue 43 of International Socialism,
quarterly journal of the Socialist Workers Party

ISBN 0 905998 67 7
ISSN 0020 8736

The cover shows Marat being carried through the street in
triumph after his acquittal by the Revolutionary Tribunal.
Designed by Ken Olende

Printed by BPCC Wheatons Ltd, Exeter, England
Typeset by East End Offset, London E3

The Socialist Workers Party is one of an international
grouping of socialist organisations:
AUSTRALIA: *International Socialists*, GPO Box 1473N,
Melbourne 3001
BELGIUM: *Socialisme International*, 9 rue Marexhe, 4400
Herstal, Liege
BRITAIN: *Socialist Workers Party*, PO Box 82, London E3
CANADA: *International Socialists*, PO Box 339, Station E,
Toronto, Ontario M6H 4E3
DENMARK: *Internationale Socialister*, Morten Borupsgade
18, kld, 8000 Arhus C
FRANCE: *Socialisme International*, BP 189, 75926 Paris
Cedex 19
GREECE: *Organosi Sosialistiki Epanastasi*, Menandrou 50,
Omonia, Athens
HOLLAND: *International Socialists*, PO Box 9720,
3506 GR Utrecht
IRELAND: *Socialist Workers Movement*, PO Box 1648,
Dublin 8
NORWAY: *Internasjonale Sosialister*, Postboks 5370,
Majorstua, 0304 Oslo 3
UNITED STATES: *International Socialist Organization*,
PO Box 16085, Chicago, IL 60622
WEST GERMANY: *Sozialistische Arbeiter Gruppe*,
Wolfgangstrasse 81, D-6000 Frankfurt 1

Marxism

and the

Great French Revolution

**Paul McGarr, Alex Callinicos
and John Rees**

Contents

Editor: John Rees. **Assistant editors**: Pete Binns, Alex Callinicos, Chris Harman, John Molyneux, Lindsey German, Pete Green, Pete Alexander, Steve Wright, Ann Rogers, Costas Lapavitsas, Colin Sparks, Mike Gonzalez and Sue Clegg.
Editorial Address: PO Box 82, London E3.
Phone 01-538 1626.

Distribution and subscriptions: Bookmarks, 265 Seven Sisters Road, Finsbury Park, London N4 2DE.
Phone 01-802 6145.
Subscription rates: Britain and overseas (surface): individual £8.50 / institutional £17.00. Air speeded supplement: North America nil / Europe and South America £1.00 / elsewhere £2.00.

Note to contributors: The deadline for articles intended for issue 45 of International Socialism is 31 July 1989. All contributions should be double-spaced with wide margins. Please submit two copies. If you write your contribution using a computer, please also supply a disk, together with details of the computer and program used.

Chronology of Events

1774	Louis XVI becomes king of France
1775	Grain riots ('The Flour War') in France
1776	American Declaration of Independence
	Adam Smith's *Wealth of Nations* published
1778	France enters American War
1783	End of American War
1786	French 'free trade' treaty with England

1787

February-May:	Assembly of Notables
August:	Exile of Paris Parlement
September:	Recall of the Parlement

1788

May:	Renewed attack on Parlements by government
June-July:	Provincial revolts by Parlements
8 August:	Estates General summoned for 1 May 1789

1789

January:	Emmanuel Sieyès' *What is the Third Estate?* published
January-May:	Preparation of *cahiers de doléances* (lists of grievances) and elections to Estates General
March onwards:	Peasant revolts
27-28 April:	Réveillon riots in Paris
5 May:	Opening of Estates General at Versailles
17 June:	Third Estate declare themselves the 'National Assembly'
20 June:	Oath of the Tennis Court
23 June:	King tries to intimidate Assembly
9 July:	National Assembly proclaims itself the Constituent Assembly
12-13 July:	Riots in Paris grow into insurrection
14 July:	FALL OF THE BASTILLE
15-31 July:	'Municipal' revolutions across France
20 July-6 August:	Rural revolts known as THE GREAT FEAR
4 August:	CONSTITUENT ASSEMBLY VOTES TO ABOLISH FEUDALISM
26 August:	DECLARATION OF THE RIGHTS OF MAN AND CITIZEN
5-6 October:	Parisian women march on Versailles followed by National Guards. King and court taken back to Paris
2 November:	Church lands nationalised

22 December:	Local government reform

1790

January:	Renewed peasant risings
	Jacobin Club formed
17 April:	Assignats issued
27 April:	Cordeliers Club formed
21 May:	Paris municipal government reorganised into Sections
12 July:	Civil Constitution of the Clergy voted by Assembly
14 July:	Festival of the Federation in Paris
18 August:	Counter-revolutionary assembly at Jalès
November:	Edmund Burke's *Reflections on the Revolution in France* published

1791

March:	Pope condemns the Civil Constitution of the clergy
May-June:	Le Chapelier laws outlawing unions and strikes
20-21 June:	Flight of royal family halted at Varennes
13-16 July:	Assembly reinstates king
16 July:	Feuillants separate from Jacobin Club under banner 'The revolution is over'
17 July:	Massacre of the Champ de Mars: troops led by Lafayette shoot down republicans. Repression of democratic movement
27 August:	Assembly votes to raise property qualification for franchise
September:	King accepts new constitution. Constituent Assembly dissolves
1 October:	OPENING OF THE LEGISLATIVE ASSEMBLY
December-January:	Debates at Jacobin Club between Brissot and Robespierre over war

1792

23 January-March:	Food riots begin in Paris and other towns and peasant revolts grow again
15 March:	Pro-War Brissotin administration formed
20 April:	FRANCE DECLARES WAR ON AUSTRIA (Prussia joins war too)
April-May:	Military defeats
12 June:	Girondin administration sacked by king and Feuillants reappointed
20 June:	Demonstration against the king, crowd invade Tuileries
27-29 June:	Lafayette bids for power—but National Guards refuse to follow him

11 July:	Assembly declares 'the fatherland in danger' (decree proclaimed 21 July)
17 July:	Fédérés now in Paris demand removal of the king
25 July:	Duke of Brunswick, commander of the invading armies, threatens Paris with total destruction Paris Sections declare themselves in permanent session
3 August:	Paris Sections demand dismissal of the king
9 August:	Assembly rejects petition for republic 'Insurrectionary Commune' set up in Paris
10 August:	INSURRECTION IN PARIS OVERTHROWS THE MONARCHY National Convention summoned, dismissed Girondin ministers are reinstated (with the addition of Danton)
11 August:	Universal Male Suffrage introduced
14 August:	Lafayette flees after trying in vain to persuade his army to march against Paris
23 August:	Longwy taken by Prussians
2 September:	Elections for National Convention begin. Verdun falls to invading armies
2-6 September:	'September Massacres'— as volunteers enrol for the front, popular tribunals set up to deal with counter-revolutionaries
20 September:	French victory at Valmy Convention meets to elect its officers
21 September:	Convention votes to abolish the monarchy. Later this day is declared the beginning of Year I
25 September:	Republic declared "One and Indivisible"
October-November:	French military victories culminating in occupation of Belgium
11 December:	Trial of king opens

1793

21 January:	King executed
1 February:	Declaration of war against Britain and Holland.
24 February:	Decree ordering levy of 300,000 men for the army
25-27 February:	Food riots in Paris
7 March:	War declared on Spain
10 March:	Creation of Revolutionary Tribunal Outbreak of Vendée rebellion Riots against Girondin government in Paris
18 March:	French army defeated at Neerwinden
6 April:	Committee of Public Safety set up (includes Danton)
24 April:	Marat, tried by order of the Convention after summoning 'patriots' to Paris to defend the revolution, is acquitted

29 April:	Anti-Jacobin rising in Marseilles
4 May:	Decree allowing Départements to impose price controls on grain and flour
29 May:	Anti-Jacobin insurrection in Lyons
31 May-2 June:	PARISIAN UPRISING OVERTHROWS GIRONDIN LEADERS
7 June:	'Federalist' revolts begin
24 June:	Convention votes a new, more radical, constitution and Declaration of the Rights of Man
27 June:	Paris stock exchange closed
10 July:	Danton removed from Committee of Public Safety and Jacobin influence on it increased
12 July:	Successful royalist rebellion in Toulon
13 July:	Marat assassinated by Charlotte Corday
17 July:	All feudal and seigneurial rights and dues abolished
26 July:	Death penalty decreed against food hoarders
27 July:	Robespierre elected to Committee of Public Safety
23 August:	*Levée en Masse* decreed
25 August:	Republic recaptures Marseilles
27 August:	Royalists hand Toulon over to British
4 September:	Workers demonstrate in Paris demanding higher wages
5 September:	Paris Commune and Jacobins back march on Convention, which makes Terror 'the order of the day'
9 September:	Decree establishing Parisian Armée Révolutionnaire
11 September:	National price controls on grain
17 September:	Law on Suspects
29 September:	Maximum General: National price controls on commodities and wages
5 October:	Revolutionary Calendar adopted

YEAR II

Vendémiaire:	De-christianisation campaign opens
18 (9 October):	Lyons retaken by Republic
19 (10 October):	Government declared revolutionary until peace
25 (16 October):	Marie Antoinette executed
Brumaire	
10 (31 October):	21 Girondin leaders executed
16 (6 November):	Municipalities allowed to renounce Catholic worship
20 (10 November):	Festival of Liberty and Reason
Frimaire:	Government steps up campiagn against popular movement
	Women's societies suppressed

1 (21 November):	Robespierre attacks de-christianisation and atheism
3 (23 November):	Paris Commune closes churches
16 (6 December):	Ban on 'revolutionary taxes' on the rich
22 (12 December):	Vendéens crushed at Le Mans
29 (19 December):	Toulon recaptured
Nivôse:	
1 (21 December):	Collot D'Herbois defends the Terror, marking start of swing back to left by government
28 (17 January):	General Turreau's 'infernal columns' begin to ravage the Vendée
Pluviôse:	
13 (1 February):	Ten million francs allocated for poor relief
16 (4 February):	Slavery abolished in French colonies
Ventôse:	St Just's Ventôse decrees
14 (4 March):	Abortive revolt by Cordeliers Club and Hébertists
Germinal:	
4 (24 March):	Execution of Hébertists
7 (27 March):	Armée Révolutionnaire disbanded
16 (5 April):	Execution of Danton
Floréal:	
11 (20 April):	Austrians take Landrecies
22 (11 May):	National Welfare Register created
Prairial:	
20 (8 June):	Festival of the Supreme Being
22 (10 June):	Revolutionary Tribunal reorganised ('Great Terror' instituted)
Messidor:	
7 (25 June):	Toussaint L'Ouverture, leader of slave revolt in Saint-Domingue, comes out in favour of the French Republic
8 (26 June):	French defeat Austrians at Fleurus
20 (8 July):	French enter Brussels
Thermidor:	
4-5 (22-23 July):	Attempts to reunify government fail
9 (28 July):	FALL OF REVOLUTIONARY GOVERNMENT
10 (28 July):	Execution of Robespierre and supporters after failed insurrection by Paris Commune
Fructidor:	
7 (24 August):	Government reorganised, power of 'great' committees curtailed

Year III

Brumaire:
22 (12 November):	Closure of Jacobin Club

Frimaire:
18 (8 December):   Surviving Girondin deputies, excluded on 2 June 1793, return to Convention

Nivôse
4 (24 December):   Abolition of the Maximum

1795

Pluviôse:
1 (20 January):   French occupy Amsterdam
20 (8 February):   'Depantheonisation' of Marat
Germinal:
12 (1 April):   Popular rising in Paris fizzles out
Floréal:
15 (4 May):   Massacre of imprisoned Jacobins in Lyons
Prairial:
1-4 (20-23 May):   Last popular revolt in Paris, crushed.
17 (5 June):   Massacre of Jacobins in Marseilles
Messidor: English invasion routed

YEAR IV

Vendémiaire:
1 (23 September):   Proclamation of new constitution
9 (1 October):   Annexation of Belgium
13 (5 October):   Royalist rising in Paris crushed
Brumaire:
9 (31 October):   Election of the executive Directory
25 (16 November)   Opening of the Club du Panthéon

1796

Ventôse:
9 (28 February):   Closure of Club du Panthéon, carried out by Bonaparte
12 (2 March):   Bonaparte appointed commander of Army-in-Italy

Germinal:
10 (30 March):   Formation of Babeuf's 'Insurrectional Committee of Equals'

Floréal:
21 (10 May):   Arrest of Babeuf and supporters
Fructidor:
23 (9 September):   Jacobins shot while trying to incite mutiny

YEAR V

Vendémiaire:
25 (16 October):   Proclamation in Bologna of the Cispadane Republic

1797

Germinal:
1-12 (20-31 March): Elections to the Legislative Body result in royalist majorities
28 (17 April): Anti-French rising in Verona
Prairial:
7 (26 May): Royalist Barthélemy elected as Director
8 (27 May): Babeuf guillotined
Fructidor:
18 (4 September): Anti-royalist coup

YEAR VI

Vendémiaire:
26 (17 October): Bonaparte signs Peace of Campo Formio
Pluviôse:
27 (15 February): Roman Republic proclaimed
Floreal:
22 (11 May): Invalidation of newly elected Jacobin deputies
30 (19 May): French fleet leaves for Egypt
Fructidor:
5 (22 August): Formation of Second Coalition against France

YEAR VII

French forced onto defensive in war, losing ground in Italy and Germany, Bonaparte cut off in Egypt
Vendémiaire:
21 (12 October): Start of the 'War of the Peasants' against the French in Belgium
30 (21 October): Anti-French rising in Cairo

1799

Pluviôse:
7 (26 January): Neapolitan Republic proclaimed
Prairial: Councils demand explanation of situation from Directory. Final revival of Jacobinism
Messidor:
18 (6 July): Jacobin Club refounded
Thermidor: Royalist uprisings in south-west

YEAR VIII

Vendémiaire: Bonaparte arrives in France
Brumaire:
19 (10 November): Bonaparte's coup. Bonaparte, Sieyès and Roger-Ducos designated consuls

1800   New Constitution with Bonaparte as First
                            Consul
                            Foundation of Bank of France
1800-1803   Bonaparte's major reforms in France
1801   Concordat signed with Pope
1803-8   Period of Bonaparte's major 'revolutionary'
                            reforms in Europe
1804   Bonaparte crowned Emperor of the French
1805-7   Bonaparte's sweeping military victories in central
                            Europe
1806-12   French economic blockade of England—the
                            Continental System
1812   Bonaparte's disastrous Russian campaign
1814   Bonaparte's first abdication and exile to Elba
1815   'The Hundred Days' ending in Bonaparte's defeat
                            at Waterloo and exile to St Helena
                            Congress of Vienna

The Great French Revolution

PAUL McGARR

Introduction

'From this place and from this day forth commences a new era in the world's history, and you can all say that you were present at its birth' [1]

With these words the poet Goethe consoled his dejected Prussian companions after their defeat by the French revolutionary army at Valmy on 20 September 1792. Massenbach, a Prussian officer, agreed: 'We have lost more than a battle. The 20 September has changed the course of history. It is the most important day of the century' [2]

The invading Prussian army was disciplined and respected throughout Europe and its commander, the Duke of Brunswick, the most renowned general of the day. But at Valmy they faced a force of a new type: a mass popular army where enthusiastic volunteers fought alongside seasoned veterans. [3] All were fighting not for a king but for *La Patrie*—their 'homeland'—an idea with a power new in history. The Prussians complained: 'Their unbelievable enthusiasm and above all their exasperation against us are beyond all measure and exceed the means at their disposal', and were shocked when civilians hid in woods and set up ambushes—quite outside the normal rules of 18th century warfare. [4]

The spirit of the French was fired by the words of the revolutionary leader Georges Danton, speaking in Paris a few weeks earlier, 'We need audacity, more audacity, always audacity and France will be saved.' [5] A month earlier the Parisian masses had risen, for the third time in three years, and finally overthrown the monarchy. On the very day of victory at Valmy, a National Convention elected on new democratic principles met in Paris. The next day it declared a republic.

The revolution then unfolding in France represented a sharp break with the past—and the participants knew it. The revolutionaries adopted a new calendar. Years were no longer counted from Christ's birth. They declared September 1792 the beginning of Year 1—the start of a new era in world history (see appendix on revolutionary calendar). Less symbolically, the links with the old order were cut when the king, Louis XVI, was sent to the guillotine in January 1793.

The impact of the French Revolution was immense. Just as the Russian Revolution of 1917 is the pivotal event of the 20th century the French Revolution shook the world a century earlier. And 200 years later it still has special importance for Marxists. Firstly, it was the event, above all others, which shaped the political world in which Marxism developed. A glance at the works of Marx, Engels, Lenin or Trotsky will illustrate the point. Secondly, it was the first real *mass* revolution in modern history, and the 'forcible entrance of the masses into the realm of rulership over their own destiny'[6] not only reshaped French society but spread internationally. Finally, the French Revolution was the decisive political conflict in the birth of the modern bourgeois world. To understand it can help us look forward to and work the better for the international revolution which will send that society to its grave.

The aim of this article is to present in an accessible form the main events and developments of the revolution. This means a number of important arguments will be left to one side—those interested in pursuing them can find signposts in the footnotes.

Absolutism

On 14 July 1789 a mass insurrection swept Paris. Between 180,000 and 300,000 people were under arms.[7] At the height of the insurrection the Bastille, the ancient royal fortress and prison, was stormed. Its fall marked the victory of the uprising—but only the beginning of the revolution. Why was there a revolution?

France in 1789 was an absolute monarchy. All power was, in theory, centralised in the person of the king, Louis XVI. From his palace at Versailles he presided over a myriad of officials. Although the king supposedly ruled by divine right, in practice there were a host of checks and balances on his power. Nevertheless it was still immense. He could summon a *lit de justice*, where he lay on a bed of cushions and read his orders out which then had the force of law. And he could issue *lettres de cachet*, warrants by which he could imprison anyone indefinitely without charge.[8] This 'absolutist' state, which had arisen across much of Europe but reached its peak in France, had grown out of a profound crisis in feudal society.

Feudalism in Europe was essentially based on local production and, therefore, a decentralised political structure. Local lords battened on a peasantry who were usually (though not always) serfs—legally tied to the land and compelled by the use, or threat, of force to hand over part of their labour or produce to the lord. The Catholic Church was the ideological cement in this society and a feudal landowner in its own right. No centralised state was possible. Kings had to balance the rival claims of local rulers who had a monopoly of armed force in their domains. Land was the central form of wealth, and warfare as a means of acquiring land, was endemic.

Though not as dynamic as capitalism, feudalism was not a totally stagnant society. Trade, commerce and new techniques *were* slowly developed.[9] This had two important consequences. Firstly it increasingly knitted together, economically and socially, larger regions. Alongside this the decentralised political structure of feudalism meant the towns which developed as centres of trade and commerce were able to become *relatively* independent of local feudal lords—new classes, political structures and ideas began slowly to develop in them.

Such changes clashed with a political structure which had grown on the basis of fragmented, feudal, local production. This coupled with revolts from below to produce a series of profound crises and social upheavals across Europe. The Black Death, Hundred Years War, Reformation and Counter-Reformation, Thirty Years War and a wave of massive peasant revolts (in England in the late 14th century, Germany in the early 16th century and so on) were expressions of this.

Feudal rule was restabilised after these upheavals, but on a new basis with the growth of centralised absolute monarchies. In France this process began in the aftermath of the violent civil wars of the late 16th century, known as the Wars of Religion, in which the whole social order had threatened to disintegrate. These conflicts naturally took the ideological form of religious differences—splits within the then dominant ideology. To restabilise society the king, Henry IV, began to construct a centralised state and curb the independent power of the local nobles. The process was continued under Cardinals Richelieu and Mazarin in the first half of the 17th century before its completion by Louis XIV and his chief minister, Colbert. The civil wars called the Frondes (1648-53) were the last fling of the local feudal lords against this centralisation.

Economic and social life had begun to outgrow the local horizons of feudalism and to lay the foundations for a 'national' economy. Absolutism was a partial recognition of this. The monarchy's curbing of much of the independent power of local feudal rulers was the price paid for maintaining their political domination in society. But absolutism was much more than a simple reconstitution of feudal rule. It also incorporated elements of the growing bourgeoisie, as the new class based on trade and commerce in the towns was called in France.[10]

The French state under Loius XIV pursued vigorous 'protectionist' economic policies (called mercantilism) designed to serve the interests of the state in its conflicts with its rivals. But they were also designed to help French trade, commerce and manufacture—and thus the bourgeoisie. Significant elements of the bourgeoisie used their wealth and influence to obtain lucrative positions within the growing bureaucracy of the absolutist state. These positions often conferred noble status on the holder, and therefore increased their political influence.

In short, the absolutist state was an adaptation to, and partial incorporation of, the bourgeoisie but within a reshaped and restabilised feudal political structure. It is worth looking at this structure in more detail.

The Church

On the eve of the revolution French society was legally divided into three 'orders' or 'estates'. The first order was the (Catholic) clergy. They were exempt from paying the most important direct taxes—instead meeting once a year in an assembly to vote a 'voluntary gift' to the state. The ideological role of the Church was vital, especially in the countryside where most people had few other sources of ideas and information than the pulpit. The Church had a monopoly on education and it was also a central part of the state apparatus through its functions of registering births, deaths and marriages.

But the clergy were not a homogeneous block. The upper echelons, bishops and so on, were part and parcel of the nobility. All bishops were nobles in 1789. They were enormously wealthy, owned vast amounts of land and collected various dues and taxes from the peasants. At the bottom were parish priests, many little better off than the peasants they served. For instance the Bishop of Strasbourg had an income of 400,000 livres, and a typical parish priest only 1,000. The resentment of the lower clergy against the bishops is well summed up by one parish priest's comment: 'While the Bishop plays the great nobleman and spends scandalous sums on hounds, horses, furniture, servants, food and carriages, the parish priest has not the wherewithal to buy himself a new cassock. The burden of collecting the tithe falls on him, but the Prelates, not he, pocket it. The Bishops treat their priests, not as honest footmen but as stable-boys.'[1]

The Church was riven with ideological conflict rooted in these social divisions. One split was between the Gallicans—loyal to the emerging national state— and the Ultramontanes—loyal to Rome and the Pope, who was still an important though dwindling temporal power. Resentment among some lower clergy and the bourgeoisie at the ostentatious wealth and privileges of the top of the Church plus opposition to royal power from a section of the nobility around the legal corporations called Parlements joined behind the austere Jansenist heresy. In essence this was an expression of emerging French nationalism and had much in common with Calvinism, which had played such an important ideological role in the earlier bourgeois revolutions in England and the United Provinces. When the Jansenists secured the expulsion of the Jesuits from

France in 1764 it was a major blow against one of the pillars of the Catholic Church and the old order.

Another important split in the Church, the Richerist heresy, was based on the division between poor parish priest and rich bishop. This had a democratic edge in its insistence on the right of ordinary priests to play an equal role in Church decision making—a political point not lost on the flocks of Richerist priests! Such conflicts within the Church began to erode the ideology of the old order.

The Enlightenment

The attack was deepened and a new ideology fashioned in its place from another quarter—the Enlightenment. It is worth a break from the survey of the social structure to consider it. There were many different aspects within this current of ideas which grew in the 18th century, but the general thrust was to argue for the reconstruction of society on more 'rational' lines. The roots of the Enlightenment lay in the 16th and 17th century revolution in understanding the world—the scientific ideas that culminated in Newton's theories and the breakdown of the old religious view of the world which had dominated feudal society. Of course this shift in ideas had material roots. The economic and social changes already mentioned created the conditions in which this transformation of ideas could take place. The new ideology and new social reality found expression in philosophy in the ideas of people like Locke. Growing knowledge of the world on the back of trade and commerce further undermined the idea that the world and society were uniquely ordered according to a divine plan.

Centred in France in the 18th century a group of *philosophes* (as they called themselves) began applying what they saw as rational, scientific principles to social and political questions.[12] The key figures were Voltaire, Diderot and D'Alembert, who were the force behind the *Encyclopedia*, Montesquieu, Beccaria and Rousseau. Their attack on the old ideas was summed up by Diderot in a letter to Voltaire—'Our motto is: No quarter for the superstitious, for the fanatical, for the ignorant, for the foolish, for the wicked and for the Tyrants.'[13] Much of their work was negative—an attack on what existed, above all religion as represented by the Catholic Church. Despite this they all (apart from a few deterministic atheists like Helvétius and D'Holbach) thought that some form of religion, usually one based on nature, was necessary for the mass of people, or else social order would be threatened.

There were many variations in the positive ideas put forward. Voltaire advocated an enlightened monarchy as the force to construct a more rational society. Montesquieu—whose book *Spirit of the Laws*, published in 1748, was probably the most influential of all— looked to a balance of powers between the king and the aristocracy as the best way to ensure a reformed rational society. What they all had in common was a belief in natural, rational law before which all were equal. Previously, natural legal inequality of people and arbitrary justice were the hallmark of society. The clearest example of this shift is Beccaria whose approach to law outlined in his *On Crime and Punishment* is the foundation of modern bourgeois law, so much so that it is now common to refer to pre-Beccarian justice, meaning that which existed before modern bourgeois society.

The *philosophes* were intermittently persecuted by the authorities—occasionally imprisoned, their books banned and burnt. But over the course of the 18th century they gradually battered down the ideological defences of the old order. Though many of the individual *philosophes* were clergy or nobles, their ideas as a whole represented the coming of age of the bourgeoisie. The social and political order evisaged by the *philosophes* was one which would be free—in the sense of freedom from abtitrary power, freedom of speech, freedom of trade, freedom to realise one's talents, in other words, a bourgeois freedom. Their ideas filtered down through the new academies, reading societies and public libraries that sprang up in most towns across France and in the salons of fashionable Parisian society. When the crisis which resulted in revolution came, the ideology of the old order had already been fatally undermined by the *philosophes*. The outlines of ideas that fitted a new bourgeois society were already at hand.

Rousseau

A special mention should be made of the Genevan philosopher Jean-Jacques Rousseau. His ideas, more than any others, were to be the ideological weapon of the future revolutionaries. In particular the Jacobins and Robespierre fashioned the ideas of Rousseau's *On the Social Contract* into a revolutionary ideology. The opening sentence of Rousseau's work gives an indication why: 'Man is born free, and everywhere he is in chains.'[14] Rousseau argued that the basis of the social order is a conditional contract between the rulers and the citizens. There is no divine right or any other justification for a particular form of rule. The citizens each have an equal say in formulating the General Will, which is the only legitimate basis of a state. Sovereignty rests with the people, they exercise it directly, not through representatives, and they are perfectly justified in removing any form of government of which they no longer approve. He attacks all subjugation of one person by another—slavery is 'incompatible with the nature of man'.[15]

But once the General Will is expressed each citizen must submit to it. They have entered into a contract and are bound by it as long as the General Will upholds it. Rousseau does not lay down what particular form the state should take. A monarchy is possible—but not by divine right, only on the basis of the General Will. But it is clear that a democratic republic is the most favoured. 'Were there a people of gods, it would govern itself democratically.'[16] And Rousseau ideally wants a people of gods, or virtuous citizens. This virtue is to be based on a society of independent property owning individuals where no one has too little property and no one too much: 'No citizen should be so rich as to be capable of buying another citizen, and none so poor that he is forced to sell himself.'[17] But given that people can be fooled and misled Rousseau allows for 'guides' who may in certain conditions represent the General Will: 'By itself the populace wants the good, but by itself it does not always see it.'[18]

More than one political interpretation of Rousseau's ideas is possible, but it should be clear that they were profoundly subversive of the existing order. And it takes little imagination to see how they could be fashioned into a justification of revolution, popular democracy and also revolutionary dictatorship by a minority. As we will see, this is precisely how Robespierre and the Jacobins used them, and the ideas also allowed them to forge an alliance between the bourgeois class they represented and the mass movement of smaller petty bourgeois property owners, in the towns and the countryside, which was to play a central role in the French Revolution. But this is running too far ahead.

What is important is that the ideas which would be used to motivate and justify action had been developed before the revolution and the destruction of the ideas of the old order was well under way. None of the great *philosophes* of the Enlightenment lived to see the revolution—and in battle it is by no means obvious where they would have lined up—but their ideas played an important role in preparing the ground for the revolution.

The nobility

The second order in French society after the clergy was the nobility. They too battened on the peasantry and were exempt from the most important direct taxes. They also had countless other privileges, including a monopoly on higher posts in the Church, state and army.[19] They were divided into two groups. The nobility of the sword were the descendants of the old localised feudal rulers. They ranged from the grand nobles, enormously wealthy with huge amounts of land, to local *hobereaux*, many deeply in debt to the new men of wealth springing from the bourgeoisie. Little separated some of these local nobles from better off peasants—but this little they were all the more determined to hang on to. On the other hand many grand nobles were heavily involved in trade and commerce and increasingly merged with the richer commercial bourgeoisie.

The other group was the nobility of the robe. To raise money the king sold, and created specifically for sale, a whole series of positions which conferred noble status—and therefore social privileges and tax exemption. Wealthy bourgeois helped themselves liberally to this avenue of advancement. It was the central mechanism by which the absolute monarchy incorporated elements of the bourgeoisie into the feudal political structure.

Some of these nobles of the robe sat in the Parlements (not to be confused with the English parliament which, by now, was an entirely different creature). These were great legal corporations in the cities and provinces of France. They had to register royal decrees before they had the force of law and, along with a host of lesser courts, they played a role in the administration of the complex 'feudal' laws. The Parlements had, especially in times of weak central government, amassed considerable power by blocking and holding up royal edicts.

The Third Estate

The rest of society was legally lumped together in the 'Third Estate'. They paid the taxes the other two orders were exempt from. Naturally this covered a vast range of classes. At the top were rich bourgeois who, fast as the monarchy created them, had not yet secured a position which conferred nobility. They included the traders and merchants of the great cities and ports and the new industrial regions—where merchants were developing industry on a putting out basis. There were only a few factory owning 'industrialists' among them—there was little factory production as yet and many basic industries were effectively controlled by the absolutist state. They also included large numbers of professionals— lawyers, doctors, civil servants and the like. Many of these had positions connected with the state apparatus. But they often found their rise to a position merited by their talents blocked by the grip of the privileged orders.

Absolutism's centralisation, improved bureaucracy, road and canal construction, building programmes, protectionist policies, war—with lucrative supply contracts—overseas trade and colonial production formed the basis of bourgeois wealth. But in a society where land was still the principal form of wealth, and the one on which the whole political structure was based, many bourgeois used their wealth to invest in land at the first opportunity—often deserting commerce in the process. They often brought more ruthless, businesslike methods to bear on the exaction of feudal dues attached to the land.[20] Many bourgeois also became involved in operations such as tax farming. They would pay the monarchy a fixed sum for the right to collect certain taxes and dues. Then they kept as profit whatever they raised over the amount paid the king. This, naturally, made them more efficient and ruthless at squeezing taxes out of the peasantry. Peasants thus had good reason to resent bourgeois landowners and tax gatherers as much as, if not more than, traditional nobles.

Nevertheless the incorporation of the bourgeoisie within the feudal political structure only operated up to a point. Some bourgeois, those involved in tax farming or who had secured royal monopolies for instance, were totally tied to the absolutist state and the old order. But the expanding economy meant there was a real growth in a class based on new forms of wealth. Between the 1720s and the revolution French trade grew by over 400 percent, production of wool cloth by 61 percent, linen by 80 percent, iron by 300 percent and coal by over 700 percent.[21] Much of this wealth was based on overseas and colonial trade and was concentrated in the growing Atlantic and Mediterranean ports such as Marseilles, Bordeaux, Nantes and Rouen.[22] These were the great centres of the commercial and merchant bourgeoisie and, though many bought their way into the nobility, no matter how fast the near bankrupt monarchy created offices for sale, supply could not match demand. The result was the exclusion of large layers of the bourgeoisie from the privileged orders.

Towards the end of the *ancien régime* there was also a closing of ranks among the nobility. Resentful of the dilution of their privilege by the inflow of upstart bourgeois they tried to close the doors. They forced through a series of laws to restrict further access to the nobility and above all to give the existing nobility a monopoly on key positions in the Church, army, state bureaucracy and so on. One example was the *Loi Ségur* of 1781 which excluded commoners and those recently ennobled (meaning those with less than four generations of noble status behind them) from all army ranks of captain and above. This seems to have been a move by the poorer hereditary provincial nobility, for whom the army was often the chief source of lucrative employment, to maintain their privileges.[23] Similar motives, along with a reaction to philosophical attacks on the whole notion of 'orders' and privilege, lay behind the growth in the importance attached to lineage by sections of the nobility in the 17th and 18th centuries. This even extended to the invention of racial myths, like that which claimed the old nobility were descended from Frankish knights whose privileges derived from their conquest and subjugation of the native Gauls.[24]

The limits of absolutism's ability to incorporate the bourgeoisie within feudal political structures were being reached. This led to a growing feeling of resentment among the bourgeoisie against the privileges of the first and second estates. Emmanuel Sieyès, a clergyman later to play an important role in the revolution, wrote: 'In one way or another all the branches of the executive have been taken over by the caste that monopolises the Church, the judiciary and the army. A spirit of fellowship leads the nobles to favour one another in everything over the rest of the nation. Their usurpation is complete, they truly reign.'[25] And he accused the privileged orders of saying to the Third Estate, 'Whatever your services, whatever your talents you shall go this far and no further.'[26] Even some nobles—especially those whose wealth partially oriented them in a bourgeois direction—joined in on the side of the bourgeois critics. At this stage none of the bourgeoisie advocated revolution to resolve their grievances.[27] But when society was plunged into crisis in the late 1780s, elements of this class began, in the course of struggle, to articulate a programme to reshape society in their interests.

At the bottom of French society were the peasantry—the vast bulk of French people. At the top they shaded into the bourgeoisie—wealthy peasants who owned a plough and draught animals, the 'roosters of the village'.[28] Sliding down the scale we find a host of intermediary layers with varying amounts of land. At the bottom were sharecroppers and landless labourers. There were complex variations in the structure of peasant society across France. But most peasants were no longer serfs and owned at least some land, though often not enough to survive without recourse to wage labour for part of the year.[29]

All peasants resented 'feudalism'. What they meant by this was quite simple: the array of taxes and dues they were compelled to pay to their landlords, the Church and so on.[30] There were obligations to pay the lord (or 'seigneur') if you bought or sold land, or if you inherited it. Then there were compulsory labour services for road building and the like as well as direct personal taxes. And there were heavy indirect taxes such as the hated *gabelle* or salt tax. Seigneurs also had exclusive hunting rights over certain areas as well as monopolies called *banalités*. These gave them the exclusive right to operate a mill, oven or wine press in a particular area which peasants were compelled to use, and pay for. They also gave the seigneurs considerable power by giving them priority in the sale of wine and allowing them to decide the date of the harvest. The precise taxes and dues varied from region to region but the burden on the peasantry was universal.

The final area to examine is the towns. Though the French Revolution was the first in which mass urban action was central to events, it is wrong to see the urban masses in the French Revolution as the forerunners of the Russian workers of 1917.[31] In the towns the bourgeoisie shaded into a vast petty bourgeoisie who had a much greater social weight than they do today. Shopkeepers, independent artisans, small merchants and traders formed the core of this group who were of fundamental importance in the revolution. There was a large wage earning working class but it is important to be clear about its nature and the objective limits on its ability to coalesce or act as an independent force. A few factories apart, it was concentrated in small workshops. Master craftsmen and retailers made up approximately 30 percent of the population of the average town. Wage earners accounted for about the same proportion but few of these were in 'industrial' establishments and about one third of them were domestic servants.[32]

There *were* a few large workplaces. For instance in Paris Réveillon's wallpaper factory in the Faubourg St Antoine employed 350 workers and there were three textile factories in the north of the city employing

279, 314 and 800 workers. More typical was a blanket manufacturer who employed 400 workers—but only 80 of these were in his factory the rest were outworkers in Paris and the surrounding countryside. But all of these were exceptional, the average number of workers per employer in Paris was about three.[33] Workers often lived in the same house—though on separate floors—as the 'boss'. The ambition of many, and not yet an altogether impossible dream, was to become an independent master in their own right. At some points in the revolution the particular demands and struggles of wage earners *did* come to the fore, but this was always temporary. It was impossible for this diffuse and embryonic working class to act independently in any consistent fashion. Wage earners' conditions of existence, both numerical and social, and their relationship to the petty bourgeoisie meant that they acted largely under its political leadership and ideological sway.[34]

Wages were fairly stable and people's immediate concern was shaped by their position as consumers rather than producers. So the supply and price of bread was the key issue in fomenting mass discontent. In a largely pre-industrial society with poorly developed agriculture and transport the supply of grain to the towns was fragile and the price therefore volatile. And this was an issue which blurred class lines between the petty bourgeoisie and wage earners. The result was a common hostility to hoarders, speculators and the big bourgeois who profited at the expense of ordinary people and threatened to drive small workshops and the like out of business. The petty bourgeois layer became known as the *sans-culottes*—so called because of their habit of wearing trousers buttoned onto their coat as opposed to the aristocratic (and bourgeois) habit of wearing knee breeches—and developed a distinctive ideology which was to profoundly influence the revolution.

The political division of society into estates had arisen on the basis of old class divisions under feudalism but now no longer fitted the real class structure of society. But the privileged orders were not about to simply surrender their privileges and political power.

Class divisions and division into estates were not the only ones in France. It is wrong to speak of France as a nation state in any modern sense before the revolution. The state was dependent on the person of the king—people owed allegiance to him not some largely undeveloped idea of the nation. This of course had a material basis. Absolutism *had* begun to construct a unified national economy and state but France was still internally divided. Whole chunks of the country spoke different languages with about one quarter of the population unable to understand French. And various groups, usually the nobility, resolutely defended their particular regional privileges. This was especially so in areas like Brittany, and others recently added to the French crown. This localism was also reflected in innumerable internal tolls and customs barriers. These included the hated gates around Paris erected by the tax officials.

All goods passing through these had a variety of dues levied on them. There were around 360 different legal codes operating in different parts of France and a bewildering variety of weights and measures. The centralisation of the absolutist state and the growing economic unity inside France only served to make all these divisions and barriers even more irksome to those engaged in trade and commerce as well as the mass of urban people who paid higher prices as a result.

The crisis

The years leading up to 1789 saw this society slide into a crisis which opened the path to revolution. Why? The world in which this French absolutism had developed was already changing still further. In England and the United Provinces (the Netherlands) revolutions had swept away the central aspects of the old order and reshaped society in the interests of the bourgeoisie.[35] The French state—the largest and most populous in Europe—was locked into a developing global conflict with these powers. The problem for France was that its political structure increasingly limited its ability to match its rivals.

The Seven Years War (1756-63), perhaps the first global conflict, underlined the problem. It was fought, in essence, between England and France, the world's two main powers by then. France lost out badly in India, the West Indies, Canada and Europe. This seriously undermined the French ruling classes' confidence in the exisiting regime. The Comte de Ségur was reflecting a general view when he commented: 'The government no longer possessed any dignity, the finances any order and the conduct of policy any consistency... The French monarchy ceased to be a first-rank power'.[36] The strain of such conflicts plunged the French state into enormous debt.[37] French intervention (1778-1783) in the US War of Independence—because of rivalry with England—was helpful to the Americans but pushed the French state debt to unprecedented levels.[38]

The monarchy was forced to look to reforms to try and sort out the approaching bankruptcy. On several occasions king's ministers pushed reforms through but the king backed down after the privileged orders mounted opposition. The most determined efforts were spearheaded by Turgot, a leading physiocrat. The physiocrats were a group of economists influenced by the dynamic (compared to France) example of English agriculture. They believed that the products of the land were the only source of new value and in the free use of landed property. This meant they wanted to do away with restrictions on individual landowners pursuing their self interest and they favoured free trade in grain. The state's job was to create the environment for efficient production of wealth, which in turn would fill its coffers. Free trade, a market free from restrictions and privileges, was their aim, 'Laissez faire, laissez passer' their slogan. In 1776 Turgot, the king's chief minister, made proposals to open up trade, abolish guilds and spread the tax burden more evenly—including introducing a land tax on the privileged orders. The outcry from the privileged orders coupled with popular revolts against the consequences of free trade in grain forced the king to drop the reforms and sack Turgot. The monarchy had first gone along with the reforms but, at the first sign of serious opposition, backed off. It wanted reform but was tied to the existing structure of society. As the Queen, Marie Antoinette, put it, 'The nobility will destroy us but it seems to me that we cannot save ourselves without it.'[39]

This inability to carry through reforms in France should be put alongside three other events in 1776. That year saw the American Declaration of Independence which, with its talk of universal rights and republican government, was an example which began to influence those seeking an alternative to the growing crisis of the existing French regime. Meanwhile in the same year, across the Channel in Britain, Adam Smith published his *Wealth of Nations* and James Watt unveiled his new steam engine. The new industrial capitalist world these heralded stood in stark contrast to the *ancien régime* with its privileges and orders in France. Though the French economy was growing rapidly, as fast as the British in fact, the growth in quantity was not matched in qualitative change. In 1789 Britain had over 20,000 spinning jennies, 9,000 of the newer mule jennies and 200 Arkwright mills. The equivalent figures for France were: fewer than a thousand, none and eight![40] The strain created by this qualitative gap was growing and was brutally exposed by the imposition of a 'free trade' treaty with England in 1786 which opened up French markets to English textiles. This had a catastrophic effect on French industry, and the textile centres of Lyons and the north of the country were badly hit by their inability to compete with the more efficiently produced English products.

This inability of the French state to match the bourgeois states in England and Holland, militarily and economically, is a fundamental cause of the crisis which resulted in the revolution. A more immediate factor, which was partly a result of this underlying problem, was the severe crisis which hit the French economy on the eve of the revolution. Economic growth meant the periodic and devastating famines of the previous century had largely disappeared during the first half of the 18th century—though for most people it meant the replacement of famine with hunger. But this improvement ended some 20 years before the revolution, partly because of the external factors discussed above and partly due to limitations imposed by the relatively backward nature of French agriculture. The increased hardship which resulted was keenly felt by those who remembered the slightly better times.

Then, on the eve of the revolution, the economy lurched into sharp crisis. Prices of essential items rocketed. Bread alone accounted for 58 percent of the budget of the bulk of the Parisian population at the beginning of 1789. This rose to 88 percent during the summer. At the same time wheat hit record prices across most of the country. The uprising of 14 July came at the highest point reached by prices over the entire 18th century.[41]

Such conditions led to riots and risings before the revolution. The most significant was the 'flour war' of 1775 where urban riots involved a score of cities.[42] The movement focused on mass invasions of markets and fixing the price at fair levels, but it did not become a revolution. The reasons why are important. Firstly, it did not spread to the vast mass of the peasantry. Secondly, the movement was not supported by any significant section of the bourgeoisie. Without the peasantry and a challenge by the bourgeoisie to the existing order there could be no French revolution.

The monarchy had repeatedly backed down from pushing reforms through. But by the late 1780s the desperate financial situation gave it no choice but to try once again. Calonne, a noble and now Finance Minister, said France was 'in its present condition, impossible to govern'[43]. The old order could no longer continue to rule in the old way and the political and social tensions, growing in response to the economic crisis, were to prove an explosive mix when the king's renewed attempt to reform aggravated them. As the 19th century historian Alexis de Tocqueville commented, 'experience shows that the most dangerous moment for a bad government is generally that in which it sets about reform.'[44]

The revolt of the nobles and the calling of the Estates General

In 1787 the king made another attempt to increase the state's revenue by spreading the burden of taxation to the privileged orders. He even went so far as to exile the Paris Parlement, but he had to back down after it mobilised popular support by posing as the defender of liberty against royal and ministerial despotism. A similar attempt to browbeat the nobility (convened in a special Assembly of Notables) in 1788 was again blocked and the king agreed to summon the Estates General to break the deadlock. This body had last met in 1614 and consisted of three assemblies, one for each of the orders. The king hoped to use it to sort out the financial mess by pushing through changes in the tax structure.

But the summoning of the Estates General provided a focus for all the grievances and discontent beneath the surface of society. And it forced various classes and groups to begin to define programmes for the resolution of the impasse in France. Crucially, there were to be national 'elections'. In effect the vast bulk of the population were entitled to attend primary assemblies where they would draw up lists of grievances and elect delegates to a higher body. There was, naturally, a property qualification on those eligible to be elected. These delegates in turn elected delegates to the Estates General, who were subject to a further property qualification. This procedure was for the Third Estate. The nobility and clergy of course elected their own delegates. It meant people in every town and village were drawn into a discussion on the problems facing society, and possible solutions. Expectations were awakened among millions of people that change for the better would be the outcome of the Estates General. An English traveller in France at the time reports a peasant's comment: 'People say that the great ones are going to do something for us poor people now, but may God send us something better for all these dues and taxes are crushing us.'[45]

Opinion polarised over an argument about the constitution of the Estates General. Would the three orders meet and vote separately, as in the past, or together? And should the Third Estate (in effect the bourgeoisie because of the electoral procedure) have double representation compared to previous occasions? The latter was conceded—a telling reflection of the growth of the bourgeoisie over the previous century and a half. But the nobility of the Parlements and the king insisted that the three orders should meet and vote separately.

At once the pretensions of the nobility to defend 'liberty' were stripped bare. Despite general agreement by the nobility on the need for some reform their insistence on separate voting meant a commitment to the old structures. They blocked any possibility of ending their privileges. The double representation of the Third Estate was useless unless a common assembly allowed them to use it to outvote the other orders. This deepened the grievances of the bourgeoisie against the privileged orders and united popular opinion behind the 'Third Estate'. A journalist wrote in January 1789: 'A change has come over the public dispute... now the main thing is a war between the Third Estate and the other two orders.'[46]

The argument forced the bourgeoisie to begin to put forward clearer ideas. They were, in common with the nobility, part of the exploiting classes, but they were an oppressed class as long as the old structures remained intact. Pamphlets started to appear in unprecedented numbers. The sharpest was *What is the Third Estate?* written by the Emmanuel Sieyès—a clergyman rejected by his own order for the Estates General who went over to the Third Estate: 'What is the Third Estate? Everything. What has it been until now? Nothing. What does it demand? To be something.'[47]

In this heightened political atmosphere the mass of the population began to stir. A poor harvest in 1788 led to hunger in early 1789 which provoked peasant rebellions. Peasants had revolted before of course, but now the arguments over reform and the Estates General gave their '*jacquerie*' a political focus.[48] The rising was directed at the taxes, dues and monopolies of seigneurs. The revolt grew and by July 1789 from Normandy to Alsace peasant bands were storming chateaux and burning the rolls on which lists of their dues were kept. They also began attacking capitalist minded farmers who had been enclosing common land.

The lists of grievances (*cahiers de doléance*) drawn up for the Estates General made peasant discontent on these questions clear. The lists of the nobility and the bourgeoisie were agreed on the need for reforms which spread the burden of direct taxes more equally—the nobility were prepared to concede this much. But when it came to abandoning 'feudal' rights and privileges the split between the bourgeoisie and the privileged orders was clear—the nobility were not prepared to surrender their privileges.[49]

Discontent was not confined to the countryside. The high price of bread led to riots in towns in the spring of 1789. In April a particularly serious outbreak occurred in Paris. Réveillon, a wallpaper manufacturer employing 350 workers in his factory, made a speech attacking the level of wages. Thousands of workers rioted in protest—storming Réveillon's house in fierce fighting with troops sent to protect it. The majority of those involved were wage earners, though not Réveillon's own workers. This was the only 'day'—as the major urban uprisings became known—of the revolution when wage earners were in a majority. Significantly, though, their demands focussed on the price of bread.[50]

From the National Assembly to the storming of the Bastille

When the Estates General finally met on 5 May the old feudal structures were flaunted in the bourgeoisie's face. The king insisted that each order march in separately, appropriately attired—with the Third Estate bringing up the rear of course. For five weeks a slow manoeuvre was played out. The Third Estate demanded that all should meet in common but the others refused. The king vacillated. This, coupled with the growing sense of crisis, encouraged the bourgeoisie. So too did the signs that the assembly of the clergy, where parish priests outnumbered bishops by five to one, was beginning to rally to the Third Estate.

On 10 June the bourgeoisie grasped the nettle. They formally invited the other orders to join them. A few priests did so and on 17 June, on the proposition of Sieyès, they declared themselves the National Assembly. This was accompanied by defensive measures—a decree that if the Assembly was dissolved all taxes would become invalid. Three days later the Assembly found itself locked out of its usual meeting place (apparently by accident!) and marched to a nearby indoor tennis court where all but one of them took a solemn oath not to disperse until a constitution was granted. This defiance now won over the bulk of the clergy (pushed by the parish priests) who voted to join the Assembly.

The bourgeoisie were still only demanding reform—but reform from a system not prepared to concede it. After his earlier vacillations the king now moved. He called a special session to order the estates to resume separate assemblies and hoped to overawe the Third Estate by a show of force. On 23 June the meeting took place, in a hall ringed with royal troops, and the king's orders were duly read out. They made it clear he was determined to block any real change: 'The king wishes the ancient distinction between the three orders of the State to be preserved *in its entirety* as being *essentially linked* to the constitution of his kingdom.'[51]

Meanwhile, rumours of the king's action had fed discontent in Paris and thousands now marched to Versailles, the royal residence a few miles outside Paris where the Assembly was sitting. The troops refused to fire on them—a sign that the armed force of the state was crumbling. Emboldened by this, Mirabeau, a noble who had gone over to the Third Estate and been elected for that order, rallied the Assembly: 'We are here by the will of the people, only bayonets will force us from our seats.'[52]

Faced with this defiance the king backed down—but only in order to play for time. The defiance also won over a minority of the nobility; 47 of them led by the Duc D'Orléans joined the National Assembly. The conflict at Versailles had further heightened popular expectations of change. And the swelling discontent over bread supplies and prices in Paris now began to be shaped and directed by more militant and clear sighted sections of the bourgeoisie. The Duc D'Orléans—a claimant to the throne who, for a variety of reasons, opposed the existing monarchy—owned gardens and cafes called the Palais Royal. These were frequented by popular bourgeois orators and journalists such as Georges Danton and Camille Desmoulins who were now stirring up the thousands who flocked there. The 'extreme revolutionary party'[53] was still diffuse and unorganised, but beginning to emerge. Meanwhile the 407 bourgeois electors—who had decided the Third Estate's Paris delegates for the Estates General—began to meet at the city hall. They constituted themselves as a Commune, or city council.

The king now moved to crush the growing defiance. He summoned 20,000 troops to an area near Paris and prepared a military coup. The signal was given when he sacked his chief minister, Necker, who reputedly favoured reforms. It was a clear provocation and a sign that the king was intent on clamping down on all demands for change. This, and rumours about the troop movements, provoked demonstrations in Paris on 12 July in support of Necker and the Assembly, and over bread supplies and prices. They were spurred on by radical orators like Desmoulins, who is said to have issued a call, 'To arms, citizens', from the Palais Royal. Crowds, fearing troops were about to arrive and restore 'order', began hunting for weapons.

The bourgeois electors at the city hall faced a dilemma. They feared popular discontent might get out of hand and threaten 'law and order'— and more particularly their property. But they also feared the king and his troops. So they stepped in to form a 'national guard' or citizens' militia to defend themselves against both threats. Thousands were quickly enrolled—the poorer petty bourgeois and wage earners were excluded. In the words of Assembly deputy Barnave it was composed of 'bonne bourgeoisie'.

But the upsurge from below continued. The search for arms was the key impulse, but also the hated toll barriers around Paris were attacked and burnt down. Then 30,000 muskets were seized at a monastery— along with flour. This turned the focus of the developing insurrection to the Bastille on 14 July. The fortress was a hated symbol of despotism, but as there were only seven prisoners more immediate matters were involved.[54] Muskets are not much use without powder, and it was thought there was plenty of that stored in the Bastille. And the fortress's guns were trained on the Rue St Antoine—leading to the large popular quarter of that name in the east of the city. They would cause havoc if used.

The bourgeois electors had no intention of taking the Bastille by force and wanted to negotiate its surrender. The governor invited a delegation to breakfast while they negotiated terms but, when they were slow to return, the crowd swelling outside feared a trap. They surged forward into the outer courtyard whereupon the defending troops opened fire, killing 98 people. The battle was settled when two regiments of mutinous soldiers turned up with cannon. The fortress surrendered and the governor was killed by the crowd as he was escorted away. The insurrection had won.

The bourgeoisie had been pushed from below. Their fear of the monarchy meant they did little to oppose, and some grudgingly encouraged, the insurrection. But what was the class basis of the revolt from below? A look at the composition of those involved in the storming of the Bastille reveals this[55]: respectable family men, average age 34, overwhelmingly composed of artisans, tradesmen and shopkeepers. Some wage earners are present, but vastly outnumbered by such petty bourgeois. The leading figures were often rather more than 'petty' bourgeois. For instance Santerre (later to lead the insurrection which overthrew the monarchy in 1792) was a wealthy brewer.

The news of the fall of the Bastille had an explosive impact in the country. In city after city 'municipal' revolutions took place. Old noble dominated authorities were swept aside or simply disappeared and new bourgeois dominated forces took over.[56] In many cases the new authorities were forced to concede a reduction in the price of bread to popular movements which brought them to power. Bourgeois National Guards were formed in most places, again to deal with the twin threat of the old order and to prevent popular mobilisations going too far. The events of July struck the first decisive blow in the transformation of society. The king was forced to recognise the National Assembly and even to go to Paris and accept the tricolour cockade—the symbol of the victorious insurrection—from the mayor.

Unrest continued in Paris after the storming of the Bastille, mainly around the question of bread. On 22 August two leading officials of the city—hated as speculators in grain—were seized by a crowd and killed. Some sections of the bourgeoisie were outraged. But Barnave, at this point the most clear sighted of the bourgeois leaders, defended the action, saying, 'Was then the blood which was shed all that pure?'[57] Some of the nobility understood very well the significance of what had happened—they emigrated and began plotting counter-revolution.

The Great Fear and the 'abolition of feudalism'

Rural revolt was already under way before the July insurrection. But the uprising in Paris and its local imitations deepened the rebellions. Many peasants thought the news gave them legal authority to put an end to feudalism. Manors and *chateaux* were invaded, hedges and ditches of enclosing landlords destroyed, tax rolls and deeds burned. Out of this exploded the Great Fear.

The itinerant bands of hungry wandering the country and worries about disbanded troops fuelled rumours that 'brigands' were about to descend on the villages. This now exploded into a certainty that their arrival was imminent. Peasants responded first with panic and then with armed defence against the brigands. The Fear rolled from village to village along six well defined routes across the country between 20 July and 6 August. Towns, fearful of brigands and armed peasants, responded by strengthening their organisation and National Guards and in some areas bourgeois National Guards violently suppressed peasant revolts. The brigands never came, but the impulse of organisation reaching down to the lowest village was immense. After the Fear passed the armed peasants put their organisation to good use. They often went on to attack local chateaux.[58]

It was against this background of 'fires of sedition'[59] that the Constituent Assembly (as the National Assembly had renamed itself) met on 4 August. The deputies voted to 'destroy the feudal regime entirely', but in the weeks that followed the reality was less clear cut. The decrees which emerged fell far short of abolishing what the peasants meant by feudalism. Some things were abolished outright—including the surviving pockets of serfdom—and legal equality of all individuals before the law was decreed. But a distinction was drawn between rights and privileges which were considered 'feudal', including the hated *banalités*, and those which were considered 'property' rights, such as rents and dues held to derive from a lease. The bourgeoisie was most reluctant to interfere with the latter. They were not abolished but, instead, made redeemable. Peasants could have them annulled if they paid 20 times the annual due in cash or 25 in kind. This they could rarely afford to do. It was a cruel disappointment to most peasants.

But many only heard the first words of the decree abolishing the 'feudal regime'. Over the next few years until 1793 (when all dues were abolished without compensation by the Jacobin revolutionary government) the peasantry conducted a long drawn out fight to turn these words into reality. Sometimes this involved open resistance and refusal to pay, at other times less spectacular defiance such as delayed payment, refusing to transport payment in kind to the landlord's barn and so on.[60] For the bourgeoisie 4 August was an attempt to disentangle property rights dependent on contract and money, which were very dear to them, from relics of feudalism or rights positively harmful to bourgeois interests, such as noble monopolies. The attempt failed largely due to the resistance of the peasantry.

Liberty, Equality, Fraternity

The new order emerging after the July insurrection was reflected in the Declaration of the Rights of Man and Citizen on 26 August. The form of this was partly inspired by the American example—Thomas Jefferson was then in Paris and Lafayette, who played an important role in drafting it, had fought in the US War of Independence. The Declaration was also based on the 'natural law' philosophy of people like Locke, Montesquieu and Rousseau. Such general principles were, though, tailored to fit the specific needs of the French bourgeoisie—and the right of rebellion was implicitly sanctioned, a recognition of the real basis of the Constituent Assembly's power.

Based on the principles of Liberty, Equality and Fraternity the Declaration has become one of the central legacies of the revolution. Most of its principles were enshrined in laws and the constitution over next two years. These principles and measures illustrate precisely the bourgeois basis of the new order.

Liberty meant, above all, freedom to dispose of property, engage in trade and the like without restriction. Guilds and monopolies were abolished—including trading monopolies and privileges such as noble *banalités*. Internal tolls in most of the country were also abolished. External trade was freed from restriction by cancelling most of the trade monopolies that existed under the old regime. Liberty included 'freedom to work'—ie no strikes or unions. The *Le Chapelier* law (passed in June 1791) banned unions or workers' associations and forbade strikes—of course this did not stop them happening.[61]

Liberty also meant personal liberty, in the sense of a guarantee of freedom of speech, and an end to arbitrary arrest and gratuitous torture by the authorities. Strange as it may seem now, the introduction of the Guillotine, named after a doctor of that name, was a humane reaction against the barbarity of the old order. One member of the Constituent Assembly, Maximilien Robespierre, a provincial lawyer from Arras, proposed the abolition of the death penalty but was not supported.[62]

Equality meant simply equality before the law. A person's treatment should not depend on their birth—'Men are born and remain free and have equal rights'. But this did not yet extend to slaves in the colonies. At this stage only the most radical of the bourgeoisie, such as Robespierre and those who would later form the Jacobins, opposed slavery. Only when the Jacobins came to power and the slaves in what became Haiti, led by Toussaint L'Ouverture, revolted would bourgeois equality be extended that far.[63] Careers should be 'open to the talents'. But there was no question of economic equality—the right to property was enshrined in the Declaration.

Fraternity was about the creation of a unified national state and market. All were now French citizens. Internal barriers to trade and commerce were gone and class antagonism could be blurred under the patriotic ideal.

All of this is not to say the Declaration was cynically drawn up to fool people. The bourgeoisie of necessity had to present its interests as those of society as a whole, as universal. This consciousness was a necessary part of them achieving power and mobilising popular support. They certainly believed they were acting in the interests of the whole of society—and in a historical sense they were. As Marx wrote,

> *Each new class which puts itself in the place of one ruling before it is compelled, merely in order to carry through its aim, to represent its interest as the common interest of all the members of society, that is, expressed in an ideal form: it has to give its ideas the form of universality and represent them as the only rational, universally valid ones. The class making a revolution appears...not as a class but as the representative of the whole of society... It can do this because, to start with, its interest really is more connected with the common interest of all other non-ruling classes.*[64]

The October days

Louis, though forced to back down in July, was still king—and most of the bourgeoisie wanted him kept there as a guarantee of order. There were few republicans yet. But he would not accept the direction of the bourgeois Assembly. He refused to ratify the August decrees 'abolishing' feudalism: 'I will never allow *my* clergy and *my* nobility to be stripped of their assets'.[65]

This fed into an argument over the future structure of government. Some wanted the king to retain an absolute veto over legislation while others only wished him to have a suspensive veto—i.e. allowing him to block legislation for a time but not indefinitely. The latter position won an overwhelming majority in the Assembly.

The open monarchists and the king then started organising to restore royal authority by force. The king summoned troops to Versailles, where, on 1 October 1789, they attended a banquet intended to whip up counter-revolutionary sentiment. The king, queen and *dauphin* (crown prince) were mystically received, the national tricolour cockade trampled underfoot and replaced with the black cockade of the queen. In the charged atmosphere the event, though small, provoked an immediate reaction.

As in July, bread shortages and high prices provided the combustible material. Some bourgeois leaders such as Danton and Desmoulins had already urged action against the king. Now, faced with the threat of a royal coup, key leaders such as Barnave withdrew their previous objections to using force to compel the king to submit to the Assembly. They thus encouraged the developing movement.

The women of the central Paris markets rose on 5 October. They first invaded the City Hall demanding bread and searching for arms. Then, several thousand strong, they marched off to Versailles—where the king and Assembly still resided—'armed with broomsticks, lances, pitchforks, swords, pistols and muskets'.[66] At their head was Stanislas Maillard, who had played an important role in the storming of the Bastille and who the women had persuaded to lead the demonstration. The women invaded the Assembly and extracted a promise of bread. Louis then attempted to head off the movement by finally sanctioning the August decrees—but it was too late. In Paris 20,000 bourgeois National Guards had gathered and compelled their commander, Lafayette, to lead them after the women.

The women, joined by the National Guard, camped overnight at Versailles. Some penetrated the palace and killed a few of the defending royal troops. The crowd then took up the demand, formulated by the bourgeois leaders, that the king and his family be brought to Paris. This was an eminently sensible move which would lessen the danger of counter-revolution. The king had little choice but to comply. The National Guard and the people set off in a procession taking 'the baker, the baker's wife and the baker's son back to Paris'.[67] Some in the crowd carried loaves of bread on pikes. Others stuck the heads of royalist troops on their pikes.

This second insurrection shifted the balance of power again. The king's position was seriously weakened, as was that of the openly monarchist faction of the bourgeoisie—some of their leaders soon emigrated to add to the growing numbers of counter-revolutionaries plotting abroad.

The attempted compromise

From October 1789 until the summer of 1791 there was a long drawn out attempt by the bourgeoisie to reach a compromise with the king and the nobility. New leaders emerged in the National Assembly who headed this attempt, men like Mirabeau and Lafayette. But already a more organised coherent 'left' was developing. A new organisation called the Society of Friends of the Constitution had developed out of a group of Breton deputies to the Estates General. It was soon to be known as the

Jacobin club.[68]

Among its emerging leaders was Maximilien Robespierre who, one deputy exclaimed, was dangerous because 'he believes everything he says'. He would soon be labelled an 'incorruptible'. Then there were those radical bourgeois who spoke for the popular movement—such as Jean Paul Marat with his newspaper *The Friend of the People*.[69]

For the moment compromise looked possible. The king went to the Assembly to declare that he accepted the new set up. But the unity was weak. In May 1790 the splits were revealed in an argument over who had the right to declare war—the king or the Assembly. A fudge was agreed, but it was a sign that fundamental issues had not yet been resolved.

Lafayette, 'the hero of the old world and the new' (so called from his exploits during the American War of Independence), was emerging as the strong man of the new regime. In the National Guard he was attempting to construct a military force which would allow him to impose a settlement. Nominally he was in favour of a constitutional monarchy but many feared he was planning to become 'a new Caesar'. Both Lafayette's position and the unity of the revolution seemed strengthened by the Festival of the Federation in July 1790. Delegates from National Guards all over France attended a ceremony, on the anniversary of the storming of the Bastille, designed to emphasise national unity. Lafayette was at the head of proceedings. The federation movement had built up over the previous six months. National Guards of different towns and areas, beginning in the south east, came together to swear oaths of mutual support. It was a concrete expression of the developing national consciousness of the bourgeoisie—and was supported by the mass of the people.

But behind the facade of unity the old order was once more preparing to strike back. Despite the king's public appearance he was set on crushing the revolution and restoring the old regime. He planned to flee abroad and rally a counter-revolutionary army (foreign if need be) to march on Paris. Meanwhile supporters of the old regime began to have some success in fomenting counter-revolutionary outbreaks. One was suppressed in Lyon in July 1790 and counter-revolutionaries provoked an uprising in Nîmes by playing on divisions between Catholic and Protestant. At Jalès, again in the south, 20,000 armed National Guards assembled in August 1790 and, at the instigation of a committee of nobles, issued a counter-revolutionary manifesto.

The same month soldiers in Nancy rebelled over pay arrears and were supported by local 'patriots', as the revolutionary bourgeoisie now styled themselves. Lafayette used it as the pretext for a crackdown—ordering that 'a great blow be struck'. The revolt was crushed, with 300 killed. Marat's headline in his *Friend of the People* was 'The Awful Reveille'. The king, on the other hand, welcomed the repression. The unity of the revolution was being exposed for an illusion.[70]

Municipal change and the crisis in the Church

One of the major, but usually underplayed, changes brought about by the revolution was the wholesale restructuring of local government.

In early 1790 all the old divisions and areas with their particular privileges and structures were scrapped. They were replaced by a uniform national structure in which the country was divided into 83 *départements*, with these in turn divided into cantons and communes (the whole structure more or less survives to this day). It was the practical expression of the founding of a unified national state. Elections were held at every level. One historian writes that 'before 1789 there was not a single truly elected assembly in the country, only government officials; in 1790 there was no longer a single official, just elected bodies'. This is overstated but the point is well made.[71]

Even though the electoral procedure was in stages, with property qualifications on those eligible for election, the impact on daily life was massive. About 1 million people were elected to various posts in the localities. Parish priests summoned people to the village church and there they would discuss and elect officials. The process transmitted the revolution down to the remotest corner of the country and the smallest village.[72]

Alongside such changes the Assembly moved to sort out the financial mess which the old regime had created, by confiscating Church property in November 1789. Interest bearing bonds (called assignats) backed by this land were issued. Land could be purchased on their surrender. The sale of such land went on throughout the revolution and there is still argument among historians about who benefitted from it. In many areas the bourgeoisie crowded out the peasants and got the lion's share. These sections of the bourgeoisie thereby had a very material stake in opposing any return to the old order. This is an important factor in understanding the tenacity with which, despite all the twists and turns of the various regimes later in the revolution, all were opposed to any restoration. But though the bourgeoisie got the lion's share, peasants did gain from the sales—often by banding together to bid in auctions.[73]

Difficulties with the assignat scheme meant they soon ceased to be bear interest and became paper money circulating alongside coins. But lack of confidence in them, because the land which underpinned their value was liable to be lost in the event of a restoration of the old order, and inflation meant they depreciated rapidly. By May 1791 they were already down to 73 percent of their face value. This continual financial instability was to plague the revolutionary governments—with the partial exception of the Jacobin republic of the Year II.

But having confiscated its land and abolished tithes there remained the problem of how to finance the Church. The solution the bourgeois leaders came up with was the Civil Constitution of the Clergy. In essence this made all priests and bishops paid state officials. At first the bishops and the king sanctioned it. But the Pope, who had already denounced the Declaration of the Rights of Man, dragged his feet because he was manoeuvring over the status of the Papal enclave inside France at Avignon. Finally, exasperated, the Assembly unilaterally imposed the constitution in early 1791 and required all priests and bishops to take an oath of loyalty. This produced a violent schism in the Church. Most of the bishops and around half of the priests refused—putting loyalty to the Pope and the old order first. From then on the 'non-juring priests', as they were called, slipped into the arms of counter-revolution. In a society where the Church was of major ideological importance this was a potent force.

This crisis was coupled with a renewed surge of activity from below in both towns and countryside. In Paris there were no food shortages, due to a reasonable harvest. But now there were strikes by journeymen carpenters, farriers and printers for higher wages. The growing turmoil prompted the king to write, 'I would rather be king of Metz than remain king of France under these conditions, but it will soon be over'.[74] The main bourgeois leaders still hoped for a compromise with the old order. They were concerned above all to stabilise society. Duport, one of their main spokesmen (along with Barnave and the Lameths), put their programme clearly: 'The revolution is over. We must preserve it while resisting excesses. Equality must be restrained, liberty reduced and public opinion controlled. The government must be strong, solid and stable'.[75] Unfortunately, for them, the only force they could see to cement a stable order was the monarchy. So they leaned on the king even while he was plotting counter-revolution.

Meanwhile, as the discontent from below grew, a new type of political organisation was developing. Paris had been divided into 48 electoral divisions called sections. They were based on direct democracy—all eligible voters in the area attended a meeting to select delegates for various municipal and government bodies. Now these sections began to meet regularly and take on a range of political and administrative functions. And as they controlled the local units of the National Guard they had their own armed force. A similar pattern of organisation grew in other towns and cities.[76]

Alongside, giving political direction to these organisations, grew the clubs. The Jacobin club was fairly exclusive—its high subscription at this stage ensured that its members tended to be, typically, Assembly deputies, professionals (doctors, lawyers, writers and so on), merchants and the like. But in April 1790 a club called the Society of Friends of the Rights of Man and of the Citizen was founded. It would soon become known as the Cordeliers, after the place where it met. It was led and dominated by radical bourgeois—Marat and Danton were associated with it at first. But it had relatively unrestricted admission, concerned itself with issues such as unemployment and took an active role in the surveillance of suspected hoarders and so on. In the localities popular 'fraternal societies' of a similar nature also began to spring up. By May 1791 the Cordeliers and these societies in Paris federated and formed a central committee. A new type of organised politics from below was entering the stage.

The flight to Varennes

The King had written (in secret) to the Prussian king in December 1790 asking him to convene a 'European congress backed by an army' to re-establish his authority[77] and at Easter 1791 he took the sacraments from a 'non-juring' priest. Marat, vigilant as ever, was insisting that an attempt by the king to escape and mount an armed counter-revolution was imminent. He was right.

On 20 June 1791 the king and his family escaped from Paris in disguise. They were heading for the border where they hoped to rally troops, émigrés and foreign mercenaries, and march on Paris. The plan was foiled by Drouet, a village postmaster, who recognised the king, and the escape was halted at Varennes. Silent, sullen crowds gathered as the king was escorted back to Paris. A count who came out to pay his respects to the king was murdered by his peasants. Many old illusions were being shattered.

Faced with the king's attempted flight and the spectre of counter-revolution a section of the bourgeoisie moved sharply to the left. Danton wanted the king dethroned and a regency of the Duc D'Orléans decreed. Robespierre argued for the king to be dethroned—but fudged on whether he favoured a republic. The Cordeliers club declared the monarchy to be incompatible with liberty and demanded a republic. This was accompanied by an upsurge of similar sentiments across the country and a wave of petitions from the provinces demanded the king be dethroned. All this terrified the bulk of the bourgeoisie who wanted order at all costs. Barnave, still a key leader in the Assembly, summed up their feelings when he exclaimed, 'Are we going to stop the Revolution or are we going to start it again? To take one step further would be a disastrous and culpable act. One step further in the direction of liberty would mean the destruction of the monarchy; in the direction of equality, the destruction of the concept of property.'[78]

The right rallied behind this banner and responded to the king's flight by a crackdown on the popular movement. The story was invented that the king had been kidnapped and he was reinstated after promising to accept the new constitution in future! Electoral qualifications for the Legislative Assembly, which was to succeed the Constituent Assembly, were raised to exclude about two fifths of adult men—the poorest. The crackdown became violent in July. A petition from the Cordeliers club calling for the king to be dethroned was being signed at a mass meeting on the Champ de Mars. Some 6,000 had signed when martial law was declared and National Guards led by Lafayette shot down 50 of the crowd. Wholesale repression was unleashed. Marat, not for the first or last time, went into hiding and Danton had to flee to England for a time.

The Jacobin club, until then the central focus for all but the monarchist faction of the bourgeoisie, now split. Most of the deputies who attended the club split away to form the Feuillant club under the banner 'The Revolution Is Over'. They took with them 1,800 out of the 2,400 members in Paris. Only four Assembly deputies, led by Robespierre, remained with the Jacobins. But they held on to the organisation which had grown up around the Jacobins and so its links with the popular movement. Above all, the national network of affiliated clubs remained loyal.

The Constituent Assembly broke up after adopting the new constitution and was replaced by the Legislative Assembly.[79] And though for the moment the right appeared to be dominant the impact of two years of struggle had shifted and clarified ideas enormously. In 1789 Marat was writing only that: 'Public liberty should never depend on the virtues of the prince but on the legal controls imposed on him to prevent him abusing his power'. Now he could write: 'the King of the French people is less use than a fifth wheel on a cart'.[80]

Political organisation and the press [81]

Before moving to the crisis which resulted in the overthrow of the monarchy it is worth saying a little on political organisation and the press.

As already mentioned, the Jacobin club emerged out of meetings of a group of Breton deputies to the Estates General. As the revolution developed in late 1789 and into 1790 similar groups sprang up across the country. They went under a variety of names though usually some variant of the 'Society of Friends of the Constitution'—after the overthrow of the monarchy many changed to 'Society of Friends of Liberty and Equality'. Some of the provincial clubs actually predated the Paris club but they always acknowledged it as their 'mother society', though the bigger regional clubs such as that in Marseille and the Recollets Society of Bordeaux were important in their own right and relatively autonomous from the Paris club. The clubs mirrored the more 'official' organisations—the sections, Communes and so on. In December 1789 the Jacobins agreed to accept affiliation from such clubs. The numbers grew rapidly. From 32 such clubs in March 1790 they grew to 213 by November of that year, 543 the following March and 921 by July 1791. A central activity at the meetings, which gradually became more frequent and eventually almost daily, was the reading of newspapers—often aloud for discussion. The clubs corresponded with each other and sent out circulars. All the clubs had a host of elected committees for correspondence, surveillance, education, welfare and so on.

At first they had an exclusively bourgeois membership, maintained by a relatively high membership fee.This meant parallel structures of more 'popular' clubs grew up. Such popular clubs could be large—in Lyon the 3,000 members had their own paper by the end of 1790. Later the various Jacobin clubs admitted poorer elements and they began to hold public sessions in 1790 and 1791 as well as a host of public ceremonies. The combination of centralised organisation within the network of Jacobin clubs and the flexible relationship these maintained with the popular societies frequented by poorer elements is extremely important in understanding the relative hegemony of the Jacobins within the organised popular movement. The Jacobins partly adapted to and incorporated, but always maintained a distance and independence from, the more popular clubs. The key Jacobin leaders understood the importance of this sophisticated political operation well. Jacobin hegemony was also due to the coherent ideology they propagated in contrast to any alternatives thrown up by the popular movement. This ideology (after the successive splits with Feuillants and Girondins left Robespierre, St Just, and so on as the dominant force in the Jacobins) was inspired by Rousseau's writings. It centred on the idea of all citizens uniting in the common defence of the nation, the revolution and republic in which all should have a stake and some property.

As well as the explosive growth of political organisation the press also mushroomed. The French Revolution was the first in which the press played a central role. Newspapers such as Marat's *Friend of the People* have been mentioned but there were countless others all engaging in political debate. On the eve of the revolution there were about 60 periodicals across the whole of France. By the summer of 1792 there were 500 in Paris alone, although few had big circulations. The largest circulation was around 15,000, while Marat's had a couple of thousand at most. But public readings ensured these ideas reached far greater numbers. So the peasant oriented *Feuille Villageoise* is estimated to have reached up to 300,000 people fairly regularly.

The social basis of the Jacobins is worth stressing in the light of recent 'revisionist' questioning of the idea of a bourgeois revolution in France. The clubs were usually founded by small groups of bourgeois—four people started the Lille club—though the average was around 30. The composition of the Limoges club at its foundation is fairly typical: 11 lawyers, eight wholesale merchants, six clergy, five civil servants, four rentiers, three doctors, two administrators, two printers, one editor, one engineer, one surveyor and an army officer. In other words the bourgeoisie and professional classes—though usually the lower and younger elements of the bourgeoisie—formed the core of the Jacobins.

The size of individual clubs grew rapidly. By 1791 there were over 2,000 in Marseilles. In Tonneins nine founders grew to 204 within two weeks. Officers of the clubs were usually subject to elections every month.In Lille for instance the three principal offices in late 1790 and early 1791 rotated between a salt merchant, a doctor, a lawyer, a wholesale merchant and a lace merchant. The clubs were male, though occasionally some allowed women to attend meetings. More often women's and youth's auxiliary societies were set up—later revolutionary women's clubs such as that led by Claire Lacombe in Paris developed.[82]

The size of this politically active minority varied enormously depending on the level of struggle. In areas like the south where counter-revolution was strong so were the Jacobin and associated popular societies. At its peak the numbers were huge. Some estimates put the numbers as high as one million at various points in the revolution. For instance fairly reliable estimates claim 10 to 15 percent of the population of a city like Marseilles were involved in Jacobin or associated popular clubs at the height of the 1792 crisis. More typical seems to be a figure of around 2 to 3 percent of the population in most towns in the years 1792 and 1793. This is still a huge number. The core militants who regularly attended outside of moments of crisis was of course much less but still large, in Paris in the period 1790-2 something in the region of 3,000 to 8,000.

This mass political organisation and its press were the backbone of the revolution. We know more about the events in Paris and in the Convention, but too often the fact that behind this stood real organisation right across the country, on a historically unprecedented scale, is forgotten.[83]

From social conflict to war

The Legislative Assembly sat from 1 October 1791 until the fall of the monarchy the following August. This period began with the right seeming to have carried the day behind the banner 'The Revolution Is Over'. But the growing social conflict, the determination of the old order not to accept a compromise but rather to restore its power by counter-revolution and, finally, the outbreak of war between the revolution and the rest of Europe combined to create a profound crisis which radicalised the revolution. The intervention of the mass of people, just as in 1789, was decisive. It was this which overthrew the monarchy, saved the revolution, and set it on a new course.

The Feuillant leaders were initially dominant in the Assembly and among the bourgeoisie as a whole. They all agreed that the revolution was over, even though there were splits between those around Lafayette and those around the triumvirate of Lameth, Duport and Barnave over how this closure was to be achieved. As mentioned already, they moved sharply to the right in the wake of the king's attempted flight in the summer of 1791. They were opposed by a smaller group around the

Jacobins. The Jacobins still embraced a wide spectrum from Marat through Robespierre on the left to Brissot and Vergniaud on the right.

Renewed price rises in the winter of 1791-2 fuelled by a poorish harvest and inflation were coupled with an industrial crisis—partly due to the disruption of building and luxury trades by the revolution. This resulted in riots in Paris over high prices in January and February 1792. More worrying was a new eruption of rural revolt. Armed bands of poorer peasants began descending on markets and fixing, by force, the price of corn and bread. In some areas, especially the south, this spilled over into renewed attacks on chateaux. In March Simoneau, the mayor of Étampes, was lynched by a crowd when he refused to order a reduction in the price of grain. Significantly, in many areas National Guards played an active role in the risings.

In the towns meanwhile the *sans culottes* were beginning to formulate clearer political demands. Price controls—the demand for the 'Maximum'—became the touchstone of this movement. In Paris these demands were articulated by new spokesmen and women such as the red priest Jacques Roux, the postal clerk Jean Varlet and the actress Claire Lacombe. They formed a grouping which was known as the *enragés* (literally the madmen).[84] They represented the radical petty bourgeois of the towns. Roux thundered against the big bourgeois and their 'equality', which 'is no more than an empty shadow so long as monopolies give the rich the power of life and death over their fellow human beings'.[85] The *enragés* were not against private property but against the logic of it—to foster large scale property owners at one extreme and propertyless wage earners at the other. Theirs was a utopian programme but it was an expression of the contradictions in the *real* situation of the urban sans culottes and it motivated revolutionary action. It was in the spring of 1792 that the *sans culottes* began to frequent the sections and clubs in larger numbers. Also at this time there was a worrying increase in hostility to the revolution in some parts of the countryside—especially in areas like the Vendée and Brittany in the west. Here nobles and non-juring priests were playing an active role in fomenting anti-revolutionary feeling.

In tandem with these social conflicts there began a debate over the possibility of war. This soon dominated all political debate. The threat of counter-revolution and armed intervention by foreign powers to restore the old order was the basic reason for a growing recognition of the likelihood of war. From England Edmund Burke had already launched his vitriolic attack on the revolution in his *Reflections on the Revolution in France*. The growing number of émigrés plotting and organising for counter-revolution on foreign soil added to the fears—had not the king tried to flee to take refuge with these forces and foreign kings, no doubt to make war on France? Behind all this the humiliation of Louis by the revolution and the principles it was preaching were an implicit challenge to the basis of the old order of monarchies and aristocracies across most of Europe. In August 1791 the Austrian and Prussian emperors had made this clear with their Declaration of Pillnitz which invited European powers, if they could all agree, to unite and restore order in France. It was not a threat of immediate armed intervention but was nevertheless a clear signal.[86] All of these factors combined meant that war was more a matter of when rather than if.

But though war was likely at some stage the conflict was precipitated by a coalition of forces that emerged in France which positively advocated it. There were three strands, all with different reasons for wanting war. The most important was a section of the Jacobins led by Jacques Pierre Brissot. They had several motivations. First, they hoped that war would allow the deepening social conflicts in France to be diverted into unity behind the nation under a stronger regime and so help to stabilise the revolution—a scheme the bourgeoisie have frequently resorted to since. In doing so they also hoped to expose Feuillant leaders who were, correctly, thought to be intriguing with the king and foreign powers. Secondly, they were well connected with the commercial and financial bourgeoisie for whom war loans and supply contracts were likely to be highly profitable—they certainly had been in the past. They also hoped war would increase demand and so revive the economy, providing another stabilising factor. Thirdly, war opened up the prospect of winning control of the wealth of Belgium and Holland. 'Amsterdam will soon be your treasury', argued Pierre Cambon[87]. The war would be initially directed against Austria, which controlled Belgium. But behind this was the fact that French expansion into the Low Countries would be a challenge to the French bourgeoisie's main rival—England. Daniel Guérin rightly notes: 'When the mercantile bourgeoisie...set their sights on Vienna their ultimate target was London'.[88]

Others supported war for different reasons. Lafayette, who had recently failed in his attempt to become the powerful mayor of Paris, hoped it would allow him to emerge as a military strongman and impose a settlement. The court supported war in the hope that defeat would open the door to a restoration of their power. The Queen, Marie Antoinette, when hearing of Brissot's war plans, put it bluntly: 'The imbeciles do not perceive that they are furthering our plans'.[89] Although those around Lafayette supported war the dominant Feuillant leaders around Duport, Barnave and Lameth were lukewarm because they understood the truth of this (though the queen did not, of course, confide her feelings to them) and were busy intriguing with foreign kings and Louis to defuse the growing international tension.

But the most consistent opposition to the war came from Robespierre, who fought a long duel against Brissot in the Jacobin club.[90] He argued against any notion of the use of war to 'liberate' neighbouring countries—'no one likes armed missionaries'.[91] And he argued that the war would go badly because the country was not prepared and this would plunge the revolution into a dangerous crisis with the possibility of counter-revolution. Robespierre was right on all counts, but lost the argument. Paradoxically the crisis which ensued would bring him and his supporters to power.

The second revolution

The war party was successful and the king called a Brissotin ministry to office. At its head were Jean Marie Roland and General Dumouriez. France declared war on the king of Bohemia and Hungary (in effect this meant Austria and Prussia) in April 1792 and Robespierre's predictions were rapidly borne out. The war was a disaster. Unpreparedness and disarray in the army led to defeat and large scale desertions. We now know that the French were not helped by the fact that the queen had leaked their plans to the enemy and Lafayette was trying to persuade the Austrians to suspend hostilities so he could turn his army against Paris, disband the Jacobins and establish a strong regime—with himself at the head.

The political backlash from military disaster, and the increased threat of counter-revolution as a result, exacerbated social and political conflicts within France. The Girondins—as the Brissotins were now becoming known because several of their leading members hailed from the Gironde region of south west France—thus found that the war they had advocated, far from stabilising the situation and helping them, was having exactly the opposite impact. The left, after losing the argument over war, now began to speak out again. Many, such as Marat, suspected treachery among the generals and the court. Robespierre warned the Jacobins: 'I do not trust the generals.. I say almost all of them are nostalgic for the old order of things... I have faith only in the people, the people alone'.[92] The Girondins lurched from left to right desperately trying to retain control of the worsening situation. But each twist and turn simply fuelled the crisis, did nothing to improve the military situation and thus pushed the popular movement and a section of the bourgeoisie towards the conclusion that decisive measures would be necessary to save the revolution.

First the Girondins tried to compromise with the Feuillant right and the monarchy against their critics from the left and the growing demand for radical measures. But they were rebuffed. The right and the king were hoping the chaos and military defeats would strengthen their hand. So the Girondins were forced to look elsewhere for support. This meant a sharp lurch to the left. They began attacking the 'Austrian committee' (meaning those around the queen, who was Austrian) for being in league with foreign enemies and began to stoke up the popular movement. The Girondins passed a decree allowing the deportation of non-juring priests and disbanded the 6,000 strong royal guard. They then summoned 20,000 *fédérés* (National Guards from the provinces) to a camp near Paris. The Girondins intended these as a counter to the National Guards from the richer quarters of Paris which were sympathetic to Lafayette and the right. The left feared they could be used by the Girondins against the Paris masses. Future events were to show that both had badly misjudged these *fédérés*.

These measures brought the Girondins into conflict with the king. Louis, thinking he would benefit from the military defeats and counting on support from the generals, now vetoed the decrees and sacked the Girondin ministers, installing a more right wing Feuillant team. On 16 June Lafayette stirred the pot further when he wrote to the Assembly from the front denouncing the 'anarchy' in Paris, and attacked the Jacobins for being just as dangerous as the enemy abroad

Faced with the threat of a coup from both the king and Lafayette the Girondins turned to the popular movement in Paris to save them. They further stoked up the popular movement and encouraged a show of strength to intimidate the right. They were supported by Pétion, the mayor of Paris—but Robespierre and others tried in vain to prevent what they felt would be a premature move. The result was that on 20 June an armed uprising of the Parisian *sans culottes*, led by people like the brewer Santerre, invaded the Tuileries—now the king's residence. The king was forced to drink the health of the nation and wear revolutionary symbols. But he refused to give way on his decisions to veto the decrees and would not recall the Girondin ministers. The right would not back down through mere threats. Stronger action would be needed.

The temperature was raised to boiling point on 28 June when Lafayette finally made his bid for power. He suddenly appeared before the Assembly demanding measures against the Jacobins and the popular movement. A coup looked likely, but the Paris National Guard refused to follow him and the king, thinking growing divisions in the Assembly and military defeat would continue to strengthen his position, refused Lafayette's invitation to join his troops and march on Paris. The king wanted to crush the revolution, but he had no intention of becoming a puppet ruler dependent on Lafayette.

In the growing turmoil the Girondins vacillated between denouncing royal treachery and trying to find a compromise. Fearing the right they had urged the popular movement on, but they feared it getting out of control and so now recoiled from the demon they had helped to summon. The Girondin leaders were paralysed, incapable of taking any decisive initiative. They were reduced to panic as the situation slipped out of their control and the mass of people moved to resolve the crisis by direct intervention. Vergniaud, a leading Girondin, wrote to the king desperately looking for a compromise. He warned: 'A new revolutionary explosion is rocking the foundations of a political system which has not had time to consolidate itself.'[93]

Vergniaud was right. The danger to the real gains of the revolution from external and internal enemies was awakening a massive popular mobilisation. On 21 July the Assembly, in view of the worsening war sitaution, had declared: 'A large force is advancing towards our frontiers. All those who hate liberty are taking up force against our constitution. Citizens, the fatherland is in danger!'[94] and called for volunteers to defend the country. The response was massive and immediate. Over 15,000 volunteers signed up in a few days in Paris alone and after the decree was read in public squares the pattern was repeated across the country. The patriotism of the masses was not the jingoism we associate with nationalism today. Defence of the homeland in France in 1792 meant above all defence of the revolution and the newly won and real, if limited, freedoms. The war was not against foreigners but against kings and tyrants who threatened the French, and their own people's, freedoms. Help and protection were offered to those who fought for liberty in their own countries.[95]

'Passive' citizens were now flooding into the clubs and sections everywhere. The movement did not confine itself to debates. In Marseilles and Toulon popular demonstrations and riots erupted and local officials were lynched. In Paris on 25 July the sections declared themselves in permanent session and on 30 July 'passive' citizens were admitted to the National Guard, radicalising this force and arming the more militant elements in the popular movement. Meanwhile, despite the king's veto of the Assembly's decree summoning them to Paris, *fédérés* were converging on the city from the provinces. Their temper was quite different to that expected by most in the Assembly. Many of them raised the demand for a republic and at the forefront were a group from Marseilles with their new marching song—the Marseillaise. The clubs in Paris also began to focus on the question of the king. The Cordeliers Club passed a motion demanding a convention to give France 'a constitution' and at the Jacobins Billaud-Varenne demanded the deportation of the king and elections on the basis of universal male suffrage. Links between the *fédérés* and the movement in Paris were cemented by providing officers for the provincial National Guards from Parisian clubs and setting up a central committee of *fédérés* (Robespierre was involved in these moves). Then, following the lead of the *fédérés*, the Paris sections passed resolutions demanding a republic and Pétion, the mayor of Paris, presented a petition in the name of 47 of the 48 sections to the Assembly on 3 August. It was clear that a decisive conflict was approaching.

The need for action had been made imperative by the manifesto issued by the Duke of Brunswick on behalf of the invading armies rapidly advancing on Paris. It warned of 'exemplary vengeance' and of 'handing over the city of Paris to the soldiery and punishing the rebels as they deserved'[96]. But the Girondins and the Assembly continued to vacillate. Others however were organising—a co-ordinating committee from the Paris sections and the *fédérés* had been set up to prepare for a rising. The leading Jacobins gave varying degrees of approval, often after much vacillation. Robespierre did not commit himself publicly until 29 July but then he said, 'The state must be saved by whatever means, and nothing is unconstitutional except what can lead it to ruin.'[97] The message was clear enough—a section of the bourgeois leadership would back an insurrection. The other side however were also organising and thought they could win the fight. Nobles gathered with royalist troops at the Tuileries and were counting on National Guard units from the richer quarters of the city. On 9 August the Assembly, still looking for a compromise, rejected the sections' petition for a republic. This put insurrection firmly on the agenda. That night an 'insurrectionary commune', composed of delegates from the sections, was set up—replacing the official commune.

On the morning of 10 August 1792 National Guards from the more militant sections led by the *fédérés* with the *Marseillais* at their head marched on the Tuileries. At first things went well. The defending National Guards defected and joined the insurrection. This left only the nobles and the royal troops defending the king's residence—the king himself had fled to take refuge in the Assembly. The royal troops opened fire and held off the insurgents for a while. At last the *Marseillais* led the *fédérés* and armed *sans culottes* in a direct assault and after a bloody struggle the king ordered his troops to surrender—600 royalist troops and 390 revolutionaries had been killed but the insurrection had won.[98]

When the victory of the insurrection was clear the Assembly voted to suspend the king and recognised the insurrectionary commune of Paris. The commune was enlarged and assumed effective power, at least for the moment. It was composed of hitherto largely unknown faces from the ranks of the popular movement with a sprinkling of bourgeois leaders, including Robespierre, who was elected to it. It allowed the Legislative Assembly to remain until a National Convention, elected by universal male suffrage, could decide on the fate of France, the revolution and the king.

But the victory of the insurrection was only one half of the battle. There were still other dangers to be overcome. Lafayette had tried in vain to lead his troops against Paris a few days after the insurrection and then deserted to the enemy. And the enemy was still advancing on Paris. On 23 August Longwy fell to the Prussians and on 2 September Verdun too. The Prussians were now within striking distance of Paris and many expected their imminent arrival. Few had any illusions as to the consequences if this should happen—there were already reports of local officials being summarily executed by the invading armies.

The nominal government leaders after 10 August were the old Girondins, such as Roland, recently ousted by the king and now restored on the back of an insurrection they had tried to avoid. But alongside the Commune the real power in the government was the newly installed provisional minister of justice, Georges Danton—whose appointment was meant to reassure the commune and *sans culottes*. He set about tapping the enthusiasm of the popular movement, rallying volunteers to march and halt the invaders. But as the volunteers set off for the front there was the still present problem of the counter-revolutionary forces in the rear. The king had been overthrown but was still in Paris. The city was full of ex-nobles and others who were ready to rise up, free the king and join with the advancing Prussians to crush the revolution. In particular the prisons were stuffed with royalists, often living in luxury despite their imprisonment, openly proclaiming their counter-revolutionary sentiments and under fairly lax security. It was, with good reason, feared they could break out and attack the revolution in the rear. In addition there were murmurings that the Girondin government planned to withdraw to the south of the country and leave Paris to the invaders, while the court set up to try royalists involved in opposing the insurrection of 10 August began acquitting them, which infuriated the popular movement. Already Danton had ordered a general search for arms in the houses of royalists and priests. Now as thousands set off for the front they decided that more decisive steps were needed.

In the first few days of September the gates of the city were closed, the tocsin, or alarm bell, rang, and well organised bands invaded the prisons and set up popular tribunals to deal with potential enemies behind the lines. Prisoners thought to be a danger to the revolution were executed on the spot—among them a large number of common criminals—while those not suspected of being a threat to the revolution were freed. In Paris around 1,000 to 1,400 prisoners are known to have been killed in early September. The tribunals were a popular initiative from below and were led by many of the key militants in Paris—Maillard, famous from the storming of the Bastille and the October Days in 1789, for example. And the Watch Committee of the Commune, of which Marat was now a key member, guided the movement. In the provinces similar reactions occurred and as the volunteers advanced to the front the same scenes were repeated with the support of local people in towns on the route. The motivation behind the executions is illustrated by events in Alençon, where wives of *sans culottes* went along and encouraged the tribunals to get rid of 'all those bloody aristocrats', saying, 'That gang would have taken up arms to slit our throats after the departure of our valiant youth.'[99]

Though almost all bourgeois leaders later disowned the September Massacres, it is clear that many tacitly encouraged them by not attempting to intervene—this is particularly true of Danton as minister of justice. But the fact that the tribunals had come from below and operated outside the direct control of the bourgeois leaders was an experience they were determined not to repeat. Some like Marat defended the actions. 'What is the duty of the people?', he wrote in his newspaper. 'To present itself in arms before the Abbaye (a major prison in Paris), snatch out the traitors...and put them to the sword'[100]. Referring to the government's failure to take any action against the royalist threat, he argued it was 'because the conspirators have escaped the sword of justice that they have fallen under the axes of the people.'[101] However grisly the event there is little doubt that Marat was right. To have left the rear exposed as volunteers marched to meet the invaders risked disaster and the far more brutal vengeance of the counter-revolution which would have followed.[102]

The internal threat had been dealt with. Now the external threat was halted when the revolutionary army met the Prussians at Valmy on 20 September. Meanwhile the political significance of the second revolution was demonstrated, as elections, for the first time based on universal male suffrage, took place across France. The new National Convention met in Paris on the very day of victory at Valmy.[103] The next day the monarchy was formally abolished on the proposal of the Parisian Jacobin Collot D'Herbois. Shortly afterwards France was declared the 'Republic One and Indivisible'. Year One had begun. There was no turning back—the revolution had entered a new phase.

Girondins and Montagnards

The impact of the developing revolution and the war forced the clarification of at first vaguely defined programmes, and divisions in the Convention thus crystallised. Increasingly these corresponded to the diverging interests of different classes and elements of classes. The Girondins were the largest 'organised' group in the Convention—a testimony that the mass movement which had triumphed in August and September still represented a minority in the country. They represented the interests of the higher sections of the bourgeoisie—in particular the merchants and traders of the great Atlantic seaports.[104] Their politics were based on a profound hostility to economic controls and regulation, an intense anglophobia fuelled by commercial rivalry with England and hostility to the popular movement. In the end, as the events leading up to the overthrow of the monarchy had demonstrated, this political outlook meant they were unwilling to carry through the measures necessary to successfully prosecute the war of which they had been the main advocates.

Against the Girondins were ranged the Jacobins—known now as the Mountain because they tended to occupy the upper seats in the Convention. Significantly they included 23 of the 24 deputies for Paris, the heart of the revolution, including Robespierre, Marat and, on occasion, Danton.[105] They generally reflected the interests of the lower layers of the bourgeoisie and those who had benefitted from the sale of Church and noble lands confiscated by the revolution, i.e. those for whom no compromise with, or restoration of, the old order was conceivable. They came to understand the need for centralisation and a more controlled economy if the revolution was to be defended against internal and external enemies. The central aspect of their politics was the idea of the 'Republic One and Indivisible'—the defence of the bourgeois nation state against all attempts to fragment it or restore the old order.

This position brought them close, at times, to the popular movement of the petty bourgeois *sans culottes*. 'Just look at how the rich are rallying to their support', said Robespierre of the Girondins. 'Well, they are the *honnêtes gens*, the respectable people of the Republic; we are the *sans culottes*, the rabble'.[106] The ideology of Jacobinism came to reflect this peculiar amalgam. They took on board large elements of a utopian petty bourgeois programme at the core of which was the idea of a republic of small property owners. No one should have too much property— hence a hostility to big merchants, landowners and manufacturers—but equally no one should have no property. There was no notion of collective ownership or control. This is clearly seen in the demands the Paris sections made on the Convention to 'regulate the profits of industry and commerce' and establish a maximum for personal fortunes. 'A single individual should not be permitted to own more than this maximum,' and 'No one is to own more than one shop or workshop', which 'would gradually do away with the excessive inequality of wealth and increase the number of property owners.'[107] The *sans culottes* also placed the question of a controlled economy with a maximum on prices of essential items of urban consumption at the centre of their demands.

The Jacobin bourgeoisie were prepared to acquiesce in this, partly under pressure from below but also because it came to correspond with their central policy of winning the war. For some Jacobin leaders the adaptation to this ideology was purely pragmatic. But others, Robespierre and St Just in particular, came to genuinely share the petty bourgeois dream of a republic of small property owners. In large measure it corresponded with the vision of society they, and other leading Jacobins, had derived from Rousseau. Robespierre's ideal of a 'virtuous republic' in which each citizen had some stake (i.e. property—though *not* equal amounts) but in which each was subordinate to the 'General Will' was directly derived from Rousseau's *On the Social Contract*. For a time this was the ideal vehicle for reconciling the *sans culottes* movement with the Jacobin dictatorship—representing the 'General Will'—in defence of the nation and the revolution. The whole ideology was essentially utopian. It rested upon the dream of a petty bourgeoisie upholding private property but opposing the logic of capital—which was to increasingly reduce independent small producers to dependent wage earners. But this utopianism did not prevent it from having the ability to motivate the most resolute revolutionary action.

In the Convention neither the Gironde nor the Mountain was in an overall majority. The vast bulk of the deputies were solidly bourgeois but not committed to any defined policy or faction. Rather they were prepared to back whichever seemed best to defend their interests at any time. They were known as the 'Marsh' or the 'Plain'—and were occasionally referred to as the frogs of the marsh because they hopped between various positions. The more coherent groups were always a minority of the Convention, and a smaller minority still among the bourgeoisie outside. They depended on the support, or tacit acceptance because of the lack of any immediately apparent alternative, of the bulk in the middle. This is of major importance in understanding the development of the revolution. In particular it is impossible to grasp the Terror, later in the revolution, other than in the context of a minority of the bourgeoisie imposing a programme on the bulk of their class with the backing of a popular petty bourgeois movement.[108]

The execution of the King

After the overthrow of the monarchy and the victory at Valmy the French revolutionary army won further victories. Most spectacular was the victory at Jemappes on 6 November where, even more than at Valmy, it was the unprecedented mass combat of the French which carried the day. Shortly afterwards the French army led by Dumouriez crossed the border and occupied Belgium[109].

Such successes seemed to remove the dangers which had fuelled the mass movement. Now, with the National Convention elected, the situation seemed to have stabilised. The mass movement subsided and the Girondins maintained their dominance. They even succeeded in disbanding the Jacobin dominated Parisian revolutionary commune of 10 August. The harvest was now complete, which eased the situation further, although problems could be expected later due to the shortfall caused by the disruption of the war. The Girondins, partly through money, partly through influence as the governing party, established effective control over the majority of the press. This too worked to create the impression of a new stability. Robespierre complained bitterly of this control of the press and in October launched his famous 'Letters to his constituents' to 'smuggle out the truth'.

But the stability was an illusion. First there was still the problem of what to do with the deposed king. Robespierre, on behalf of the Jacobin Club, proposed that he be brought before the Convention and sentenced to death without further ado. 'The right of punishing the tyrant and of dethroning him are the same thing; they do not take different forms.'[110] But the bulk of the bourgeoisie, though having acquiesced in 10 August for fear of a restoration of the old order or a military dictatorship, wanted to spare the king's life. Many still hoped for a compromise or partial restoration along English lines.

Circumstances, however, made this difficult. A secret chest had been discovered in the king's apartment which revealed his counter-revolutionary intrigues.[111] So the deputies had little choice but to record a unanimous verdict of guilty when Louis was brought for trial before the Convention. The Girondins then tried to manoeuvre for a stay of execution and argued for a popular referendum on the king's fate. But the Jacobins, who sensed the fundamental importance of the issue, successfully pushed for an open ballot where each deputy had to publicly record their views. This exposure to public scrutiny was sufficient to force many a reluctant bourgeois to vote for the king's death—to reprieve the king risked stirring the Parisian masses up again. Bertrand Barère carried much of the Marsh to vote with the Jacobins and by a majority of 70 a referendum was rejected and Louis condemned to immediate execution. He was guillotined on 21 January 1793.

The political significance of the execution was enormous. From now on, as publicly acknowledged regicides, the bulk of the bourgeois deputies had little choice but to defend the Republic, which was precisely what the Jacobins had sensed when they forced the issue. Robespierre's speech in favour of execution ended simply, 'Louis must die because the Motherland must live.'[112] The war now became explicitly what it had always been implicitly—a challenge to the old order of kings, queens and aristocracies across Europe. Any restoration or counter-revolution in France would now see many of the bourgeois leaders following Louis to the scaffold. 'We are on the way and the roads are cut off behind us', wrote the Jacobin Le Bas.[113]

The Girondin vacillation over the king's fate had compromised them further with the more militant elements of the popular movement. And though the temporary cessation of active combat in the war, because of the winter,[114] combined with the factors described earlier to create an appearance of stability, the problems, military and economic, were still real. In the early months of 1793 they resurfaced with a new sharpness. In February war was declared on England and then on Holland and Spain. France was now facing the combined might of all the major European powers. The opening of the spring campaign demanded still more troops, and the internal organisation of the economy to supply them, if the Republic was not to succumb.

Also towards the end of the winter the economic situation deteriorated sharply, the assignat fell to 50 percent of its face value and prices began to move up again—particularly those of colonial products like coffee, sugar, candles, soap and so on. But above all the price of bread rocketed.[115] By the end of winter grain circulation had virtually ceased and bread reached record prices, doubling in a matter of weeks. Bands of workers moved across the countryside enforcing price freezes. In the towns discontent exploded into riots in Paris, while in Lyons a movement developed in January demanding a maximum on prices. The riots usually took the form of 'popular taxation', crowds invading markets and shops and fixing prices at what they considered a fair level.

All sections of the bourgeoisie united to condemn the riots—Robespierre attacked people for fighting over 'paltry merchandise'. But the pressure forced some concessions. The Lyons Commune effectively municipalised bread supplies in the spring of 1793 and the Paris Commune agreed to fix the price of bread by subsidies[116]. By May the Mountain had declared its support for a maximum grain price in each department. The Girondins however resolutely opposed such measures, deepening the popular movement's hostility to them. This hostility took the political form of a growing demand, first formulated by the enragés, for a purge of the Girondin leaders (known as 'appellants' from their attempt to have the king's fate put to a referendum) from the Convention. The economic and political questions began to fuse once again.

The *enragés*, with some backing from the Cordeliers Club, attempted to organise a 'day' on 10 March to push through their demands. But the Paris Commune and Jacobin Club refused to give it their backing and it fizzled out. With no working class capable of acting as an independent force the petty bourgeois popular movement, however militant and radical, was incapable of acting consistently without the leadership and backing of at least some elements of the bourgeoisie. This limit on the *sans culottes* movement would be underlined again and again during the revolution.

The Vendée and the fall of the Girondins

The failure of the popular movement in early March did not remove the cause of the discontent nor lessen the demand for something to be done. In the following two months the impact of the war was to deepen this pressure from below and, most importantly, push a section of the bourgeoisie into giving it direction and leadership.

The first major development was the outbreak of full scale civil war in the Vendée region of western France. This was provoked by the Republic's attempt to recruit ever larger numbers of troops to cope with enemies advancing from all sides to crush the revolution.

The backward peasants of the wooded '*bocage*' areas in the Vendée (and other such regions) were heavily influenced by the Church. The attack on the clergy, through the Civil Constitution and the subsequent persecution of non-juring priests, had pushed many peasants into hostility to the revolution. More importantly they had benefitted little from the revolution and in particular had seen the 'republican' bourgeoisie of nearby towns grab most of the land released by the sale of confiscated property. Though this had happened elsewhere it appears to have been particularly blatant in parts of the Vendée. The attempt to drill the peasants into fighting for the bourgeois republic was the last straw. In a fairly spontaneous movement they rose across the region and stormed a number of key towns between 10 and 15 March. The rising appears to have caught nobles, plotting a rising of their own, by surprise. But they quickly assumed organisational and political leadership—revolt became counter-revolution. The Convention was panic stricken at the outbreak of civil war when it was already fighting against all Europe, but the Girondins vacillated over how to respond and it was not until May that significant military measures were taken to crush the revolt. The *Vendéens* meanwhile tried to connect the internal and external threats to the Republic by appealing to the English for help—who did not respond and so passed up what was probably their best chance of a decisive victory over the revolution. Even so, with French troops tied down on the front successive forces sent by the Republic to put down the Vendée revolt were only partially successful and the civil war in the west continued until late in the year and the advent of the Jacobin dictatorship.

The second development was a series of military disasters in the north followed by the treason of Dumouriez, the victor of Valmy and leader of the army. This was the catalyst for a new turn in the revolution. The unwillingness of the Girondins to take decisive measures to mobilise resources for the war effort was the basic reason behind the military reverses. French troops were driven out of Belgium, and Dumouriez, thinking he could succeed in the role Lafayette had failed to play, then concluded a deal with the enemy. He attacked the growing strength of the Jacobins and the popular movement in Paris as the cause of all the problems and tried to persuade his troops to follow him in a march to restore order in Paris. But for the second time the would be Caesar failed. Dumouriez' troops refused to follow him and so on 5 April he defected to the Austrians.

The treachery of the commander of the French forces, on top of everything else, provoked an enormous political crisis and a series of complex manoeuvres in the Convention. The Girondins, who had been closely associated with Dumouriez and who had basked in his earlier successes, attempted to deflect the wave of popular anger at the treachery of the general. They attacked Danton, who had been sent to negotiate with Dumouriez on the eve of his defection and was already—with some justification—suspected of wanting to make peace. But this forced Danton to defend himself and he finally broke with the Girondins and rallied to the Mountain along with his supporters—shifting the balance of forces in the Convention.

The Jacobins were rapidly coming to see that the war demanded revolutionary measures to avoid defeat. The Girondins had proved time and again they were unwilling to take such steps and so would have to be pushed aside. At first the Jacobins hoped to achieve this by 'parliamentary' means—winning the Marsh to support them. They had some success. Danton had pulled some elements behind the Mountain and now some conservative bourgeois like Lazare Carnot followed. Carnot was to become the key military organiser under the Jacobin dictatorship of the Year II, and later a key architect of Thermidor and a Director. He put the situation clearly: 'No genuine peace can be expected from our enemies, even less from those within than from those outside...we must crush them or be crushed by them.'[117] A growing awareness of the truth of this was the basis for an increase in Jacobin support among the bourgeoisie.

But the Jacobins failed to make sufficient headway in the Convention. So they had to turn to the popular movement, already demanding a purge of the Girondin leaders, to allow them to secure dominance. They had no intention of allowing the popular movement to dictate the terms of any such alliance and some voiced the fear that a too drastic purge might ensue and the 'rump' of the Convention would be powerless to resist wholesale concessions to popular pressure. The Jacobins also feared (and they were essentially correct in this) that unless the Convention was preserved as the national sovereign body the operation could leave militant Paris isolated from the provinces and threaten internal disintegration of the republic. Their opposition to the earlier attempted 'day' promoted by the enragés and the Cordeliers had underlined that their backing was essential for success. This secured effective leadership for them.

On 2 April Maximilien Robespierre proposed that charges be brought against the 'appellants' but was rebuffed. Then on 5 April Augustin Robespierre (Maximilien's brother and close associate) publicly invited the sections to present themselves at the bar of the Convention and 'force us to arrest the disloyal deputies'.[118] Within a week the sections responded by naming 22 Girondin deputies whose removal would go some way to satisfy popular demands and give the Mountain a working majority. The Jacobins had skilfully channelled popular demands into a form which would secure Jacobin leadership of the revolution.

Meanwhile a Jacobin circular to its affiliated clubs around the country, signed by Marat as the club's current president, urged them to come to the aid of Paris threatened by counter-revolutionaries and external invasion. The Girondins began to fight this orchestrated campaign against them. They used the circular as the pretext to summon Marat before the Revolutionary Tribunal—created in March. It was a move which blew up in their face. The Tribunal, under popular pressure, acquitted Marat, who was carried through the streets in triumph.

At this point Robespierre moved to further tie the *sans culottes* to Jacobin leadership by proposing a series of amendments to the Declaration of the Rights of Man. He had already argued on 3 April at the Jacobin club for a 'revolutionary army composed of every patriot and *sans culotte*' to organise and secure the supply of grain to Paris.[119] But his new proposals were more radical. They included a limit on the amount of property any one individual was allowed to own as well as a proposal for a progressive income tax, the provision of 'work or...the means of existence to those who are unable to work' and the principle that: 'When the government violates the rights of the people, the insurrection of the entire people, and of each portion thereof, is the most sacred of duties.'[120] The Convention refused to support Robespierre's proposal and the Girondin press denounced it as 'absurd and ruinous for industry'[121]. But they published it, which served to make it well known, and the Jacobin Club adopted it. The Jacobins had effectively tied the popular movement to their leadership just as conflict within the bourgeoisie was rapidly coming to a head.

But the Girondins were organising too, and round them rallied every opponent of the revolution from those favouring a restored 'constitutional' monarchy to open supporters of the old order. Richer elements began to organise in the Paris sections to back up the Girondins, while in Lyons, Bordeaux and Marseilles there were successful insurrections of 'moderates' against Jacobin led communes. The forces behind the pro-Girondin movement are illustrated by a spokesman agitating in their defence in the department of the Gard: 'Brissot, Pétion and Guadet are as much to be feared as Marat, Danton and Robespierre.'[122] Had the Girondins been victorious there is little doubt that it would have opened the door to full blooded counter-revolution.

The Girondins deepened the crisis by moving to openly attack the popular movement. Leading militants, among them the *enragé* Varlet, were arrested. Then the Girondins moved against Jacques-René Hébert, now a key figure in the Paris Commune and editor of the popular bourgeois paper *Le Père Duchesne*—named after a pipe smoking small merchant (of stoves) in popular theatre, which aptly sums up the social basis of its support. Girondin leaders threatened the popular movement of Paris with dire measures. Guadet demanded, in the Convention, the abolition of the 'anarchical' Paris Commune, which had infuriated the Girondins by ordering a progressive tax on the rich to help pay for the expenses of the war.[123] And Isnard threatened the destruction of Paris: 'People would be searching soon on the banks of the Seine to see if Paris had ever existed.'[124] The Girondins also reaffirmed their opposition to any but legal equality or any increase in economic regulation.

The ground was laid for a new trial of strength. The real fears of a right wing coup aroused by the Girondin attacks made the organising of a new 'day' an immediate question. Marat had already demanded a decree impeaching the Girondin leaders and threatened, 'If the decree is not enacted we will enact it ourselves.'[125] The Commune summoned delegates from the sections to a meeting at the Archbishop's palace and, as in the summer of 1792, an insurrectionary committee was set up. Command of the National Guard was turned over to the Jacobin François Hanriot and a militia of *sans culottes* enrolled—20,000 strong and paid by the Commune for loss of earnings while taking part in the insurrection! A first attempt to mobilise mass demonstrations on 31 May fell flat as, being a Friday, it was a workday. But then on Sunday 2 June the tocsin sounded again and this time an enormous armed demonstration surrounded the Convention. After attempting a dignified exit the deputies crumbled and accepted the expulsion of 29 leading Girondin deputies and two ministers, who were placed under house arrest.

This left the way clear for the Jacobins to assume leadership of the revolution. They were still a minority in their class and the Convention, but by allying with the *sans culottes* had pushed the majority, who shared their aim of winning the war and saving the Republic, into accepting their leadership. The revolution had moved sharply to the left on the basis of another mass 'day', the best organised of any in the whole revolution.

From crisis to the Revolutionary Government of the Year II

After the overthrow of the Girondins the revolution was faced with a near terminal crisis which was only resolved by the emergence of the revolutionary government of the Committee of Public Safety.

The civil war in the Vendée continued and 75 deputies protested against the removal of the Girondin leaders while others left Paris to organise opposition to the new regime. These forces provoked a series of effective regional secessions from the Republic and the 'dictatorship' of Paris—hence the label of 'federalists' which they were given. Normandy, Franche-Comté and much of the south, including Lyons and Marseilles, broke away. The situation in Normandy was particulary perilous given its important role in the organisation of the Parisian food supply. The Convention just managed to scrape together a force which routed a rebel group that threatened to march on Paris. But in the south the rebels went so far as to hand Toulon over to the English along with a large part of the French Mediterranean Fleet. And in the north east a string of military disasters allowed the Austrians to occupy the department of the Nord. They promptly set about restoring much of the old regime complete with feudal dues. It looked as if the Republic was disintegrating and Paris would be left isolated. The example of the Nord made clear what could be expected if the Republic fell.

The dangers of counter-revolution were graphically underlined when in July Marat, the most popular of the Jacobin leaders, was assassinated in his bath by a young royalist called Charlotte Corday. The economic situation was little comfort to the Republic either. Prices were rising again and the assignat continued to depreciate—helped by the British government's attempts to destablise the economy by sending forged assignats into France.

At first the Jacobin leaders hesitated and were indecisive in the face of this crisis. But then the revolutionary government began to take shape as a series of measures were pushed through. The Convention had set up a Committee of Public Safety following the treason of Dumouriez. Its 12 members were re-elected every month by the Convention and it was rapidly becoming the central body of government. It drew up a new constitution which was ratified in a referendum. It did not go as far as Robespierre's earlier proposals—though it did enshrine the right of insurrection against a government which 'violates the rights of the people'.

It made general welfare the aim of society, made poor relief an obligation of the state and insisted that education must be 'put within reach of every citizen'. It enshrined universal male suffrage, guaranteed 'asylum to foreigners banished from their homelands for the sake of liberty' and extended the vote to 'every foreigner who shall be judged by the legislative body to have merited well of humanity'. Finally it flung down a defiant challenge to the old order in the rest of Europe by declaring: 'The general force of the Republic is composed of the entire people. All Frenchmen shall be soldiers; they shall all be trained in the use of arms', and concluded that the Republic 'does not make peace with an enemy occupying its territory.'[126]

The constitution was put into cold storage until the return of peace. (This was not done formally until 14 Frimaire Year II, 4 December 1793, when the government was decreed 'revolutionary' until peace). But its central political purpose was achieved: to act as a rallying point against the prospect of a successful counter-revolution. On a more practical level peasants who were still conducting a fight to end the remnants of seigneurial dues, including those commuted to cash payments, had to be won to support the Republic. The civil war in the Vendée showed the danger of alienating them. So émigrés' property was confiscated, divided up into small lots and put up for sale. Common lands were allowed to be divided into small private plots. These measures were never fully implemented, not least because the division of the commons was actually opposed by significant elements of the peasantry[127].

More important was the decision of 17 July 1793 to abolish all feudal or seigneurial dues and rights completely with no compensation. At a stroke what the peasants had fought for since 1789 had been won by a combination of their own efforts and the needs of the bourgeois republic to secure itself. These measures were accompanied by the emergence of a new leadership. First Georges Couthon and Louis-Antoine St Just, militant Jacobins associated with Robespierre, joined the Committee of Public Safety. Then, in late July, Robespierre was added. These and other Jacobin leaders were joined on the committee by former members of the Marsh who had rallied to the Mountain because of their growing awareness of the need for exceptional measures if the Republic was to be saved. These included Carnot, who took charge of military organisation. The support of such people and Pierre Joseph Cambon, who took charge of finances, although not on the committee, was crucial in constructing the Jacobin dictatorship. But they only went along with it out of necessity. When the threat to the revolution seemed to be lifted by the very success of the revolutionary government, they would withdraw support.

The Committee of Public Safety was re-elected every month by the Convention, but its real strength came from the political backing won for it by Robespierre, St Just, Barère and others at the Jacobin Club and from the network of affiliated clubs across the Republic.[128] In the summer of 1793 it suppressed stock companies, raised forced loans, forbade the export of capital and made bondholders pay the price of sorting out many of the state's debts. Such measures were, of course, none too popular with the class whose interests the Jacobin dictatorship was defending. Cambon was hated by his own class as the 'executioner of bondholders'[129] and for his comment, 'War on the *chateaux*, peace to the cottages.'[130]

The popular movement was also rapidly developing in the crisis ridden summer. The *sans culottes* conducted a long fight to gain the upper hand over the richer elements in the section assemblies. They were largely successful over the summer of 1793.[131] The sections were meeting almost daily and direct democracy—through attendance at meetings, accountability of representatives to the section assembly and so on—was a distinctive characteristic of the sectional movement.

The sections demanded Terror, to root out speculators, hoarders and so on. They also demanded a more controlled economy, in particular a maximum on consumer products—above all grain and bread. There was a degree of ambiguity in demands for price controls, as many artisans, retailers and small merchants did not want controls on their own products. For them the demand was aimed against big merchants and traders and the peasants whose produce supplied the towns. The demand for 'the maximum' grew ever louder from the Paris sections. Bread became more and more expensive, when it was available at all. By late August resolutions demanding price controls and action against hoarders and speculators were flooding into the Convention.

Matters were brought to a head when massive street demonstrations erupted in Paris on 4 and 5 September. But while the dominant petty bourgeois core of the popular movement focused on prices and their position as consumers, there were some who had the beginnings of a different set of priorities. On the morning of 4 September meetings of arms workers, building workers and workshop journeymen took place demanding higher wages. The workers invaded the commune's assembly rooms, whereupon the bourgeois leaders of the commune, Hébert and Chaumette, stepped in. They proposed that there should be a demonstration the next day to the Convention to demand measures against hoarders and political suspects. The Jacobin Club and Robespierre agreed to back *this* demonstration. That evening the commune gave orders to disperse the building workers. But it instructed all workshops in the city to close the next day so that small masters and workers could attend the demonstration together.

A mass demonstration surrounded the Convention on 5 September. In response the Committee of Public Safety pushed through a series of measures which partially conceded the *sans culottes'* demands. Terror was made 'the order of the day'. On 17 September the Law on Suspects was passed. It institutionalised the sections' revolutionary watch committees power to check on possible counter-revolutionaries, speculators, suspected hoarders and the like.[132]

Within days the wearing of the tricolour cockade—symbol of he revolution—was made compulsory. Then price controls on grain and fodder throughout the Republic were announced. On 21 September a Navigation Act was passed, bringing external trade under a degree of government control. By the end of September the demands of the *sans culottes* seemed to be met when the Convention decreed the 'general maximum', regulating the prices of a whole range of basic commodities.[133]

The Terror was an integral part of this policy of a controlled economy. Much of the bourgeoisie (and the better off peasantry) were opposed to such control and regulation and had to be compelled to submit by the threat, or use, of force. In the words of the proclamation issued by Collot D'Herbois and Fouché at Lyon, 'The time for half measures and for beating about the bush is past. Help us to strike great blows or you will be the first to feel them. Liberty or Death: Reflect, and Choose.'[134] In part the Terror was directed against those who could become the focus for counter-revolution. So Marie Antoinette (the former queen) was sent to the guillotine on 25 Vendémiaire Year II (16 October 1793). Two weeks later 21 of the Girondin leaders, including Vergniaud and Brissot, followed.

The decisive measures taken by the Comittee of Public Safety began to have an effect. Slowly the tide was turned against the counter-revolution. Lyons was retaken by the Republic in Vendémiaire Year II (October 1793) and in Frimaire (December) Toulon was recaptured from the British—after a siege in which a young artillery officer, Napoleon Bonaparte, played an important role. Finally Marseilles was recaptured by the republic in Nivôse Year II (January 1794). In all cases wholesale repression followed. Some 2,000 people were shot out of hand in Lyons, for instance. Marseilles was renamed 'Town Without a Name', while Lyons was called 'Freed City' and the houses of the rich were demolished.

Meanwhile the revolt in the Vendée was finally brought under control in Frimaire and Nivôse (December 1793). And then in early 1794 the region was 'pacified' with ruthless repression. In Nantes thousands of rebel prisoners were drowned in the river on the orders of Carrier—the infamous 'noyades'. And Turreau unleashed his 'infernal columns' across the region. Thousands were killed as the Republic's troops criss-crossed the Vendée adopting a 'scorched earth' policy designed to crush any further resistance and serve as an example to other would-be rebels.[135]

Another aspect of the Terror was the organisation of the Revolutionary Armies (*Armées Révolutionaires*). These had first been mooted back in April but had come to nothing. But now, after the September days, an army of Parisian petty bourgeois *sans culottes* were recruited. It consisted of some 6,000 men—including infantry, cavalry and artillery units. They were paid for service in the Revolutionary Army but remained an essentially civilian political militia. They were composed—especially the artillery units—of stalwarts of the Paris sections and often remained under the effective political direction of the section assemblies. Commanded by Charles-Phillipe Ronsin, their function was to ensure the compliance of the countryside in the controlled economy and maintain the food supply of Paris. They spawned some 56 other similar armies around the country whose total strength amounted to something like 30,000.

As well as their economic role they spread republican propaganda wherever they went and were heartily detested by the bourgeois merchants and traders and better off peasants against whom they were directed. The armies also repressed attempts to form 'combinations' and strikes for higher wages by carters and agricultural day labourers. Their central concern was to subordinate the economy to the war effort and above all to keep the food supplies coming to the towns. In this they were largely successful, often more by the threat of their intervention than anything else—their numbers were simply inadequate for any systematic supervision of grain supplies.[136]

But if all these measures seemed to indicate that the government had conceded to the *sans culottes*' demands, there was another side to the picture. Many of the *sans culottes*' demands fitted the needs of a war economy. Winning the war was the overriding concern of the Jacobin bourgeoisie and the Committee of Public Safety. The rising of 4 and 5 September had the backing of the Jacobins, who channelled it into strengthening the central government. Robespierre put the Jacobin aim clearly:

> *What we need is a single will. This rising must continue until the measures necessary for saving the Republic have been taken. The people must ally itself with the Convention, and the Convention must make use of the people.*[137]

The war

It is worth breaking the narrative to examine the question of the war and its connection with the internal development of the revolution in more detail. As Engels noted, 'the whole French Revolution is dominated by the war... all its pulsations depend upon it.'[138]

With the revolution confronted by all the major European powers the war could only be successfully prosecuted on the basis of an unprecedented mobilisation. It was this which, in the end, enabled the French to beat off the invasions. Mallet du Pan explained the European powers' defeat simply: 'They feared their subjects almost as much as they feared the enemy.'[139] So they refused to match the French in arming the mass of their people and making the war a 'popular' fight. For the revolutionary army it was not a war to gain bargaining counters in a future peace conference, as was the norm. Outright victory and total defeat were the only options. This altered the character of the conflict. Mallet du Pan wrote at the time, 'It is a war to the death.'[140] St Just, when invited to parley with the enemy, replied, 'All that the French Republic receives from its enemies and sends them back is lead.'[141] These were the basic reasons for French victory.

The revolutionary character of the war was dramatically underlined on 23 August 1793 when a *levée en masse* of the entire nation was decreed. In memorable terms the Republic announced,

> *Young men will go to war, married men manufacture arms and transport supplies, women make tents and uniforms and serve in hospitals, children turn rags into bandages, and old people repair to the public squares, stimulate the courage of the warriors and preach the unity of the Republic and the hatred of kings.* [142]

Army battalions were instructed to march into battle carrying banners inscribed 'The French people rise up against tyrants'.[143] In all approaching one million men were enrolled in the army by early 1794—a number which dwarfed any previously mobilised in Europe. Mobilisation on this scale implied the transformation of the way the army was organised. 'Always use massive troop strength and be on the offensive…and keep pursuing the enemy until his complete destruction,' insisted Carnot.[144] It became a political force fired by ideas of nationalism. St Just told the army commanders, 'You must not expect victory from the numbers and discipline of soldiers alone. You will secure it only through the spread of the republican spirit within the army.'[145] And the real attachment to such ideas among at least part of the troops is shown by reports of wounded men blowing their brains out rather than surrender. Others, if captured, preferred to be shot rather than shout 'Long Live the King.'[146] Nor were such sentiments confined to the army. At Strasbourg St Just appealed for shoes for the army and the local population responded by handing over 20,000 pairs![147]

Of course the support for Republican ideas had a material basis. The largely peasant soldiers only had to look back and remember the old regime to see what the Republic meant to them. A foreign observer noted ruefully at the time,

Any attempt to detach the soldier from the cause of the Convention would be fruitless. Nowhere else could he find what he finds in France: liberty, pecuniary benefits and rapid promotion, subsistence, relief of all sorts... Despite their poor organisation, and their mediocre commanders, and despite their inexperience and indiscipline, they are holding their own against the best armies in Europe.[148]

Effective leadership in the army often rested with the 'representatives on mission'—Convention deputies dispatched by the Committee of Public Safety to carry through its orders. Many of these representatives led the columns of troops into battle. On several occasions they were decisive in rallying the troops and turning potential defeat into victory. St Just at Charleroi and Carnot at Wattignies were particularly important in this respect. Soldiers participated in local political clubs, and revolutionary newspapers were widely read—in particular Hébert's *Le Père Duchesne*, distinguished by its coarse language. There was also a real degree of democracy within the army at the height of the revolution in 1793 and 1794. Officers were often elected by the rank and file they led, though this did not always happen and usually only applied to the lower officers.[149]

The necessary counterpart of such a force was the total mobilisation of the economy. Troops had to be enrolled and organised; food to be produced and requisitioned along with material for uniforms, transport and other raw materials. This job was made doubly difficult by the enemy blockade which cut off vital external supplies. This task, not political vindictiveness (or some eternal law that revolution must, like Saturn, devour its own children), was the real basis of the Terror.

Church bells were confiscated for making cannons. Saltpetre needed to make gunpowder, formerly imported, was collected from walls and floors in every village. Potassium salts were refined from household ashes and soda distilled from sea salt. All businesses were placed at the disposal of the Republic and the state initiated new factories, clothing workshops, munitions factories, tanneries and saltpetre refineries where needed. New agricultural techniques, the suppression of fallow, new crops and the like were encouraged. To help with food supplies pleasure parks and gardens such as the Luxembourg in Paris were ploughed up. Labour was effectively militarised. Despite this, military demands meant there was a labour shortage and so workers were often able to push up their wage rates. Scientists too were mobilised to help the war effort. The first airborne warfare occurred when the French revolutionary army used a company of balloonists at Fleurus on 8 Messidor Year II (26 June 1794) and a semaphore telegraph was installed between Paris and the north eastern front.

To mobilise such resources and to suppress internal counter-revolution 'representatives on mission' were sent to all areas of the country. Many behaved in a bloody fashion—Carrier at Nantes, Fouché at Lyons, for example. But their central role was to organise the war economy. In this they relied on the local Jacobin Clubs and associated popular societies whose ranks formed the real backbone of the Republic and the revolution. One representative on mission(Dubois-Crancé) , when deciding on who to rely on in a particular locality, simply asked local Jacobins, 'What have you done to be hanged if the counter-revolution were to arrive?'[150]

I have already given examples of the size and composition of these clubs in the earlier part of the revolution. The numbers grew even larger in the summer and autumn of 1793. Some historians estimate there were over 1,000 clubs across the country directly connected with the Jacobins in Paris and this does not include the countless local and 'popular' societies. For instance in six south eastern departements alone (out of 83 in the country) there were over 1,000 such clubs in October 1793.[151] Total numbers involved in the clubs are difficult to estimate but a figure of over half a million is probably a reasonable guess. The *core* of Jacobin activists in the localities were middle class landowners, merchants and professionals. But as the size and number of the clubs expanded they drew in more petty bourgeois layers—shopkeepers, artisans and small tradesmen. Wage earners and peasants also flooded into some clubs at the height of the revolution.

It is important not to overstate the effective degree of control and centralisation the revolutionary government achieved. The Jacobins were bourgeois and preferred to deal with private contractors wherever possible rather than rely on direct state control. Many of the supplies to the army were organised by inviting contractors to tender and many made a healthy profit from the operation. Some areas, such as livestock sales, were never controlled at all. Again, despite the Terror, house to house searches for provisions in Paris were forbidden. And the Committee of Public Safety made almost no attempt to curb the developing black market in which the better off could buy at higher prices. Partly these limits to control and centralisation stem from the objective situation. The level of economic development, poor transport and communications and the like, set a limit to the degree of centralisation. An indication of the difficulties is that it took around two weeks to transport goods from Paris to Lyons, and 25 days to reach Marseilles.[152] Despite the immense difficulties over the winter of Year II the revolution succeeded in mobilising its resources, halting the invasions and crushing internal counter-revolution. It was a feat which astounded Europe.

It is worth putting the violent side of the Terror into context, as it has become exaggerated by counter-revolutionary mythology. Later reactionaries accused the Jacobins of being 'drinkers of blood' and of eating pies filled with human flesh—and they meant it to be taken literally. Around 40,000 people were executed during the Terror (i.e. not counting lives lost in military conflicts). The vast bulk of these were executed in regions of civil war—71 percent in the west (Vendée) or south east (Lyons, Toulon etc). Around three quarters of executions were for armed rebellion. In two thirds of the 83 departements less than 25 people were executed during the whole course of the revolution. In Paris about 2,500 people were guillotined during the revolution—over half of these during the two months of the Great Terror, Messidor and Thermidor Year II. Interestingly the biggest single 'batch' sent to the guillotine on a single day in Paris was when the reactionaries of Thermidor sent Robespierre and the Jacobin leaders of the commune to the guillotine. Of course far larger numbers, estimated up to around half a million, were killed in military conflicts in regions of civil war. The Terror in the French Revolution arose out of the fact that a minority of the population (a large minority) was imposing measures to defend the Republic in a situation of internal and external war. And, it must be said, it was the work of amateurs compared to the violence of the modern bourgeoisie.[153]

The bourgeoisie and the popular movement

Though the Jacobins were prepared to harness and use the popular movement to achieve these results they had no intention of surrendering to it. At all times they retained their central purpose of subordinating everything, including the popular movement, to the war. So the measures outlined above were accompanied by an offensive against the independent initiative of the *sans culottes*.

In September just as the government instituted the Terror and the Maximum it made the first moves against the popular movement. Section assemblies which had been meeting 'in permanence' were reduced to meeting twice a week—twice a *décade* when the new calendar was introduced. *Sans culottes* were now to be paid for attendance. This was the first step in the incorporation of a layer of *sans culottes* militants in the bureaucracy of the revolutionary government. The multiplication of official positions brought about by the Terror and the revolutionary government turned a layer of these militants into state functionaries subordinate to the Committee of Public Safety.

At the same time the government launched an attack on the enragés, the leading spokesmen of the popular movement. Jacques Roux was arrested and, after rotting in jail for months, committed suicide. Jean Varlet was arrested and then released but forced to remain silent. Theophile Leclerc too was silenced under threat of arrest. Women's societies—such as that led by Clare Lacombe which stood on the left of the movement—were suppressed. In Frimaire Year II (December 1793) the departmental revolutionary armies were suppressed and Ronsin and Vincent—leading figures in the Parisian revolutionary army and associated with Hebért—were temporarily arrested.

The popular movement was slowly being subordinated to the Jacobin dictatorship by a combination of granting those demands that coincided with the war economy, incorporating a layer of the militants in the machinery of the government and removing the movement's independent spokesmen and women. The process was uneven and slow. For instance, the suppression of the 'permanent' sectional assemblies simply led to the setting up of sectional 'societies' which met on the days when the assemblies were not allowed to meet. In effect the assemblies continued to be active under this guise for a long while.[154]

A further conflict between the revolutionary government and the popular movement arose over the issue of de-Christianisation. This has to be understood against the background of the increasing identification of the Christian religion with the old regime and counter-revolution—and there was plenty to base that identification on. The revolution and the 'Republic One and Indivisible' were about breaking from the past, creating a unified state free from local particularism, superstition and identification with Rome (or any other idea but the nation). This was what lay behind the introduction of the revolutionary calendar and a host of other proposals such as the metric system of weights and measures, hostility to dialects, banning Latin in schools and so on.[155] The role of the Church was undercut by measures such as the introduction of divorce rights and rights for illegitimate children. Local communes were given the right to renounce the Catholic religion.

But despite hostility to Catholicism most of the bourgeois leaders were convinced of the need for religious ideas of some form as an ideological cement. Whatever their own private views they followed Enlightenment thinkers such as Voltaire in recognising the social function of a mass 'religion'. The main Jacobin leaders were profoundly hostile to atheism—Robespierre had the bust of Helvétius banned from the Jacobin Club. It was out of this contradiction between anti-Catholicism and wanting a mass religion that a new civic religion began to grow. In August 1793 a ceremony venerating the 'Holy Mountain' had taken place in Notre Dame. A girl played the role of the 'goddess' Liberty, revolutionary martyrs like Marat were idolised and Notre Dame was renamed the Temple of Reason. This had the approval of the key Jacobin leaders, as did the development of patriotic festivals with processions, speeches and singing where Republican and Jacobin virtues would be celebrated.

An example of ambiguous attitude of the *sans culottes* to religion is the new version of the prayer *Our Father* they used:

> *Our father who are in heaven, from whence you protect in such an admirable manner the French Republic and the Sans Culottes, your most ardent defenders.*
>
> *May your name be blessed and sanctified among us, as it always has been.*
> *May your steadfast will, making men live free, equal and happy, be done on Earth as it is in Heaven.*

Give us today the daily bread which we eat despite the vain efforts of Pitt, Coburg and all the Tyrants united to keep us hungry.

Forgive us the faults which we have committed in supporting for so long the Tyrants from which we have purged France, as we forgive the Enslaved Nations, when they imitate us.

Do not suffer them any longer to endure the fetters which restrain them and from which they are strenuously seeking to free themselves

But may they deliver themselves, as we have done, from Nobles, Priests and Kings. So be it.[156]

Some of the Terrorists—those bourgeois leaders allied to the popular movement who demanded more systematic attacks on the old order, stricter economic controls and more ruthless repression of counter-revolutionaries, hoarders and so on—wanted to take things much further. Leading figures began banning public religious ceremonies in areas they visited or where they had influence. They often replaced them with Republican celebrations in which figures such as Brutus from the Roman Republic were idolised. Fouché and Chaumette began this process in September 1793 at Nevers and then Chaumette pushed for similar measures in Paris where he was a key figure in the commune. They secularised funeral processions and cemeteries, posting signs such as 'Death is an Eternal Sleep' on graveyards. These measures had the support of many of the urban *sans culottes* who were profoundly hostile to the Catholic Church—identifying it with counter-revolution. In Paris the commune ordered the closure of all churches on 3 Frimaire Year II (23 November 1793). Other areas followed suit.

The factions

This seemed to the Jacobin leaders to be going too far. They sensed the de-Christianisation movement was headed by forces wanting to carry economic control and Terror further than the revolutionary government wanted. These forces were also identified with a greater degree of independent initiative for the popular movement than the revolutionary government would tolerate. So to attack de-Christianisation was to attack these forces and further strengthen the government. More immediately such outright hostility to Christianity ran the risk of pushing peasants under the influence of priests and into the arms of counter-revolution. One Vendée was quite enough.

Robespierre and the Jacobins began attacking the de-Christianisers from the beginning of Frimaire (21 November 1793). Many of the leading de-Christianisers, and certainly those advocating the extension of controls and Terror, were associated with the Paris commune and Hébert— through his newspaper *Le Père Duchesne*. And so this opposition to the Committee of Public Safety began to be labelled Hébertist.

Meanwhile an opposition to the revolutionary government was

developing from another quarter. It was centred around Danton and Desmoulins and became known as the Indulgents. In contrast to the de-Christianisers and Hébertists, the Indulgents wanted an end to the Terror and economic control. They reflected the interests of those bourgeois who, though they supported the revolutionary government, were resentful of the price they were paying. Danton in particular was believed to be intriguing for peace with England (he was). The Indulgents were increasingly hostile to the Hébertists and the popular movement's constant demands for regulation and control. Desmoulins founded a new paper, *Le Vieux Cordelier*, in which he attacked the Terror and the de-Christianisers, while Danton appealed to Robespierre to 'put up the barriers' against further concessions to the Terrorists and *sans culottes*.[157]

Faced with growing opposition from the Hébertists on the 'left' and Indulgents on the right, the Committee of Public Safety vacillated. At first they swung to the right and allied with the Indulgents to curb the popular movement and its Hébertist spokesmen.

In Frimaire (November-December) a decree was issued defending freedom of worship—though in practice most churches remained closed until after Thermidor. Ronsin and Vincent—associated with the revolutionary armies—were arrested and Robespierre gave Desmoulins' new paper his blessing. On 16 Frimaire (6 December) 'revolutionary taxes' on the rich, which some local communes and revolutionary committees had been using, were banned and shortly after some food speculators were released. These moves indicate that behind issues like de-Christianisation lay more material questions. These attacks on the popular movement encouraged the Indulgents. It looked as though Danton would return to centre stage as the representative of a united bourgeoisie clamping down on the popular movement and those wanting to carry the revolution further. By the end of Frimaire there were proposals from the right in the Convention for a purge of the Committee of Public Safety and an automatic rotation of one third of its members each month.

The Committee of Public Safety saw that its attacks on the Hébertists were strengthening the Indulgents to the point where they threatened to enforce their programme of winding down the Terror and the controlled economy and suing for peace. With the winter deepening, bread and other commodities were once again becoming scarce, fuelling discontent. There was a rash of strikes in the arms factories. Any relaxation of economic control threatened massive hardship and social discontent. With the decisive battles in the war awaiting the opening of the spring campaign any such disruption, or an attempt to sue for peace, would only encourage the Republic's enemies and threaten catastrophic defeat.

So following a robust defence of the Terror by Collot d'Herbois at the Jacobin Club on 1 Nivôse Year II (21 December 1793) the Committee of Public Safety veered back to the left. Ronsin and Vincent were released in Pluviôse (January/February 1794) and Robespierre began denouncing Desmoulins' paper. St Just attacked the speculators (many were implicated in all sorts of shady financial dealings) who stood behind the Indulgents, 'Those who want to tear down the scaffolds are those who are afraid they might be forced to mount them.'[158]

The Jacobin leaders' gyrations reflected the real dilemma they faced. They were a minority of the bourgeoisie and rested on an uneasy alliance with the popular movement. They used this to impose a barely tolerated discipline on large sections of their own class to defend the bourgeois republic against counter-revolution and the restoration of the old order. The operation was inherently unstable, and it became more so the more the revolutionary government was successful in subordinating the popular movement to itself and the more successful it was in defeating counter-revolution and invasion.

The new swing to the left encouraged the Hébertists. And the Committee of Public Safety pushed through a series of measures which seemed like concessions to Hébertist demands. On 13 Pluviôse (1 February 1794) 10 million francs was voted for poor relief. Slavery was abolished outright in French colonies on 16 Pluviôse (4 February—the motion for abolition was moved by a black deputy from Santo Domingo and a black woman in the public gallery was invited to take the Assembly President's chair). Then on 3 Ventôse (21 February) a new General Maximum was decreed. Following these measures a series of decrees were announced which seemed to go further still—indeed further than many of the Hébertists or enragés had demanded. They are associated above all with St Just who presented the key report to the Convention and certainly inspired many of the ideas behind them.

The Ventôse decrees included the seizure of suspects' property for distribution among 'indigent patriots' and stiffer sanctions against food hoarders. They set out a scheme of pensions for the aged and infirm, allowances for mothers and widows with children to support and free medical assistance in the home. A scheme for poor relief in the countryside was devised—but this did not become a decree until 22 Floréal (11 May). Many of the decrees were never fully implemented—and the final versions were watered down by the Convention. But they achieved their primary purpose which was to secure wider support for the revolutionary government and the Republic at a time when it was becoming clear that the decisive battles in the war were soon to be fought. 'An unhappy people has no homeland,'[159] said St Just, spelling out the political importance of the decrees. 'Let Europe learn that you no longer wish French soil to harbour oppressors or oppressed.'[160] The decrees also partly reflected the dream of creating a republic of small property owners which was shared by the *sans culottes* and Jacobin leaders such as St Just and Robespierre.

The immediate political effect of the measures was to encourage the

Hébertists and the Cordeliers Club to believe that with only one more push they could come to power and implement their programme. Hébert began attacking Robespierre by name and Ronsin, leader of the Paris revolutionary army, began talking of the need for an insurrection. It is fairly clear that a lot of this was empty rhetoric, but when the commander of a military force talks of insurrection it is not surprising if people take him seriously! Yet again a new 'day', which would bring the Hébertists to the fore and push the revolution leftwards, looked on the cards.

But the imminent opening of the military campaign impelled the Committee of Public Safety to decisive action after their long drawn out manoeuvring between the Hébertists and the Indulgents over the winter. The war demanded 'a single will' and the factions undermined this necessary unity. But it was clear, from the experience of the winter, that to attack the left alone could strengthen the right to the point where they could impose their programme on the Republic. Similarly, the only solution to the government's dilemma was to crush both oppositions simultaneously. They carried this out successfully in late Ventôse and early Germinal Year II (March 1794), but it left the revolutionary government dangerously isolated on all sides when the emergency of the war appeared to pass.

First the government turned on the left. Hébert, Ronsin, Vincent and others were arrested and hurriedly executed on 4 Germinal (24 March) after a brief trial. Three days later the Paris revolutionary army was disbanded. Shortly afterwards the Paris Commune was purged and had its powers sharply reduced and the Cordeliers Club reduced to insignificance. Similar attacks on the 'Hébertists' took place across the country. Popular newspapers were burnt and from Lyons to Le Mans and Le Havre local communes and popular societies were purged and Hébertists arrested. The *sans culottes* did not respond to this attack on their spokesmen and their 'army'. Why?

Partly, the Hébertist leaders were not connected with the popular movement to the same degree as the enragés, whose leading spokesmen the revolutionary government had curbed several months earlier. The Hébertists were bourgeois whose difference with the main Jacobin leaders was one only of degree. True they articulated many *sans culottes* demands, but they were not *of* the popular movement itself. This difference is well illustrated by the fact that Hébert had denounced Jacques Roux at the Jacobin Club during the government's campaign against the enragé leaders (Marat too, shortly before his assassination, had attacked Roux). Secondly, the *sans culottes* agreed with the importance the Jacobin leaders placed on prosecuting the war. With the spring campaign about to open everything must be subordinated to that, the Jacobin leaders argued—the only hope of winning the war and defending the revolution was to preserve the authority of the revolutionary government. It was a powerful argument. Thirdly, the attacks on the popular movement of the previous months had a real effect. The removal of key spokesmen such as the *enragés*; the curbing of the sectional assemblies; the incorporation of a layer of section militants into the administrative machinery of the revolutionary government; the thinning of the militant *sans culottes* ranks caused by the *levée en masse*, all these had sapped the will and independent initiative of the popular movement.

The victory of the revolutionary government over the popular movement was underlined when, under government pressure, a succession of sectional popular societies 'voluntarily' pronounced their dissolution in Floréal (April-May). The popular movement which had driven the revolution forward was exhausted. When the bourgeoisie decided the Jacobin dictatorship was no longer necessary, the Jacobins could no longer look to the popular movement for support against their own class, as they had done in the past. St Just prophetically noted the change in atmosphere around this time: 'The revolution is frozen solid.'[161]

But, more immediately, after crushing the 'left' the real danger was that the Indulgent right would now be irresistible. So six days after the execution of the leading Hébertists the leaders of the Indulgents, including Danton and Desmoulins, were rounded up. After a hurried trial—largely on trumped up charges like the Hébertistes—they were dispatched to the guillotine. Thus the Committee of Public Safety crushed all opposition and strengthened its authority in time for the decisive battles of the spring. But as Mallet du Pan wrote at the time, 'its tyranny will be forgiven by the bourgeoisie only as long as it is successful'. He could have said 'and only until it is successful'.[162]

Victory and Thermidor

When the military campaign of 1794 opened it went badly for the Republic at first. The strain of the total mobilisation was beginning to tell. Carnot expressed the general feeling when he said that the war must be finished that year or 'we should die of hunger and exhaustion'.[163]

Meanwhile despite successes against the counter-revolution in the south and west the internal threat was still present. On 26 Germinal (15 April) nobles and foreigners were banned from residing in Paris and fortified towns out of fear of counter-revolution. Then in Prairial (May) royalists attempted to assassinate Robespierre and Collot d'Herbois. This was followed by the two months of the Great Terror—which accounted for more than half the 2,500 victims of the guillotine during the revolution in Paris. It is often suggested that this was a measure of desperate vindictiveness, in revenge for these assassination attempts, by the isolated dictatorship of the Committee of Public Safety. Though the assassination attempts undoubtedly fuelled the atmosphere, the real reasons were rather different.

Firstly, as in September 1792, the enrolment of troops to go to the front led to real fears about a 'fifth column' at home. In particular these fears were encouraged by the large number of suspected hoarders, *ci-devants* (as the former privileged orders were called) and the possibility of mass prison escapes. The nightmare was that internal rebellion would link up with the foreign invader. The consequences of military defeat were spelled out by the British prime minister, Pitt, who had 'concluded in favour of the total destruction' of the Republic—it was to be 'wiped off the face of the earth'.[164] Robespierre claimed he did not have the will to live and the situation looked desperate for the revolutionary government, so much so that St Just was summoned back to Paris from an important mission to the front.

Secondly, the decrees of Ventôse required a stepping up of the Terror in all its aspects. To identify suspects, assess their property and confiscate it and to identify the means of satisfying the other decrees meant using the state apparatus against a largely resentful bourgeoisie. Though the decrees were only implemented to a very limited degree, they had enough impact for St Just to be bitterly attacked by the richer bourgeois for 'despoiling the rich to shelter and clothe the poor'.[165]

On 22 Prairial (10 June) the Revolutionary Tribunal was reorganised to speed up the processing and sentencing of suspects. The only possible verdicts became not guilty or death. Couthon justified the new law because of the exceptional circumstances the beleaguered revolution found itself in: 'It is a matter less of punishing them (enemies of the revolution) as of annihilating them...it is not a question of making a few examples, but of exterminating the implacable satellites of tyranny or of perishing with the Republic.'[166]

But suddenly the entire situation was decisively altered when the French repelled the Austrians at the Battle of Fleurus on 8 Messidor Year II (26 June 1794). A French defeat would have been catastrophic and opened the way to Paris and counter-revolution. But victory turned the tide and the French resumed the offensive in the war. Within weeks they had cleared all the invading armies from France. The Spanish were forced back across the Pyrenees, while in the north French troops swept the enemy out of the Republic and reached Liège and Antwerp on 9 Thermidor (27 July)—a significant date. The subordination of the entire economy to the war effort by the revolutionary government had borne fruit. But with victory, the rationale for the revolutionary government had gone. The bulk of the bourgeoisie no longer felt the need to submit to the discipline of the controlled economy and the Terror. They felt safer in beginning to question the revolutionary government now that the popular movement and the 'wild men' of the Paris Commune had been curbed by the revolutionary government itself. The bulk of the bourgeoisie tolerated Jacobin dictatorship only while the alternative—defeat and the restoration of the old order—seemed worse. With that threat now, temporarily, lifted it only needed a suitable political crisis to open the way to a decisive shift in the balance of power within the bourgeoisie.

The immediate cause of the crisis which led to the downfall of the revolutionary government was the growing division within the government itself. Robespierre, backed by St Just and Couthon, was moving to curb the most zealous Terrorists. This was not because he was against the Terror, far from it, but because he saw it as subordinate to the needs of the war. Controls on the economy and the like were an expedient, not an end in themselves. Already Robespierre and his allies had recalled a number of the most notorious Terrorists from the provinces, such as Fouché, Tallien and Barras, to account for their excessive zeal. They were attacked as rascals 'whose hands are full of the wealth of the Republic'[167]—Tallien, at Bordeaux, was widely suspected of corruption. On 26 Messidor (14 July) Fouché was expelled from the Jacobin Club and three days later Tallien suffered the same fate.

Alongside this development members of the Marsh were regaining confidence and increasingly resented the revolutionary government. And inside the Committee of Public Safety itself there was a growing split. Carnot, who rallied to the Mountain when the war demanded exceptional measures, was now rapidly moving away from the Jacobin 'ideologues' like St Just and Robespierre. On the other hand Collot D'Herbois and Billaud-Varenne within the committee identified with the threatened terrorists. Added to this was a series of squabbles over who was responsible for 'police' matters between the Committee of Public Safety and the other 'great' committee, that of General Security. Of course all these personal differences within the government reflected larger currents of opinion within the bourgeoisie.

In the face of these divisions Robespierre had withdrawn from the Committee of Public Safety at the end of June. From then until his downfall at the end of July he appeared exclusively at the Jacobin Club and, more rarely, the Convention. We still do not know precisely why he behaved in this fashion, fatal to him and the whole revolutionary government. The underlying explanation, whatever the immediate motives, is that he was paralysed by the situation itself. The revolutionary government had outlived its use and the 'virtuous Republic' he advocated was utopian.[168]

But what is certainly true is that Robespierre's behaviour allowed the various factions to present him as responsible for all the ills of the country and as harbouring ambitions for a dictatorship. In his role as President of the Convention he had overseen the Festival of the Supreme Being in Paris on 20 Prairial Year II (8 June 1794). This was an attempt to substitute an official 'natural' religion, based on reverence for nature, virtue and so on and derived from Rousseau's ideas—for Christianity. It was politically designed to mediate between the still powerful de-Christianisers and Catholicism. But Robespierre's presiding role and his withdrawal from the Committee of Public Safety's day to day business allowed his opponents to present him as the would be 'Pope' of the new religion. They claimed that this was all part of his scheme to become a dictator.

As news of further French victories came, the lifting of the siege mentality further encouraged the divisions and squabbles within the bourgeoisie. Matters were suddenly brought to a head on 8 Thermidor (26 July) when Robespierre, after a long absence, appeared at the Convention, denounced his opponents and demanded unity of government. He called for the removal of a few people who were threatening the unity of the Republic and undermining the revolutionary government. His targets were almost certainly the Terrorists. When he repeated the same speech that evening to the Jacobin Club the 'few people' were easily identified by the Jacobins. They drove Collot d'Herbois and Billaud-Varenne—the leading Terrorists within the Committee of Public Safety—out of the club.[169] But in appealing to the Convention Robespierre made the bourgeoisie of the Marsh the arbiters of the fate of the revolutionary government, just at the time when they were coming to the conclusion that they need submit to it no longer. Though his speech in the Convention was well received at first, his obstinate refusal to name the 'few people' fuelled fears among the Marsh that a drastic purge of the Convention was intended. This threw the Marsh and the threatened Terrorists together in an alliance against Robespierre and his closest colleagues.

It was clear that the next day would be decisive. Robespierre and St Just prepared a lengthy report to the Convention. The Terrorists decided that unless they acted they were in danger of elimination. The Marsh was now ready to throw off the shackles of the revolutionary government. When Robespierre and St Just tried to speak in the Convention on 9 Thermidor (27 July 1794) they were drowned out by an organised disruption led by Tallien and Collot d'Herbois. Then, following a well organised plan, a motion was moved (by an obscure former Dantonist) to arrest Robespierre, St Just, Augustin Robespierre and Couthon. With the backing of the newly confident Marsh this was passed. Phillipe Lebas, a young associate of St Just, leapt to his feet: 'I will not share in the infamy of this decree. I demand to be condemned with my colleagues.'[170] They were all led away under arrest.

But the fight was not over. The Robespierrist Paris Commune declared itself in a state of insurrection and appealed to the sections to come to its aid. The Convention issued a similar appeal. All during the day conflicting orders to the armed force of the sections flew around the city and arguments and debates raged. At first it looked as though the Robespierrists were gaining the upper hand. The warders of the prisons refused to accept Robespierre and the other prisoners. They were set free and by the evening the accused Jacobin leaders reached the City

Hall and were joined by around 3,000 National Guards with 30 cannons—a formidable force. The Convention had also imprisoned the Jacobin commander of the National Guard, Hanriot, but he was released by a military raid.

The force defending the Jacobin leaders was confused and less than enthusiastic. And the leaders vacillated—the only way to save themselves and the revolutionary government would be to launch an outright attack on the Convention and disperse it altogether. But this would destroy the very body the revolutionary government existed to defend against counter-revolution. More immediately, to disperse the Convention threatened the unity of the Republic. Federal disintegration and civil war would surely follow and Paris would be left isolated. While the Jacobins' leaders vacillated, many sections rallied to the side of the Convention and more stayed neutral.[171] Why?

The government's attacks on the popular movement had taken their toll and have already been mentioned. Secondly the Maximum, demanded by the *sans culottes*, had in practice hit many of them as much as those they intended it to be used against. And the revised Maximum scales published in the spring of 1794 had increased the profits allowed to merchants and traders, undercutting popular support. Thirdly, on the eve of Thermidor the Robespierrist commune had finally applied the Maximum to wages after holding off for several months. Many workers had pushed wages up due to the labour scarcity created by military demand. To apply the Maximum would mean a real cut in wages of up to half for a large part of the population. The commune finally imposed the new rates on 5 Thermidor—a particularly ill chosen moment for the government.

The lack of popular enthusiasm for the revolutionary government and the lack of decisive leadership allowed the initiative to pass to the other side. They rallied many of the sections, particularly from the richer western half of the city. Slowly, after hours of inactivity, the force defending Robespierre and his colleagues began to melt away. By two in the morning of 10 Thermidor Paul Barras and a force loyal to the Convention entered the City Hall without resistance. Lebas and Augustin Robespierre committed suicide, while Maximilien Robespierre tried to shoot himself but only succeeded in shattering his jaw. He, Couthon and St Just were bundled away and executed. The next day the Jacobins were purged from the Paris Commune by the 'Thermidorians'—71 people were executed, the biggest batch on any day of the revolution. The revolution lurched sharply to the right after Thermidor. Robespierre, in one of his last speeches, had, prophetically, warned, 'Slacken the reins of the revolution for one moment and you shall see military dictatorship take over.'[172]

The meaning of Thermidor

Considerations of space mean the five years from Thermidor to Napoleon
Bonaparte's coup d'etat of 18 Brumaire Year VIII (9 November 1799)
will be dealt with more briefly than the earlier phases of the
revolution.[173]

Many on the left of the popular movement welcomed the overthrow
of Robespierre—including Varlet, the former *enragé*, and Babeuf (of
whom more in a moment). They thought that now it would be possible
to return to greater direct democracy and the promises of 'the constitution of 1793'. When Robespierre and his supporters were guillotined
eye-witnesses report the crowd shouting, 'Down with the Maximum',
thinking that an end to the controls of the revolutionary government would
benefit them.[174] Equally the Terrorists who had been centrally involved
in the direct organisation of Thermidor thought things would develop
to their advantage. Barère argued on 10 Thermidor that the previous
day's events were 'a slight commotion which left the government intact'.[175] Both groups were soon disabused of such illusions.

Whatever the immediate causes and forces involved, Thermidor
represented the reassertion of power by the bulk of the bourgeoisie—the
Marsh and former Dantonists and Girondins. They soon showed their
dominance by dismantling the revolutionary government.

They moved cautiously and slowly. Gestures to the popular movement
were made, such as placing Marat's remains in a place of honour in the
Panthéon. But the real work of the Thermidorians proceeded
systematically. The power of the two great committees was severely cur-
tailed (7 Fructidor Year II—24 August 1794). An offensive against the
Jacobins culminated in the closure of the Jacobin Club on 22 Brumaire,
Year III (12 November 1794). This was accompanied by the return of
the surviving Girondin deputies to the Convention (18 Frimaire Year
III—8 December 1794). Meanwhile revolutionary committees and the
like in the sections were sharply curbed and sans culottes systematically
excluded and on 4 Nivôse, Year III (24 December 1794) the Maximum
was finally abolished, giving free rein to bourgeois merchants and
speculators again. The confidence of the new regime was bolstered further by the French occupation of Amsterdam on 1 Pluviôse, Year III
(20 January 1795). Just over two weeks later the new order was symbolised when Marat's remains were removed from the Panthéon—one
of the most powerful symbols of the radical phase of the revolution could
be trampled on with impunity.

The right drew confidence from all this. They were further encouraged
by the release of former 'suspects'. The *jeunesse dorée* (gilded youth)—
bands of thugs composed of the sons of the richer bourgeois—began to
systematically harass and beat up Jacobins. The Terrorists who had con-
spired to overthrown Robespierre had the reality of the new balance of

forces sharply brought home to them when on 12 Ventôse Year III (2 March 1795), Barère, Billaud-Varenne, and Collot d'Herbois—former members of the Committee of Public Safety—were arrested.

The dismantling of the controlled economy caused increasing hardship for the mass of the population in the winter of the Year III. Combined with the clearly reactionary nature of the new regime this began to awake the sans-culottes from the passivity with which they greeted the overthrow of the revolutionary government. Many began to regret the fall of Robespierre. An arrested carpenter put the growing feeling clearly: 'While Robespierre reigned blood flowed and no man went short of bread.'[176]

In the spring of Year III (March-May 1795), the popular movement rose for the last time in the revolution in an attempt to challenge the dominance of the Thermidorian bourgeoisie. First on 12 Germinal Year III (1 April 1795) thousands of *sans culottes* demonstrated in the Faubourg St Antoine and then marched on the Convention. They demanded 'bread and the constitution of 1793', the reopening of the popular societies and release of imprisoned Jacobins. But now the limitations of the petty bourgeois popular movement were graphically exposed. In the past such 'days' had been successful because a section of the bourgeoisie, albeit under pressure, had allied itself with the popular movement and given it leadership and a programme for government action. But with the overthrow of the Jacobins and the now united opposition of the bourgeoisie it was incapable of going beyond revolt. With no clear programme and leadership the movement fizzled out after briefly invading the Convention. The same night a decree was passed deporting Billaud-Varenne, Collot d'Herbois and Barère to the 'dry guillotine' of Guiana. The arrest of Cambon, another former member of the revolutionary government, was ordered. The bourgeoisie was destroying any possible rallying point for the popular movement.

But the conflict was still unresolved and the discontent which had fuelled the revolt continued. Growing hunger and food riots in many towns made it clear that a final and decisive trial of strength between the popular movement and the bourgeoisie was still to be fought. The bourgeoisie prepared well. Thousands of regular troops were brought into Paris—significantly, for the first time since 1789. The conflict erupted on 1 Prairial Year III (20 May 1795). The tocsin sounded and the *générale* was beaten in St Antoine for what was to be the last time in the revolution. Hungry crowds gathered and were joined by the armed force of the sections. An enormous crowd set off for the Convention. The crowd invaded the Convention and killed a deputy—sticking his head on a pike to try and impress the urgency of their demands on the deputies. But once again without the backing of a section of the bourgeoisie the movement was paralysed. The movement was demanding measures *from* the government. It did not have any notion of *overthrowing* the government and taking power.[177] After a stalemate lasting several hours the Convention summoned troops and National Guards from the richer western sections and dispersed the crowd.

The next day was quiet but the Convention was assembling troops to crush the movement and the Faubourg St Antoine once and for all. Over 20,000 National Guards (selected from among those 'who had a fortune to lose'[178]) joined with regular troops and on the morning of 4 Germinal (23 May) marched on St Antoine. They were met with barricades and it looked as though a bloody battle was on the cards. But the same paralysis which prevented the movement from going forward also crippled the possibility of real resistance. After a few hours stand-off the troops were able to dismantle the barricades and occupy the Faubourg without resistance. It was the end of the popular movement in Paris and marked the consolidation of the new bourgeois order.

Following Prairial a White Terror was unleashed against Jacobins and *sans culottes*.[179] In Paris alone 1,200 were imprisoned in a single week and 36 sentenced to death for their part in the Prairial rising. In the provinces the reaction was even worse—tens of thousands of Jacobins were rounded up. In the south east Companies of Jesus—right wing terror groups—hunted down Jacobins 'as though they were partridges'.[180] At Lyons, Marseilles and Nîmes and a host of other towns there were massacres of Jacobins, while in Toulon an attempted *sans culottes* insurrection was brutally crushed. The tide of reaction was now in full flow. The National Guard was purged to make it solidly bourgeois and the churches were allowed to reopen. Former federalist rebels were pardoned and property restored to many counter-revolutionaries who had been sentenced to death or deported. Non-juring priests flooded back into the country to foment open counter-revolution until 'they swarmed like the locusts of Egypt in every department'.[181]

The real danger of full blooded counter-revolution was shown when in Messidor Year III (June 1795) the English finally mounted an invasion at Quiberon in the counter-revolutionary stronghold of western France. Though this was quickly routed by the Republican armies, led by the former 'Maratiste' Lazare Hoche, attempts at royalist uprisings were made in Franche-Comté and the south, while the rebels in Vendée and the Chouans in Brittany once more took up arms. But now the real nature of Thermidor was revealed. It was reaction, not counter-revolution, a sharp move to the right, but on the basis of bourgeois rule, *not* a restoration of the old order.

In the face of the growing strength of openly counter-revolutionary forces the Thermidorian bourgeoisie began to change tack. They released former Terrorists and passed a series of decrees in early Vendémiaire Year IV (late September 1795): against anyone attacking the sale of 'national property' (church and other confiscated property from whose sale many bourgeois had benefitted); against anyone advocating a restoration of the monarchy; confirming sanctions against émigrés and non-juring priests. These measures quickly brought matters to a head by provoking a royalist uprising in Paris, based mainly in the richer western sections and backed by a motley collection of landlords, racketeers and rentiers.

On 13 Vendémiaire (5 October 1795) 25,000 joined an armed royalist demonstration which marched on the Convention. Significantly, the *sans culottes* refused to join the movement. Despite their suffering at the hands of the Thermidorean regime they knew that a restoration would be far worse. The defence of the Convention was entrusted—as in Thermidor— to Barras. He was assisted by General Bonaparte—who until then had been kept out of any real role in the army after he was briefly imprisoned as a Robespierrist sympathiser following Thermidor. The 5,000 defenders were heavily outnumbered by the royalist insurrectionaries, but the troops stood firm and dispersed the insurrection with artillery fire—Bonaparte's 'whiff of grapeshot'. Around 300 were killed and the rising crumbled away. But repression was limited and most of the leading elements were allowed to slink away unmolested. Paris, however, remained under military occupation. The Convention had survived thanks to, and now depended on, the army—a telling pointer to the future.

Prairial Year III and Vendémiaire Year IV between them sum up the basis of the post Thermidor regime—the bourgeoisie firmly in the driving seat, dismantling the controls of the revolutionary government, crushing the popular movement but also still maintaining the gains of the bourgeois revolution.

The Directory

The Thermidorian bourgeoisie attempted to give shape to their new order through a new constitution, adopted on 1 Vendémiaire Year IV (23 September 1795). Boissy d'Anglas, introducing it in the Convention, summed up its basic arguments: 'A country governed by men of property belongs to the social order, whereas one governed by men of no property reverts to a state of nature.'[182] The Convention must 'guarantee the property of the rich' and resist 'the fallacious maxims of absolute democracy and unlimited equality which are without doubt the most serious threats to true liberty'[183].

The constitution was accompanied by a new declaration of Rights and Duties—the addition of duties is significant. The right of insurrection was withdrawn and, it declared, 'the maintenance of property is the foundation of agriculture, production, every kind of labour and the entire social order'[184]. The universal male suffrage of the Year II was withdrawn and the franchise restricted—though not as much as it had been in 1791. And it was still far wider than elsewhere in Europe. The Assembly was divided into two chambers: a Council of 500, all aged 30 or above, and a Council of Elders, 250 deputies aged 40 or above.

This was a deliberate attempt to shift control to older, more conservative elements in reaction to the memory of the youthful leaders of the Year II. Executive authority was vested in five Directors, each holding office for five years. The first Directors were Barras, Reubell, La Révellière, Letourneur and Carnot. All were regicides, a clear indication that restoration of the old order was out of the question. To guard against a royalist 'coup' through parliamentary means the Convention decreed that two thirds of the members of the new councils had to be existing Convention deputies.

But the new order remained chronically unstable. Though the war had moved from the defensive to a war of expansion fought outside France, it continued to feed financial and economic crisis at home. The instability was compounded by the election of one third of the deputies in the Councils each year. The constant series of elections amplified any shifts in the balance of forces. In the winter of Year IV (1795/96) the assignat finally collapsed, and its successor, the *mandat territorial*, suffered the same fate within six months. Even beggars refused paper money which was, literally, worth less than the paper it was printed on. Prices rocketed and the new rich flaunted their wealth during a winter that was unbelievably miserable for the poor. The bread ration in Paris fell to 75 grammes and the rice it was supplemented with could not be cooked for lack of firewood. In such circumstances the regime veered wildly from left to right, trying to balance between Jacobin revivals and royalists. Increasingly the regime relied on the army. The generals became the ultimate arbiters of political disputes.

Immediately after the crushing of the royalist uprising of Vendémiaire the Directory swung to the left. Many former Jacobins were released and the Club du Panthéon was founded—a new umbrella for Jacobins. Though its high subscription meant it remained solidly bourgeois, with around 7,000 members in Paris, it attracted growing numbers of ordinary people to its debates. But after their swing to the left the Directory now worried that the desperate economic situation would allow the revived Jacobins to connect with popular discontent. So, in Ventôse Year IV (February 1796), they clamped down and ordered the closure of the Club du Panthéon. The orders were carried out by General Bonaparte, despite his proclaimed Jacobinism. This display of loyalty to the regime played no small part in securing the position of Commander of the Army of Italy for Napoleon, from where he increasingly dictated the foreign policy of the Republic.

Babeuf and the Conspiracy of the Equals

Within the brief Jacobin revival of the winter of Year IV a radically new set of ideas developed. At the time it was only a minor episode but it is important as it pointed to the future. The key figure was Gracchus Babeuf, a parish clerk from Picardy, and his newspaper *Le Tribun du*

Peuple. Babeuf had earlier been attracted by the idea of the agrarian law—the equal division of the land into small private plots, supposedly based on the laws of the ancient Roman Republic. But now he argued that private property meant this would not help 'even for a day, since, on the morrow of the enactment of that law inequality of possessions would reassert itself.'[185]

Babeuf had grasped that private property and equality were incompatible and now argued that only a system of collective ownership could guarantee social equality. It was necessary

> to establish the communal management of property and abolish private possession, to place each man in the craft for which his natural abilities fit him, to compel him to deposit the fruits of his labours in a common warehouse and to institute a simple method of distributing commodities in which a record would be kept of all persons and goods and the latter would be shared out with scrupulous exactitude.[186] ...a people who had no property would have no need of the large number of laws which the societies of Europe groan under.[187]

Production in Babeuf's society would still be on a largely individual basis and Georges Lefebvre correctly describes Babouvism as 'distributive communism'. Nevertheless it marks a decisive step beyond the utopianism of the popular movement in the French Revolution. But Babeuf is not just important for the revolutionary nature of his ideas. He had learnt the lessons of the defeat of the *sans culottes* movement in the Year III—after which he was imprisoned for a time. He recognised that if the mass movement was to be successful it needed an organised, determined and clear sighted leadership with a programme for reorganising society. So he set about organising the Conspiracy of the Equals, the first attempt to build a revolutionary political organisation committed to collective ownership of property.

A small tightly knit, and secret, group of revolutionaries formed the core. Around this were concentric layers of supporters and sympathisers who were only partly aware of the full aims of the Conspiracy. The idea was to launch an insurrection based on this minority of activists and institute a popular dictatorship which would set about building Babeuf's communist society. Babeuf claimed the Conspiracy could count on some 1,700 supporters in Paris. It issued pamphlets and posters and, as well as Babeuf's own paper, it used Maréchal's *L'Éclair du Peuple* and Antonelle's *Journal des Hommes*.

In practice the Conspiracy drew in a layer of ex-Robespierrists, such as Buonarotti and Darthé. It rebuffed advances by the Director Barras and the ex-Terrorist Tallien who wanted to use it to further their own ambitions. But however new the ideas and organisation of Babouvism the social basis of the Conspiracy was still the petty bourgeois *sans*

culottes—artisans and shopkeepers.[188] This gap between the ideas of
Babeuf and the social base of the movement explains the ambiguity of
the stated politics of the Conspiracy[189] and the gap between the nucleus
of leaders and the followers.

In the winter of Year IV Babouvism briefly became a real force
attracting the support of those driven to revolt by the harsh conditions.
After the closure of the Club du Panthéon Babeuf decided that action
was needed or the chance would be missed. He formed an Insurrectional
Committee to prepare for a rising.

But the Conspiracy was smashed before it could put its plans and ideas
to the test. The Babouvists had paid special attention to the military and
had won influence in some regiments. This alarmed Carnot, who knew
more than anyone the importance of the army, in particular and he played
the central role in crushing Babouvism. Also in the eyes of many of the
bourgeoisie Carnot was still tainted by his role at the centre of the
revolutionary government of the Year II. He hoped to bury his 'black
legend' by showing his class he would guarantee their order. A police
spy betrayed the Babouvists' plans to Carnot and on 21 Floréal Year
IV (10 May 1796), the key leaders were arrested.

In the aftermath of this repression those, mainly Jacobins, who had
been waiting for the signal to action fell into confusion. A few months
later some of them made one last desparate attempt to change the course
of events by trying to initiate a mutiny in the army. In Fructidor Year
IV (September 1796), a few hundred of them approached an army camp.
Carnot knew of the plan and let it proceed. The Jacobins were met with
a hail of bullets as they drew near. Thirty were shot out of hand and
widespread repression followed. Finally, after a long drawn out trial
Babeuf and Darthé were guillotined on 8 Prairial Year V (27 May 1797),
while Buonarotti and six others were deported.[190]

It was impossible for Babouvism to bridge the gap between the notion
of collective control of society and the real social forces which existed.
But it was a pointer to the future and, in that sense, forms part of our
tradition. Its limitations could only be overcome with the development
of a new social force, the proletariat, which the success of the French
Revolution helped create.

From the Fructidor Coup to Brumaire

The crushing of both Babouvism and the Jacobin revival fuelled a royalist
upsurge. In the partial elections of Germinal Year V (March 1797),
constitutional monarchists won most of the seats. The Assembly, born
of the revolution, now had a royalist majority! Royalists were elected
to preside over both Councils. It looked as if a restoration by
parliamentary means was possible.

The bourgeoisie was still deeply split and many who had kept their
heads down in the revolutionary storms of 1792 and the Year II now

re-emerged. The divisions were paralleled among the Directors. Carnot, rapidly moving right and now a near royalist, was joined as a Director by the constitutional monarchist Barthélemy. Barras vacillated while the remaining two Directors, Reubell and La Réveillère, favoured strong action to preserve the Republic. But what action? An appeal to the people conjured up the horrors of the Year II for the Thermidorian Republicans. And now the Jacobins were too weak to tip the balance. The generals were the only force the Republic could rest on. Generals Bonaparte and Hoche (both former Jacobins, the former an 'ex-Maratiste' the latter an 'ex-Robespierrist') backed the Republicans. Hoche sent part of his army to Paris, while Bonaparte sent his lieutenant, Augereau. Meanwhile Barras finally threw his lot in with his more determined colleagues on the Directory.

On 18 Fructidor Year V (4 September 1797), the Republic was saved by a military coup against the royalist majority in the Assembly. Barthélemy was imprisoned while Carnot escaped. Over 200 royalist deputies were purged from the Councils and dozens deported to Guiana. Hundreds of priests were deported and returned émigrés had to flee again. Bonaparte's role in the coup combined with his military victories in Italy to strengthen his hand further. He persuaded the Directory to send him on a mission to build a French Empire in the eastern Mediterranean by invading Egypt. He had already signed a peace treaty with Austria at Campo Formio on his own initiative and was slowly becoming the real master of the Republic's foreign policy.

But for the moment, with the royalists crushed and Bonaparte safely on his way to Egypt, the Directory looked to have stabilised the revolution. The financial system was reorganised on a sounder basis and a series of decent harvests eased the economic situation. The apparent confidence of the Directory was underlined when in the elections of the Year VI (1798) a new Jacobin revival was summarily dealt with by excluding over 100 deputies from the Councils.

But the war continued and the internal divisions, though temporarily subdued, were still there. French expansion in Egypt allowed England to pull together a new coalition of Austria, Turkey, Russia and Sweden which soon threatened the Republic once again. There was a series of military defeats and the Belgian provinces revolted against French control. In the west civil war erupted with the Breton Chouans again. The renewed danger revived the Jacobins for the last time in the elections of the Year VII (March/April 1799). Demands for 'public safety' were heard once more. Sieyès was elected as Director and Lindet, a former member of the great Committee of Public Safety of the Year II, even became Minister of Finance. Jacobin Clubs and the press reopened, while suspects were rounded up. Mass conscription was introduced and forced loans were imposed on the bourgeoisie once again. Echoes of the Jacobin dictatorship began to sound.

But then, as after Fleurus, the whole situation was shifted by military victory over the Coalition. The bourgeoisie heaved a massive sigh of relief that revolutionary measures were no longer needed to safeguard their Republic. But the problem was how to ensure some measure of stability? The Republic seemed condemned to an endless oscillation between the rock of the royalist counter-revolution and the hard place of the Year II. This looked to be confirmed when, once again, the royalist threat revived. In Thermidor Year VII (August 1799), there was a rising in the south west fuelled by resentment at conscription. The rebels almost seized Toulon before they were beaten and the Chouans briefly seized Le Mans and Nantes before they were defeated.

This continual instability could only be resolved by a strong regime capable of imposing a settlement after the years of revolution. And the military was now the only force capable of delivering that. The Directory had ceased to be credible even among the business circles which were its social basis. In this situation came news that Bonaparte had secretly returned to France. He appeared to many to offer a way out of the instability and as he now progressed towards Paris he whipped up support as the 'saviour' of France. He summed up the situation well: 'On my return to Paris I found division in all sources of authority and agreement on only this one truth, that the Constitution was destroyed and could not save liberty.'[191]

Sieyès, 'the mole of the revolution', had drawn similar conclusions and turned to Bonaparte. The Councils were persuaded, on the pretext of a terrorist plot, to meet outside Paris at Saint Cloud under the 'protection' of Napoleon's troops. The coup plot almost backfired. When the Councils met on 19 Brumaire Year VIII (10 November 1799),[192] they were reluctant to succumb to the demand to strengthen the executive. When Napoleon marched in uninvited and started haranguing the deputies, he was greeted with shouts of 'Outlaw him! Down with the dictator!'[193] Bonaparte lost his nerve and had to be helped out of the hall. But his brother Lucien, conveniently in the chair of the session, kept cool. He rallied the troops and they drove the Council of Five Hundred out of the hall. The Council of Elders then agreed to set up a strong executive of three Consuls—Bonaparte, Sieyès and Roger-Ducos.

In effect, and soon formally, Bonaparte was the new master. Robespierre's warning of five years earlier had been borne out—the bourgeois Republic could now only survive under a military dictator. The curtain had come down on ten years of upheaval. Three days after the coup the Consuls proclaimed: 'The revolution is established upon the principles which began it; it is ended.'[194]

Napoleon and the balance sheet of the revolution

Napoleon gradually consolidated his power and in 1804 the Republic finally ended when he had himself crowned Emperor. But whatever the form, the content of Bonaparte's regime remained bourgeois, consolidating the essential gains of the revolution. The founding of the Bank of France in 1800 symbolised this.

Three years later the structure of the new society was laid out in the Civil Code—renamed the *Code Napoléon* in 1807. It was a charter for bourgeois society. In around 30 countries is still the basis of the legal structure today. The *Code* preserved the 'principles of '89', but with a heavy emphasis on property rights. It was a unified national system compared to about 360 local legal codes in France before the revolution. This creation of a unified national state was the central legacy of the revolution.

The destruction of feudal privileges and structures was confirmed in the *Code*. So too was freedom from arbitrary arrest and liberty of internal trade and commerce. A modern educational system was established, including the Lycées—selective schools with provision for scholarships for the 'talented', whatever their social origins. In the Lycées there was a strictly secular curriculum controlled by the state. Workers, needless to say, were still denied the right to organise and a new law, in 1803, compelled them to carry passbooks stamped by the boss. But workers too had gained from the revolution. Despite the restrictions, wages were now between one quarter and one third higher than before the revolution.[195] The gains of the peasantry during the revolution were left intact, while measures to limit grain exports (and a revived Maximum in 1812) ensured stability in the towns and countryside. This meant Napoleon retained strong popular support throughout most of his rule.

Napoleon sought to stabilise society by compromising with forces which had opposed the Republic. In 1801 a Concordat was signed with the Pope, re-establishing the Catholic Church as the dominant religion in France. Napoleon put his motivation bluntly: 'In religion I do not see the mystery of the Incarnation, but the mystery of the social order.'[196] The Concordat, by incorporating the Church with the bourgeois state, did much to undercut an important source of opposition and helped prevent a renewal of revolts such as those of the Vendée and the Breton Chouans. It also helped pave the way for a compromise with émigrés who had opposed the revolution, many of whom now returned.

But this series of compromises were all conditional on acceptance of the new political and social order. On signing the Concordat, Napoleon insisted that the re-established religion 'must be in the hands of the government'.[197] There was to be no return to the *ancien régime*, and there was no question of returning confiscated Church property. The bourgeoisie (and the peasantry) were keeping the spoils of victory. Not even Napoleon, even if he wanted to, would have survived in power if there had been any attempt to take them away. Napoleon represents a further retreat, after Thermidor and the Directory, from the high watermark of the revolution, but it is still a retreat which rests on a consolidation of the essential gains of the revolution.

Outside France Napoleon's armies were a historically progressive force—uprooting much of the old order across Europe.[198] After a short peace with England in 1802, war resumed in 1803. It was soon, once again, general and would remain so until Napoleon's final defeat at Waterloo in 1815. The French armies were spectacularly successful. At its height the Empire stretched from Hamburg in the north to Rome in the south, and beyond this were a host of satellite and vassal states.

Virtually everywhere this resulted in irreversible blows to the old order. These were largely carried through from above—democracy was denied. There was no question of unleashing the mass forces which had pushed through social change in France itself. Across much of Europe variants of the Civil Code became the cornerstone of constructing new regimes. Serfdom was abolished wherever it survived and feudal dues were done away with. Single customs areas were created. Unified systems of justice and of weights and measures were constructed. Equality before the law and an end to feudal privileges were pushed through in many places. The Church was weakened, and civil marriages and secular education were introduced. In short, the spread of the revolution on the bayonets of Napoleon's armies laid many of the foundations of the modern bourgeois state in much of Europe.

With Napoleon's defeat at Waterloo the victorious European powers, led by England, met at the Congress of Vienna and attempted to unscramble the legacy of 25 years of upheaval. They restored monarchs, old state boundaries and divisions and many of the old structures. They agreed to maintain their new order in Europe by force against liberals, democrats and nationalists.

Yet the changes wrought by the revolution and the French armies were irreversible. In Germany, for instance, the old Holy Roman Empire was gone and the patchwork of 396 petty states and 'free' cities before the French Revolution was now reduced to 40, and many of these remained united in a customs union. In Naples the restored king did not dare restore feudal structures and retained the *Code Napoléon* intact. There was much unfinished work to complete the creation of a unified bourgeois state, but many important steps had been taken. In Rome the Pope was restored to his temporal power but he too had surrender this barely 25 years later as a united Italian state emerged.

In France itself the old monarchy was restored and it certainly attempted to turn the clock back. But the changes were too deep and all the essential gains of the revolution stayed intact. There was no return of feudal privileges, dues and monopolies, no return of the internal tolls and divisions. In France, and elsewhere, these had been irrevocably destroyed. To be sure, there were further revolutions in France. In 1830 the July Revolution brought in a new monarchy—one prepared to accept that the changes were there to stay. A new bourgeois Republic emerged from the revolution of 1848 and then a Second Empire under Napoleon's nephew. These revolutions and regimes were all important in completing the victory of the bourgeoisie and facilitating the development of industrial capitalism in the middle of the 19th century. But the essential work of destroying the old structures and clearing the path ahead had been achieved by the Great Revolution.

As the 19th century progressed, the development of industrial capitalism, first in England and then France and elsewhere, also created a force which could look beyond this revolution and the limitations on the mass movement which had driven it forward. When the masses of Paris took to the streets in the 1848 revolution, they now called themselves not *sans culottes* but *proletaires*.

Marx and Engels, Lenin, Trotsky and the Bolsheviks all learned much from the Great French Revolution. It showed that revolution was at the very heart of social change. In particular Lenin praised the Jacobins for showing that conscious revolutionary organisation could be decisive in changing history[199] so, though they fought for a different class, a class which is our worst enemy today, we should not forget the Jacobins but, rather, learn from their example. In so doing we should remember the words of Gracchus Babeuf in *The Manifesto of the Equals* shortly before he was executed: 'The French Revolution is only the forerunner of another, greater, more serious and impressive revolution, which will be the last.'[200]

Appendix: Historians and the French Revolution

Many of the current arguments within, and challenges to, the Marxist view of the French Revolution have been dealt with, explicitly or implicitly, in the text and footnotes. But it is worth adding a few points. The French Revolution has been the subject of fierce debate for 200 years. The debate has *always* been a political one. In England the reactionary Edmund Burke first took up the cudgels in 1790 with his *Reflections on the Revolution in France*. In it he damned the revolution and all its works. He attacked the whole notion of social change and urged that the revolution be crushed by force. His worst venom was reserved for the 'swinish multitude' which a conspiracy of ambitious men had unleashed in France. Thomas Paine's *Rights of Man* was written in reply to Burke and was enormously influential in English radical circles and in the embryonic working class movement. But reaction had the upper hand in England and Paine had to flee to France to avoid arrest. There he was elected to the National Convention—though as a Girondin he narrowly avoided losing his head as the revolution moved on. The story is worth telling because, though today's arguments are conducted in a more subdued and academic manner, they remain profoundly influenced by the politics of the participants.

For much of this century the idea that the revolution was a bourgeois revolution, driven by class conflict, which swept away the political structures of feudalism and cleared the way for the development of capitalism, was generally accepted. This idea was first fully formulated by Marx, though earlier figures, above all Barnave during the revolution itself, had partly developed a similar view. Not all those who advocated this view considered themselves Marxists, but their interpretations of the revolution drew heavily on Marxism.

Beginning with the Second International leader Jean Jaurès and then developed by people like Georges Lefebvre and Albert Soboul, the Marxist approach grew into the accepted orthodoxy.[201] These last two contributed, along with others such as George Rudé, to our understanding of the revolution through their research on the movements from below in the revolution (Lefebvre on the peasantry and Soboul and Rudé on the urban sans culottes). In recent years, though, this 'orthodox' tradition has come under sustained attack by what have become known as 'revisionist' historians. There are many parallels, both in the political background and the historical arguments to the similar trend in the interpretation of the English Revolution.[202]

The 'orthodox' tradition had its weaknesses. In particular the 'Marxism' it drew on was Stalinism. This meant a tendency towards a mechanical, deterministic approach. Reading some of their work one gets the impression that all was preordained, that history inevitably progresses and that, at the appointed hour, a revolutionary bourgeoisie with a fully formed consciousness of what it is fighting for springs up and seizes power. Too little room is left for conscious human intervention in making history. Not enough attention is paid to the fact that the consciousness of those engaged in the revolution developed in response to a crisis over which they had little direct control—and then went on developing in response to conflict and battles.

Fortunately Lefebvre, Soboul and others were good enough historians not to be totally derailed by these influences. Their work, especially on the movements from below, pulled in the opposite direction. Yet there was a tension between the real history and the distorted theoretical framework within which they tried to locate it.

Another weakness was a tendency to overplay the unity of the Third Estate against the old order. Again the real history uncovered showed all the conflicts and divisions wonderfully. The limitations on different movements and how they affected the revolution were brought out. Yet this sat in a framework which stressed Republican unity to an unwarranted degree. This is not an accident of course. It takes no leap of imagination to see how such an idea of an all class alliance of the Third Estate against the old order fitted Stalinist Popular Front politics.[203] Despite these weaknesses, though, the tradition is one which is worth defending, if not uncritically. But these weaknesses undoubtedly made the job of the revisionists easier. In the article I have tried to present a view which overcomes some of these weaknesses and rebuts the main revisionist arguments. I will not therefore repeat the arguments here.[204]

The assault on the Marxist interpretation began with the English historian Alfred Cobban in his *Myth of the French Revolution* in 1955 and then his *Social Interpretation of the French Revolution* in 1964. Cobban had a peculiar view—that the revolution was led by an anticapitalist bourgeoisie against a capitalist nobility. Needless to say this has found few supporters even among later revisionists.[205] But since then the attack has gathered pace through the work of George Taylor, Elizabeth Eisenstein, William Doyle and François Furet among others.[206] Their argument that the Marxist view of the revolution is wrong is fast becoming the new orthodoxy. Even many on the left who have taken up the arguments concede most of the revisionist case. This is true of Georges Comninel, for instance.[207] Comninel sums up the new consensus 'Virtually all non-Marxist historians have now been won away from the social interpretation (i.e. the orthodox Marxist account) essentially because its supposed historical foundations have simply been found wanting when subject to scrutiny... It must now be accepted that the long-standing claims to historical validity of the Marxist interpretation of the French Revolution have been exploded.'[208]

What is the argument which has 'exploded' the Marxist interpretation? Much of it is nakedly and unashamedly political and is a simple reflection of the general right wing trend of recent years. This should be seen for what it is and dealt with as such. The historical arguments vary. But the essence of it is that though the revolution was led by the bourgeoisie (most still accept this—facts can be stubborn things even for right wing historians) it was not a bourgeois class revolution against a feudal ruling class. They argue that in fact the nobility and bourgeoisie were part of a single ruling elite. Both were primarily landowning classes and there was no fundamental social divide or conflict between them. Indeed they were all in favour of reform and if only people had been a little more sensible political reform, without social upheaval, was possible. The revolution thus becomes a squabble over political power among this relatively homogeneous elite, not any kind of class conflict between the nobility and the bourgeoisie. It is now seen as a struggle fuelled by the 'autonomous political and ideological dynamic' of struggle between 'sub elites' (Furet).[209]

Some of the revisionists make the identification between the bourgeoisie and capitalism and industrial capitalism. They look for a class of factory owners leading the revolution and then claim Marxism is nonsense when, naturally, they can't find one. Much of this argument is easily refuted. Marxism does not argue that a class of industrial capitalists fought a class of landowning nobles in the revolution.

But what of the main revisionist argument? The revisionists are right to say the bourgeoisie in France was partly a landowning class, but there was a real growth in wealth based on commerce, manufacture and trade. And all landowners, noble or bourgeois, were increasingly producing for the market. Of course this all took place within the existing structures of society. How could it be otherwise? So a landowner could be involved in commercial grain production, for instance, yet still be involved, directly or indirectly, in exploiting the range of feudal dues and privileges, internal tolls, taxes, monopolies and so on, to extract surplus, rather than accumulating through investment in technical improvements. The same is true of non-landowning bourgeois. In seeking to increase their wealth and position within society they would naturally attempt to exploit the existing structures in whatever way possible.

Nevertheless, for significant elements of the bourgeoisie, this process was hindered by the privileges and restrictions imposed on them by those very structures. Many bourgeois, hit by noble monopolies, internal tolls, unequal tax burdens and so on, had a very material interest in the destruction of these structures. Of course until a crisis in society opens the possibility of real change and throws people into struggle these interests can remain, at best, half formed. People will rather look for ways to adapt, not believing fundamental change is possible. Only in response to crisis and struggle do they become fully understood and expressed. So, for instance, Barnave, a good example given the relative clarity of his ideas by 1792, wrote that 'ideas which had engaged me when they were still the object of fruitless curiosity absorbed me totally when public events began to suggest that there was some hope for them.'[210]

New forms of wealth, new or growing classes and changing social relations meant that the real content within the feudal forms was changing. Eventually the old structures, which could adapt to new social relations up to a point, became an obstacle to further growth—the economy was in crisis. It could not match the more modern states of England and Holland either economically or militarily. In the crisis the old order attempted to reform without undoing the essential political structures of society. The attempt opened a space in which movements of all groups— and particularly from below—deepened the crisis further.

The monarchy was unable to push through reforms without attacking the whole basis of its power, while the nobility, though agreed on the need for change, was not prepared to surrender its power. Some of the bourgeoisie too was tied into defending the existing structure of society, but a large part of the bourgeoisie had everything to gain from breaking these structures and rallied around a programme for change. Buffeted by opposition from the old order and pressure from below, this spilled over into revolution. As the conflicts deepened, classes and parts of classes rallied around diverging programmes, some seeking to halt change, others seeking to carry it further.

The revisionists reduce the political conflicts to 'elites' fighting for power. This makes a nonsense of history. Millions of people were engaged in real social conflict. Programmes for social and political change put forward by minorities grew out of such conflict and developed through it. They could only gain support if they reflected the real interest of significant social forces. The revisionists fail to ask why some programmes were taken up and others not—after all, there were countless schemes put forward. Robespierre's comment on the Girondins, 'Just look at how the rich rally to them', when generalised, is close to the truth.

The bourgeoisie *was* part of the exploiting classes in *ancien régime* France. Yet despite partial integration within the old order they remained oppressed. The destruction of the structures which oppressed them (i.e. their class interest) combined with the class demands of the peasantry and urban masses to push the revolution forward. The peasants and urban poor were not capable of forming an independent force capable of taking power in society. Only the bourgeoisie had the potential to be a new ruling class. This gave them hegemony in constructing the new order. So the urban *sans culottes* were incapable of imposing their programme, other than as a junior partner in a temporary alliance led by a section of the bourgeoisie.

In fighting for their class interests the different factions of the bourgeoisie were not always fully conscious of their actions. Some, Barnave for one, were—though of course even these necessarily saw their class interests as those of the vast majority of society. But once battle was joined the objectively clearer class consciousness of Barnave, for instance, was a block to mobilising the forces needed to win against the old order. It required a minority of the bourgeoisie—the Jacobins—whose ideas reflected a utopian mixture of bourgeois interests and petty bourgeois dreams, to do this.

The victory of the revolution elevated the bourgeoisie from an oppressed junior partner in the exploiting classes to the dominant class in society. With this went a state, legal structure and so on that reflected their interests, which were central in clearing the way for capitalism to develop fully. Those who reject the connection between the political conflicts in the revolution, class struggles, the outcome of these and the further development of capitalism should set themselves a simple test: try and imagine the mid-19th century industrialisation of France taking place with the essential structures of the *ancien régime* still intact.[211] One gets the impression reading much of the revisionists' work that the revolution had nothing to do with the future development of capitalism. Somehow it just came along in the 19th century, but the Great Revolution had nothing to do with this. I hope it is clear from the arguments in the article that this is nonsense.

The most sophisticated of the revisionists, and the most influential, is François Furet, associated with the *Annales* group of historians in France.[212] He was a member of the French Resistance during the war and is an ex-member of the Communist Party. He is thus well placed to find the weaknesses in the orthodox tradition—which, it must be admitted, he does in a skilful way.[213] Furet argues that, while it may make sense to talk of a bourgeois revolution in describing the long transition from feudalism to capitalism over the course of several centuries, the Great Revolution is not a decisive part of this process. The long-term economic and social changes and the short-term political battles are separate and one should not try to relate the two. He does make a number of accurate criticisms of the orthodox tradition for compressing the two and overstating the degree of economic change brought about in the years of the revolution.

When discussing the events of the revolution, Furet introduces the now very fashionable notion of the *dérapage*—'skidding out of control'—of the revolution during the Year II.[214] This means that though the revolution was perhaps undertaking necessary political reform (but this is not about class interests and struggle) the fact that it was a revolutionary change had disastrous consequences. The revolutionaries tore 'France away from its entire past', 'revoked' everything that had been done in previous centuries and set out on 'the immense and utopian ambition to create an entirely new social order and a new set of institutions'.[215] This opened up a rupture in which the 'autonomous political and ideological dynamic' of struggle between 'elites' allowed the mass of ordinary people—led of course by the 'elite' of political activists—to take on a role for which they were ill prepared. This meant the revolution skidded off course away from the 'liberal' period into the 'despotic' period of the Jacobins. He now claims that 'the revolution is over' because all the important ideas of the 'liberal' phase of the revolution have triumphed. He recommends the 'American' concept of 'market society' because, he tells us, competition leads to balance! And Furet is delighted that, apparently, no Frenchman any longer believes that in order to change society you have to take over the state by force.[216]

It is fairly clear, I think, that this argument has as much to do with current politics as history.[217] In fact the argument is little more than a nicely dressed up version of Burke's tirade against fundamental social change and revolution of 200 years ago. Furet wants to bury the notion of revolution, and the Jacobins and sans culottes along with it.

Albert Soboul is now dead, but towards the end of his life he replied to the revisionists and, though I do not agree with all of his arguments, he was right on two counts. He wrote, 'The problem of feudal survivals and of the seigneurial regime is at the heart of the society of the *ancien régime*: it remains at the heart of the French Revolution.'[218] And finally, 'Reform is not a revolution stretched out in time. Reform and Revolution are not distinguished by their duration but by their content. Reform or Revolution? It is not a question of choosing a longer or shorter route leading to the same result, but of specifying an end: to wit, either of the establishment of a new society, or of superficial modifications to the old society.'[219]

Note on the Revolutionary Calendar

The revolutionary calendar was decreed on 24 November, 1793, and was probably the work of the poet Fabre d'Églantine. It lasted until 1806. The calendar was backdated to the declaration of the Republic on 22 September, 1792, which was decreed to be the first day of Year I. The months all had 30 days and were named after natural phenomena. They ran as follows:

Vendémiaire, 22 September to 21 October, the month of vintage
Brumaire, 22 October to 20 November, the month of fog
Frimaire, 21 November to 20 December, the month of frost
Nivôse, 21 December to 19 January, the month of snow
Pluviôse, 20 January to 18 February, the month of rain
Ventôse, 19 February to 20 March, the month of wind
Germinal, 21 March to 19 April, the month of budding
Floréal, 20 April to 19 May, the month of flowers
Prairial, 20 May to 18 June, the month of meadows
Messidor, 19 June to 18 July, the month of harvest
Thermidor, 19 July to 17 August, the month of heat
Fructidor, 18 August to 16 September, the month of fruit

The five days 17-21 September (plus an extra one in leap year) were known as *sans-culottides*. Each month was divided into three *décades*, with the tenth day (*décadi*) a holiday. This abolished the biblically derived seven day week, Sundays and Church festivals. Of course one day off work in ten instead of one in seven is a fitting indication of the bourgeois character of the revolution!

Most writing on the French Revolution uses the revolutionary calendar for the period from the beginning of Year II (September 1793) to Bonaparte's coup of Brumaire, Year VIII (November, 1799). I have followed this, but give the dates in our current calendar in brackets.

Notes

I would like to particularly thank Paul Blackledge, Joe Hartney, Annie McMullen, Mary Black and Ian Birchall for drawing various articles to my attention, and assisting in obtaining others, and these and others for discussions and encouragement in preparing this article.

1   Quoted in J F C Fuller, *The Decisive Battles of the Western World* (Granada, London 1970), p58.

2   Ibid, p57.

3   At the time of Valmy there were about 400,000 men in the French Army. Of these only one tenth had been soldiers before the outbreak of revolution in 1789. At Valmy 34,000 Prussians faced about 52,000 Frenchmen. Despite the ferocity of the artillery fire, casualties were not high—about 300 on the French side and 184 on the Prussian. See Fuller, op cit, p56 and Marc Bouloiseau, *The Jacobin Republic* (Cambridge, 1987), p38.

4   M Bouloiseau, op cit, p42.

5   E Belfort Bax, *The Story of the French Revolution* (Swan Sonnenschein, London, 1907), p43.

6   As Trotsky characterised the 'most indubitable feature of a revolution' in his *History of the Russian Revolution*. The scale of mass involvement in the French Revolution dwarfs that in the earlier bourgeois revolutions in the United Provinces, England or the USA.

7   These figures are from G Rudé, *The French Revolution* (Weidenfeld, London, 1988), p56. France had a population of around 27 million people in 1789, by far the largest in Europe. Paris had a normal population of between 500,000 and 600,000, but in times of economic hardship large numbers of unemployed flooded in from the countryside, swelling the population. See, for instance, J de Vries, *The Economy of Europe in an Age of Crisis* (Cambridge, 1976), p156, and M Vovelle, *The Fall of the French Monarchy* (Cambridge, 1987), p44.

8   Though Louis XVI issued considerably less of these than previous rulers (Louis XV issued 150,000), he still managed around 14,000. See Rudé, *The French Revolution*, p14.

9   An indication of this process is given by the following list of innovations in western Europe: the invention of the horseshoe, padded horse collar and stirrup transformed the horse into a source of power, the watermill and windmill were introduced as productive forces at the end of the 12th century, gunpowder in the 13th century, the blast furnace—a major breakthrough—in the 15th century, the first use of magnetic compasses and navigation charts on ships towards the end of the 13th century, the invention of movable type printing in the 15th century—a development which was particularly subversive of the closed ideology of the time.

10   This whole account is a crude sketch of a process which is the subject of vigorous debate among Marxists. See the collection of articles in *The Transition from Feudalism to Capitalism* (Verso, London, 1976) and the more recent *The Brenner Debate* (Cambridge University Press, 1985).
      On the specific question of absolutism the best starting point is P Anderson's *Lineages of the Absolutist State* (Verso , London, 1974). Anderson is right to question the tendency of Marx and Engels to see the absolutist state as holding 'the balance between the nobility and the class of burghers' (Engels, quoted in Anderson, p15). He stresses that it was rather 'the new political carapace of a threatened nobility' (p18). But he underestimates, I think, the degree to which Marx and Engels were right to point to the way absolutism was not simply this but also a specific adaptation to the bourgeoisie. Engels accurately summed up the essence of the matter, 'The political order remained feudal, while society became more and more bourgeois' (Anderson, p23). Anderson's account also suffers at times from his attachment to

'structuralist' concepts and language. He also grossly overstates the importance of things such as Roman law in the transition from feudalism to capitalism in western Europe.

11   L'Abbé Michel Lavassor quoted in L W Cowie, *The French Revolution: documents and debates* (Macmillan, London, 1987), p10. There were about 130,000 clergy in France at the time of the revolution. The Church owned over 10 percent of all land outright and collected feudal dues from the peasants who leased or worked it. In addition peasants had to pay the tithe (nominally a tenth of their produce, though in practice usually less) supposedly for the expenses of worship. In reality the higher clergy creamed off much of it at the expense of local priests. See Vovelle, *The Fall of the French Monarchy*, pp18-20.

12   The Enlightenment was a European wide phenomenon but was dominated by developments in France. For a summary see, for instance, N Hampson, *The Enlightenment* (Pelican, Harmondsworth, 1968).

13   E N Williams, *The Ancien Régime in Europe* (Pelican, London, 1984), p227.

14   Jean-Jacques Rousseau, *On the Social Contract*, in *The Basic Political Writings* (Hackett, Indianapolis, 1987), p141.

15   Ibid, p145.

16   Ibid, p180.

17   Ibid, p170.

18   Ibid, p162.

19   There were about 300,000 nobles in all and they owned about 25 percent of all land outright. See Vovelle, op cit, pp7-15.

20   This was a more attractive method of increasing wealth than investment in improved agricultural methods and is an important factor in the relative lack of a layer of capitalist market oriented landlord layer in France compared with the English Revolution. The consequences were that French agriculture, with only a few exceptions, was very backward compared with English. The example of the English agricultural revolution was an important factor in the growth of the French reforming economists and philosophers known as the physiocrats.

21   Vovelle, op cit, pp46, 47.

22   Apart from Paris, which dwarfed all other cities in France in size, with over 500,000 people, there were only around 45 towns with a population bigger than 15,000. One quarter of all towns with a population over 20,000 were ports. Ibid, p38.

23   T C W Blanning, *The French Revolution: Aristocrats Versus Bourgeoisie?* (Macmillan, London, 1987), p14.

24   A Soboul, *A short history of the French Revolution* (University of California Press 1977), p11.

25   Ibid, p10.

26   In his *What is the Third Estate?* (1789) (see *The French Revolution: Introductory Documents*, ed D I Wright, Queensland, 1980, p19). Other future revolutionary leaders expressed a similar resentment. Barnave recalled how his mother was evicted from a seat at the opera to make way for a noble. Madame Roland recalled being excluded from the dining room and sent to eat in the kitchen at a noble's chateau (both Barnave and Roland were wealthy). Danton said later, 'The old regime drove us to it [revolution] by giving us a good education without opening any opportunity for our talents' (for these examples see Williams, *The Ancien Régime* p223) One of the clearest (and most enjoyable) examples though is to be found in the plays of Beaumarchais especially *The Marriage of Figaro*.

27   The only exception seems to have been Jean Paul Marat who spoke of revolution in his *The chains of slavery* in 1774, see Vovelle op cit, p72. And a nobleman, the Marquis d'Argenson, wrote in 1751 'All the orders of society are discontented together...a disturbance could turn into revolt, and revolt into a total revolution,' see Blanning, op cit, p30.

28   Eighty five percent of the French population was rural and two thirds of these were

peasants. Recently some historians such as Robin, Postal-Vinnay, Ado and Soboul have argued, though in different ways, that a layer of better off peasants, 'yeoman or kulak types' (Soboul quoted in Comninel, p45), were pushing the development of agrarian capitalism forward, and use this to draw some parallels with the English Revolution. This may have some validity in the cereal growing Paris basin but the evidence is not, yet, entirely convincing. In particular, that any such layer played a key role in the revolution has not been demonstrated. For a summary of the arguments see, for example, *The Peasantry in the French Revolution*, P M Jones, (Cambridge, 1988), p124, and G Comninel, *Rethinking the French Revolution: Marxism and the Revisionist Challenge* (Verso, London, 1987), pp34-51.

29   Only in a few areas, such as Franche-Comté, did serfdom survive. About 95 percent of French peasants had legal personal liberty. The peasantry legally owned about 40 to 45 percent of all land (but this did not mean they were exempt from all dues on this land). There were, though, enormous variations within this average. An especially marked difference was between the north and east where the peasantry generally owned a small amount of land (and the burden of taxes and dues was much heavier) and parts of the south and the highland areas from the central plateau to the Alps where they often owned the vast majority of the land. (See Vorelle, op cit, pp5-13, for an overview of the structure of peasant society. For a detailed account see Jones, op cit.)

30   Many writers on the French Revolution tie themselves in knots over whether the structure of society in 1789 can be called feudal. Of course it would be stupid to simply equate it with 'classical' feudalism. But the essential political structures were derived from feudalism and a surplus was extracted from the direct producers in the countryside by extra-economic methods—compulsion backed by force.

The peasants themselves, and other contemporaries, had little doubt what was meant when they complained of 'feudal' or 'seigneurial' dues. Alexis de Tocqueville, a 19th century historian who generally argued that there was a continuity between the old order and the post-revolutionary society put it well: 'Feudalism had remained the most important part of our civil institutions…we should observe that the disappearance of part of the institutions of the middle ages only made what survived of them a hundred times more odious' (quoted in Soboul, *A Short History…*, p23).

31   Daniel Guérin in his *Class Struggles in the First French Republic: Bourgeois and Bras Nus 1793-1795* (Pluto, London, 1977—an abridged translation of his *La Lutte des Classes sous la première République: bourgeois et bras nus*, Paris, 1946) falls into precisely this ahistorical lapse. Much of Guérin's argument *is* true and a valuable corrective to most accounts of the French Revolution which tend to downplay the significance of conflicts between the Jacobin bourgeoisie and the mass movements in the towns. So, for instance, he rightly draws attention to the curbing of the popular movement by the Jacobin dictatorship and points out that there were significant strikes by wage earners—also repressed by the Jacobins. (pp222-237).

One also has to remember the context in which he wrote the work—part of a polemic against the Popular Front politics espoused by the bulk of the French left under the influence of Stalinism. The notion of 'Republican unity' in the Great French Revolution was a useful buttress for these politics. It is true that the tradition of 'Marxist' writing on the French Revolution associated with Lefebvre and Soboul incorporated elements of such ideas in their interpretations (along with a tendency to mechanical, deterministic 'Marxism' also derived from the Stalinist orthodoxy).

However, in his polemical zeal Guérin's historical judgments go wildly astray. He comes close to arguing for 'permanent revolution' based on an embryonic working class in 1789 (he does *not* in fact argue this, but sails very close, for instance in his use of Trotsky's analysis of the Russian Revolution on p4), despite the fact that the whole notion only makes any sense after the development of a world economy and world working class. He also grossly underestimates the revolutionary side of the bourgeoisie in the French Revolution because of his blinkered concern to attack unity with bourgeois politicians in the 20th century. He bemoans the fact that the French Revolution brought 'the bourgeoisie to power in the end rather than the *proletariat*' (p2, my emphasis) and can write nonsense claiming that the French Revolution was the cradle of 'soviet democracy, the democracy of workers' councils' (p3) and refer to a situation of 'dual power' (pp29-31) in Paris in 1793!

32   Vovelle, op cit, pp56, 57.

33   see R B Rose, *The Making of the Sans-Culottes* (Manchester University Press, 1983), pp10, 11.

34   Thus on no 'day' (ie insurrection) of the revolution did wage earners amount to more than one quarter of the direct participants and they were far outnumbered by petty bourgeois. A similar balance is true for the composition of the various revolutionary committees which emerged later. It is worth stressing that though vagrants and unemployed amounted to up to 10 percent of the Parisian population at times, and no doubt played a role in mass riots and the like, they were not a central force in the revolutionary 'days' or in grass roots organisations—contrary to the myths of right wing historians. See, for instance, G Rudé, *The Crowd in the French Revolution* (Oxford University Press 1959), and Albert Soboul, *The Parisian Sans-Culottes and the French Revolution, 1793-4* (Oxford University Press, 1964). Soboul estimates that 63.8 percent of the members of the Parisian 'revolutionary committees' (the cadre of the mass movement, if you like) which developed during the revolution were independent craftsmen or shopkeepers (p40).

35   Of course England still had a king. But to contrast England under William of Orange with France under Louis XIV shows the content of the monarchy was entirely different.

36   Quoted in Blanning, op cit, p30.

37   Again by way of contrast England and Holland could marshal their wealth through institutions like the Bank of England, founded after the settlement of 1688, or the impressive and developed financial institutions of Amsterdam. Yet in France money had to be raised essentially as the personal debt of the king. A Bank of France would not be founded until after the revolution in 1800.

38   In 1788 payment of interest on the state debt accounted for 51 percent of the national income. And the state's annual expenditure exceeded its income by about 20 percent. Vovelle, op cit, p76.

39   Quoted in E N Williams, *The Ancien Régime...* p242. For a good discussion of the attempts at reform by Turgot and others see Olwen Hufton, *Europe: Privilege and Protest 1730-1789* (Fontana, London, 1980), pp299-347.

40   Figures from Blanning, *The French Revolution: Aristocrats...* pp9-11.

41   Soboul, *A short history...* pp29-33, from the work of C-E Labrousse (*La Crise de l'économie française a la fin de l'Ancien Régime et au début de la Révolution*, Paris, 1944), whose research uncovered these facts.

42   The Flour War was partly a response to the first steps at introducing a free market in grain by Turgot, discussed earlier. I have deliberately emphasised the limits on *independent* activity by wage earners to guard against ahistorical judgements (which, for socialists living in a modern industrialised society, it is easy to fall into), but this does not mean that there were none.

   In the years before the revolution there were near insurrectionary strikes by silk workers in Lyons as well as builders' strikes in Paris in 1785 and 1786 and a strike by printers and bookbinders for a 14 (!) hour day. The printing industry seems to have had a high level of conflict between workers and masters and Lyons, the most industrial city in France, seems to have had a particularly high degree of class conflict between wage earners and their bosses (see Rudé, *The French Revolution*, p34). There were repeated clashes during the revolution too.

   The crucial point about the working class in the French Revolution is that though they did often fight for better wages and conditions and did use weapons of class struggle—strikes etc—they were not capable of consistently fighting for specifically proletarian interests because of the objective conditions in which they existed. No political programme emerged representing their interests and it *could not* have done so—Babeuf's ideas were the nearest to such a development, but even these were a confused mixture which remained heavily marked by petty bourgeois ideas. The working class was not and could not be a class *for itself* in the French Revolution.

43   Quoted in L Huberman, *Man's Worldly Goods: The story of the wealth of nations* (Monthly Review Press, New York, 1963), p156.

44   Quoted in Rudé, *The French Revolution*, p14. The point is of more than historical importance in the light of current developments in the USSR and Eastern Europe. In this presentation I have somewhat separated the internal and external factors in the revolution. In reality the two were inextricably linked. Also I have deliberately emphasised the problem of French rivalry, economic and military, with England and Holland, as it is underestimated in most accounts. But this should not be taken to imply a crude parallel with the role of competition between states and national economies in the modern world of capitalist imperialism.

45   Soboul, *A Short History...* p40, quoting Arthur Young, *Travels in France during the years 1787, 1788 and 1789* (New York, 1969).

46   Mallet Du Pan, who emigrated early in the revolution and who, though hostile to the later course of the revolution remained a sharp observer. Quoted in E N Williams, op cit, p242.

47   See Wright, op cit, p2.

48   Peasant revolts were called Jacqueries from the nom-de-guerre Jacques Bonhomme (Jack Goodfellow) conferred on rebellious peasants in 1358 by nobles.

49   Much has been made by 'revisionist' historians (those who have mounted a sustained attack on the Marxist view of the French Revolution in recent years) of these lists of grievances, of which many survive. They argue that those of the peasantry do not attack 'feudalism' and that the bourgeoisie and nobility were agreed on the need for reform.

It is true that the peasant lists often do not attack 'feudalism'—though this is exaggerated by these historians. But they do complain on specific dues etc. And the electoral procedures meant that peasants were often drawing up the lists in meetings at which their lords, clergy etc were present. A flood of complaints that this meant specific peasants' grievances were omitted from the final lists descended on the government (see Jones, op cit, pp63-67).

Again, it is true the nobles were willing to reform. But when it comes to the crunch issue of seigneurial privileges the split is clear. For instance, T C W Blanning, op cit (Macmillan, London, 1987), reproduces a summary of the 'cahiers' of the nobility and the Third Estate. He comments that it shows 'if anything the nobles were more liberal than their bourgeois colleagues' and that the table 'provides the revisionists with their best evidence'. But on closer inspection this 'best evidence' is not what it seems.

On issues such as equality before the law, abolition of arbitrary arrest, establishment of a constitution, equalisation of taxes and liberty of the press there is general agreement. But, tucked away at the bottom of the table, we find that on 'more economic freedom' the Third Estate is clearly split from the nobility. And, crucially, on 'abolition of seigneurial rights' the Third Estate is against the nobility by five to one. Yet Blanning, in common with the revisionists and a few of their recent left critics, insists that 'it is impossible to infer any confrontation'! (See Blanning p35, 36 for these quotes and the table.) Also see Jones, op cit, p67, who calculates that over half the peasant lists called for the abolition of seigneurial monopolies and dues while 85 percent of noble lists were totally silent on these questions.

50   See Rudé, *The Crowd* ... pp34-44, for a detailed account of this incident.

51   See Cowie, op cit, p49, my emphasis.

52   Quoted in Vovelle, op cit, p102. Mirabeau's exact words are disputed but the general

point is clear enough.

53   As Sebastian Hardy, a bookseller living in Paris, who kept a diary of events, began
     to call it about now (quoted in Rudé, *The French Revolution*, p42).

54   The Bastille was the French equivalent of the Tower of London.

55   Rudé, *The Crowd...* p57. We know the composition of those who stormed the Bastille
     reasonably well, as they were given medals and pensions by the Republic later.

56   In some areas this took place before news of the Bastille. Rennes, and other towns
     in Brittany, as well as Grenoble and Dijon, had already had serious clashes between
     the Third Estate and the nobility earlier in the year. See Vovelle, op cit, pp106, 107.

57   Quoted in Vovelle, op cit, p106. Barnave though a leading member of the Assembly
     at this stage, would end up on the right later, as the revolution radicalised. He
     was guillotined in 1793. In 1792 he wrote his brilliant *Introduction to the French
     Revolution*, which is far and away the clearest exposition by a contemporary of
     the basis of the bourgeois revolution. His analysis is worth quoting at some length:
     'Once industry and commerce have begun to establish themselves...the way will
     be open for a revolution in law and politics, a shift in the balance of wealth leads
     to a shift in the distribution of political power. Just as the possession of land once
     raised the aristocracy to power, so the growth of industrial property now increases
     the power of the people.' Of course by people he means the bourgeoisie!
     And he went on in a striking passage—when one remembers this was written
     50 years before Marx—'One may from a certain point of view consider population,
     wealth, customs, knowledge as the elements and the substance which form the social
     body, and see in the laws and the government the tissue which contains and envelops
     them...if the tissue expands in the degree that the substance grows in volume the
     progress of the social body will occur without violent commotion. But if instead
     of being an elastic force it opposes itself rigidly there will come a moment when
     proportionality will end and where the substance must be destroyed or where it
     must break its envelope and expand.'
     For these quotes and a good discussion of Barnave's ideas see Ralph Miliband,
     'Barnave: A Case of Bourgeois Class Consciousness', in *Aspects of History and
     Class Consciousness*, ed I Meszaros (London, 1971), pp22-46. Miliband's otherwise
     excellent article is marred only by his attempt to use the contrast between Barnave's
     clear bourgeois consciousness, which ended up as an obstacle to the bourgeois
     revolution, and the 'false' consciousness of Jacobins such as Robespierre, which
     carried it through, as the basis for opposing basing clear socialist politics today,
     and in particular building a revolutionary party.

58   See G Lefebvre, *The Great Fear of 1789: Rural Panic in Revolutionary France*
     (London, 1973), for a full account.

59   As the radical bourgeois journalist Jean Paul Marat put it.

60   It is not true, as is sometimes asserted, that the peasants simply refused to pay
     any dues after 4 August. See Jones, op cit, pp86-123, for an account of the struggle.

61   This law remained in force until 1884, one of the few from the revolution to survive
     unscathed through all the upheavals of the Great Revolution, Bonaparte, the 1830
     Revolution, 1848 and the Paris Commune. For text of Declaration of Rights of
     Man see Wright ...*Introductory Documents*, pp58-61.

62   Until the revolution nobles were allowed the 'privilege' of execution by the sword,
     while commoners were subject to brutal tortures such as breaking on the wheel,
     disembowelment while still alive, having hands burnt off and sulphur rubbed in
     the wounds, and being torn apart by horses. Charles Dickens's *A Tale of Two
     Cities*—whatever its faults otherwise—has some grisly, accurate descriptions of
     such methods.

63   The Jacobins attacked slavery as 'the aristocracy of the skin' and Robespierre insisted
     that 'the moment you pronounce the word "slave" you pronounce your own
     dishonour' (see Vovelle, op cit, p148). The relation of the French Revolution to
     the colonies is complex and I have not the space to deal with it here. By far the

best book on the slave revolt remains CLR James's *The Black Jacobins* (Allison and Busby).

64 Quoted from *The German Ideology* (Lawrence and Wishart, London, 1963, pp40-41) in *Essential Writings of Karl Marx*, David Caute (ed) (MacGibbon and Kee, London, 1967), p65.

65 Vovelle, op cit, p114.

66 Maillard quoted in Rudé, *The French Revolution*, p57. Also see Rudé, *The Crowd...* pp72-78, for a detailed account of the October Days.

67 Vovelle, op cit, p117.

68 The name derives from the convent where they met, and was originally used by royalist propagandists to attack them—they accepted the label.

69 Marat was the most consistent spokesman for the revolutionary movement until his assassination in 1793, but he was a spokesman for the interests of the most revolutionary *bourgeoisie* who understood the need to ally with the mass movement and was prepared to express many of their demands. It is wrong to see him as on the side of the masses and somehow opposed to the interests of the bourgeoisie as is sometimes argued—after all he became president of the bourgeois Jacobin Club.

70 See Vovelle, op cit, pp125-128, for a summary of the counter-revolutionary movement in the summer of 1790.

71 A Métin, *La Révolution et l'autonomie locale* (1904), quoted in Jones, op cit, p168.

72 Despite the electoral restriction something like 61 percent of adult males had the right to vote at a time when about 4 percent could do so in bourgeois England.

73 See Jones, op cit, p154-161 and Bouloiseau, *The Jacobin Republic*, pp167-171 and pp184-186, for the arguments on this.

74 Vovelle, op cit, p132.

75 Ibid, p133.

76 The power and composition of the sections changed at various stages in the revolution. Initially they were dominated by the better off bourgeois, the 'active' citizens allowed to vote in the restricted franchise in the years up to the fall of the monarchy in 1792. This restricted the vote to men over 25 who paid tax equivalent to three days labour—which amounted to about 60 percent of men over 25. They were later dominated by poorer petty bourgeois sans-culottes when the suffrage restrictions were abolished and became the vehicle for their movement. In practice such poorer 'passive' citizens became active in the sections well before the fall of the monarchy. The same evolution took place in the National Guard, initially a weapon of the richer bourgeoisie used against popular disturbances. See Vovelle, op cit, pp186-189.

77 Ibid, p140.

78 Ibid, p142.

79 Under a self denying ordinance proposed by Robespierre no members of the Constituent Assembly were entitled to be deputies in the new assembly. The suffrage was based on the distinction between 'active' and 'passive' citizens (see note 76). An even higher property qualification on those eligible to be elected to the Assembly was introduced.

80 In *L'Ami du Peuple*—both quoted in Vovelle, op cit, p147.

81 Most of the information in this section is from Michael Kennedy's two volume *The Jacobin Clubs in the French Revolution* (Princeton University Press, New Jersey)—*The First Years* (1982) and *The Middle Years* (1988). Apparently a third volume is planned dealing with the later years of the revolution which should be equally valuable.

82 Condorcet's *Essay on the Political Condition of Women* had argued in 1788 for women with property to be allowed to take part in the elections to the Estates General. In late 1790 he published an essay arguing for political rights for women which sparked off widespread debate. Also the Dutch feminist Etta Palm d'Aelders was active in the 'Cercle Sociale des amis de la verité' founded in October 1790, which

published her speeches calling for women's emancipation and circulated them to the provinces.

In February 1791 some Jacobin Clubs admitted women, but the mother Jacobin Club wrote that this 'does not appear to accord to the regime of liberty suitable to the Societies of Friends of the Constitution'. Fédérés (National Guards from the provinces) proposed at the Jacobin Club on 17 August 1792 that women be given the vote but again this was not taken up. Women's auxiliary branches of the clubs began to appear from late 1790, encouraged by men as a way of spreading republican propaganda, especially against the Church. At Dijon, for instance, the women's club forced the male society to send a circular to affiliated clubs urging the creation of women's clubs. At Lille the women's club won the right to attend the male society as a body.

The size of such clubs varied, but they could be large. There were around 400 at the founding meeting in Dijon and, according to contemporaries, 3,500 at one meeting in Bordeaux. Most seem to have ranged from a few tens up to a couple of hundred. Much of the activity of the women's clubs was 'instructional'—reading newspapers and the like. The women's organisations came to play an important role in whipping up patriotic sentiment—making flags, speaking to National Guards and soldiers before they set off to fight. They also played a role in fighting against the counter-revolutionary ideas fostered by the Church. At Grenoble they declared their purpose as 'to rally around the constitution those citizens led astray by fanatical priests'. At Dijon the women's Jacobin Club had a series of clashes with associations of Catholic women—including disrupting masses and the like. In Paris the Society of Revolutionary Republican Women led by Claire Lacombe played an important role in the sans-culottes movement. It closely allied with the enragés, particularly Leclerc and Roux. It held meetings in the library of the main Jacobin Club and played a key role in the campaign for stern measures against speculators, hoarders and so on. It also played a role in preparing the ground for the insurrection of May/June 1793. The club was closed down in the winter of 1793/94 as part of the general attack on the left of the movement by the revolutionary government.

83   I have dwelt on the facts about the Jacobins at some length in view of the arguments put forward by 'revisionist' historians (such as Alfred Cobban, George Taylor and William Doyle) that there was no bourgeois revolution in France in the 18th century. Unfortunately too many of the 'left' critics of these historians, such as Georges Comninel, concede much of their argument. Those who look at the composition of the various national assemblies and complain that you don't find the actual bourgeoisie so there cannot have been a bourgeois revolution fail to understand two things. Firstly, compared to most modern bourgeois parties the actual bourgeoisie was highly prominent in the various assemblies. Secondly, by concentrating solely on the assemblies they miss the real social basis in the localities which the national figures represented or came to represent in the course of struggle.

The revisionists also claim there was little if any difference or friction between the bourgeoisie and the nobility. They have a point, in that there was a real degree of merging of the two under the absolutist state. But they overstate it and miss the fact that there was real subordination of the bourgeoisie within the social structure. This is especially clear when you look down at the base of the movement. There was a real antagonism between the ranks of the bourgeoisie, and especially its lower ranks and the privileged orders—and the participants in the revolution knew it and said so themselves. That lawyers and the like are over represented among the prominent spokesmen of the revolutionaries (another revisionist argument) should not come as a surprise. Professional advocates of causes, keenly aware of the restrictions on 'men of talent' like themselves, they were (and still are) natural spokesmen for bourgeois interests.

The evidence from any serious study of the movement which formed the backbone of the French Revolution leaves no doubt about its class character. Michael

Kennedy's massive study of the Jacobin Clubs is worth quoting on this. He is an anti-Marxist, accusing Marxist historians of 'a kind of intellectual tyranny', and commends revisionist historians such as François Furet. But he concludes: 'Nevertheless my own studies of the clubs have led me to the conclusion that there is much truth in the radical-Marxist view of the Revolution, that class conflict was, indeed, a major determinant' (both quotes from Kennedy, *The Middle Years*, p368).

84   Though 'Maratiste' was usually used at the time, see Bouloiseau, *The Jacobin Republic*, p3.

85   My emphasis. See A Soboul, *A Short History...* p86.

86   See Wright *...Documents*, p113, for text of Declaration.

87   Guérin, *Class struggles...* p50.

88   Ibid, p6. In this I think Daniel Guérin is correct. Others such as Albert Soboul (see his *Short History of the French Revolution*) think Brissot and his supporters wanted war against France's continental rivals, but not England, as this would involve naval conflict which would disrupt the trade of the Atlantic ports.

89   Wright *...Documents*, p123.

90   See speeches at the Jacobin Club by Brissot and Robespierre in Wright *...Documents*, pp114-133.

91   See Vovelle, op cit, p222.

92   Ibid, p224.

93   Ibid, p228.

94   Ibid, p229.

95   See, for example, the Sans-Culottes Paternoster (above p54) and the Decree on the Levee en masse (above p49). Also see the First and Second Propagandist Decrees quoted in Conor Cruise O'Brien, *Nationalism and the French Revolution*, in G Best (ed), *The Permanent Revolution: The French Revolution and its Legacy 1789-1989*, p32—though O'Brien's general argument, need it be said, is right wing drivel.

96   Vovelle, op cit, p230.

97   Bouloiseau, *The Jacobin Republic*, p9.

98   Figures given by Rudé in *The Crowd...* p105.

99   Bouloiseau, *The Jacobin Republic*, p12.

100   E Belfort Bax, *Jean-Paul Marat: The People's Friend*, (Grant Richards, London, 1901), p205.

101   Ibid, p210.

102   The best discussion of the aftermath of 10 August and the September Massacres is in Peter Kropotkin's *The Great French Revolution* (2 Vols, Elephant, 1986), Vol 2, pp302-329.

103   Following 10 August the right to vote was granted to all male French citizens over 21 who had a permanent residence and worked for a living—including domestics. Overnight around four million former 'passives' acquired the vote. The electoral procedure was in stages as on earlier occasions. The actual numbers voting in the election were fairly small due to the flood of volunteers to the front and the general disruption caused by the war. Around 10 percent of those eligible attended the primary assemblies. Sometimes the voting was by secret ballot, but in Paris it was conducted orally and was open to the public at all stages. The Jacobins intervened actively in the elections. They won almost all the positions in Paris, while Feuillants and Brissotins triumphed in the provinces. Some 749 deputies were finally elected to the Convention. Of these it is estimated that 142 were committed Jacobins, 178 Girondins openly opposed to the Jacobins, and the rest sat in the 'marsh'. See Bouloiseau, *The Jacobin Republic*, pp47-49, and A Patrick, *The Men of the First French Republic* (John Hopkins Press, 1972).

104   Recent historians have challenged this interpretation, usually from the right. But even George Rudé in his new book agrees with their argument, seeing the question of 'ideology' and personal rivalry as the central divide between Girondins and

Montagnards. The challenge is based on a detailed examination of the personal backgrounds of Giorondin and Montagnard deputies which allegedly reveals that there was little difference. In fact this is overstated. In general the Girondins do appear to have been more closely connected personally with the class forces referred to in the text (for instance Isnard, one of their leading figures, was a wholesale dealer in oil, a grain importer, owner of a soap factory and a silk mill).

However, the question of personnel in the Convention is entirely secondary. The key fact is that the political conflicts in the Convention can only be understood as developing in response to political and social divisions outside. Political groupings were forced by the pressure of events to define programmes which, if they were to command any real support, had to align themselves with a material force outside the Convention. In other words they had to articulate and express the real interests of a significant social group—a class or part of a class. In this light it is clear that the Girondins increasingly expressed the position of the higher layers of the bourgeoisie. St Just commented that 'the force of circumstances' was responsible for the divergent political policies of rival groups. Yes, and these circumstances were above all the conflict of different social groups in the developing revolution.

105   Danton, though earlier associated with the populist Cordeliers Club, was in effect to the right of the bulk of the Jacobins. His role in August and September in the defence of the revolution gave him real support and influence. He increasingly acted as a rallying point between the Gironde and the Mountain.

106   Bouloiseau, *The Jacobin Republic*, p50.

107   Petition of the *Jardins des Plantes* section to the Convention. See Soboul, *Short History...* pp99-100.

108   I use Terror, with a capital T, to denote the regulated, controlled economy with strict measures against counter-revolutionaries and those who sought to profit at the expense of the defence of the Republic. The use of force was part, a necessary part, of this, but not the whole. The term has a far wider meaning than it has today. Similarly Terrorist is used to describe those who advocated more controls and regulation, and the necessary force to back them up.

109   The French attempted to impose a new order on Belgium, confiscating Church property, abolishing tithes and seigneurial dues. But this was very different from a revolution and, as it was overseen by French comissioners, meant the Belgians were at best lukewarm about their new found freedom—though not desiring a return to Austrian control. No doubt the intention of the French to extract serious amounts of loot from the pockets of the Belgians to finance the occupying army etc played a role here too.

110   Rudé, *The French Revolution*, p82.

111   And implicated bourgeois leaders such as Barnave. This was to cost him his head.

112   Cowie ...*Documents and Debates*, p92. Robespierre's excellent speech in particular throws back at the right their refusal to support his earlier proposal to abolish the death penalty for ordinary crime yet now wanting to spare the king.

113   See Bouloiseau, *The Jacobin Republic*, p57.

114   The rhythm of military operation was still dictated by the seasons. Poor transport and the like meant that winter operations were all but impossible. This had a significant impact on the timing of the political crises of the revolution as the renewed demands of the war after the winter combined with the worst time of the year for grain supplies.

115   All these price rises were exacerbated by the scarcity in the markets caused by contracts and requisitions to supply the army and navy—the latter pushed up the price of firewood, essential for cooking.

116   The price was fixed at 50 percent above pre-revolutionary level, but as most wages had doubled by then it was of real benefit. The Convention hesitated to follow the example of the commune on a national scale partly out of hostility to any economic controls but also because of the financial scale of the operation. Many towns did

embark on similar schemes long before the General Maximum was imposed later in the year.

117   Lefebvre, *The French Revolution* (2 vols) (Columbia University Press, New York, 1964), vol 2, p48.
118   G Rudé, *The French Revolution*, p85.
119   R Cobb, *The People's Armies*, (Yale University Press, London, 1987), p21.
120   Wright ...*Documents*, pp155-161, for text of Robespierre's declaration.
121   Bouloiseau, *The Jacobin Republic*, p66.
122   Lefebvre, op cit, p52.
123   Wright ...*Documents*, pp165-167, for Guadet's speech.
124   Kropotkin, *The Great French Revolution*, p418.
125   Bouloiseau, *The Jacobin Republic*, p66.
126   See Wright, *The French Revolution*... pp173-180, for text of Constitution.
127   As with much of the detail of the peasant movement during the revolution, there is real disagreement on this. Partly this stems from lack of knowledge—by its nature it is difficult to penetrate the motives of a rural, largely illiterate movement. Historians such as Georges Lefebvre stress the attachment of peasants in the French Revolution to collective rights. Others such as the Russian historian Anatoli Ado emphasise partial satisfaction of the land hunger of small peasants by the revolution and argue that this turned them into a class of embryonic capitalists.
       Soboul adopted this view towards the end of his life, seeing these peasants, rather than large bourgeois landowners, as pushing agrarian capitalism forward. I think both views contain elements of truth—the peasantry was internally divided and like the urban sans-culottes had a contradictory ideology—wanting individual property *and* collective rights over the property of their well to do neighbours. But Lefebvre's arguments I find particularly strong. The defence of collective rights was successfully waged and enshrined in the Rural Code of September 1791. Despite many attempts at reform, the basic provision for collective grazing remains in force to this day. See Jones, *The Peasantry*..., pp124-166, for detailed discussion of these points.
128   The 12 members of the Committee who ruled in the Year II were remarkably young. Ten of them were under 40. Robespierre was 31 at the beginning of the revolution, while St Just was only 22.
129   Lefebvre, op cit, p67. Though Cambon was hated for the forced loans, he correctly understood that they tied the better off bourgeoisie to the Republic—if it fell who would pay their money back? In proposing the measure he made this clear: 'You are rich... I want to bind you to the revolution whether you like it or not; I want you to lend your wealth to the Republic' (quoted in Kropotkin, *The Great French Revolution*, p431).
130   A Taylor, *Glimpses of the Great Jacobins*, (Cattell, London, 1882), p66.
131   A Soboul, *The Parisian Sans-Culottes and the French Revolution, 1793-4* (Oxford University Press, 1964), for the definitive account of this movement.
132   Wright ...*Documents*, pp188-189, for Law of Suspects.
133   Ibid, pp190-192, for full details. The Maximum applied to a range of goods including meat, soap, salt, wood, coal, candles, sugar, tobacco and 'the raw materials used for manufacture'. A Food Commission was set up to oversee and enforce it. Though it was partly successful, it suffered many shortcomings. In particular transport costs were ignored and the scales tended to favour the producer and hit small retailers, which did not go down well with large chunks of the sans-culotterie. The Maximum was amended in Germinal, Year II (March, 1794) by adding profit margins and other 'costs' to the 'general' prices.
134   Ibid, p197.
135   The rebellion smouldered on in the Vendée, and in Brittany the counter-revolutionary Chouans operated right down to Napoleon's rise to power. The best insight into this guerilla war is Balzac's novel, *The Chouans*. The crushing of the counter-revolution in the Vendée is becoming the centrepiece of a right wing attack on

the whole revolution as the bicentenary approaches. The tone is summed up by Pierre Chaunu, a leading French historian with regular access to the columns of the right wing paper *Figaro* and French TV. He argues that the Jacobins mark 'the foundation of a long and bloody sequence which runs from the genocide of the French Catholic west to the Soviet Gulag, the ravages of the Chinese Cultural Revolution and the autogenocide of the Khmer Rouge in Cambodia'. He now claims that the 'Genocide' in the Vendée 'was proportionately more effective than the Holocaust' (*Newsweek* magazine, 20 February 1989, p15). For a sensible discussion of the Vendée and a rebuttal of much of this right wing nonsense see 'Genocide and the Bicentenary: The French Revolution and the Revenge of the Vendée' by Hugh Gough in *The Historical Journal*, 30, 4 (1987), pp977-988.

136   Richard Cobb's *The People's Armies* (Yale University Press, London, 1987) is the definitive account of these armies.

137   Rudé, *The French Revolution*, p98.

138   In a letter to Victor Adler quoted in Rudé, *The French Revolution*, p73.

139   G Lefebvre, *The French Revolution*, vol 2, p38.

140   Bouloiseau, *The Jacobin Republic*, p125.

141   Ibid, p123.

142   Cowie, op cit, p106.

143   Bouloiseau, op cit, p145.

144   Ibid, p125.

145   Lefebvre, *The French Revolution*, p98.

146   Bouloiseau, *The Jacobin Republic*, p148.

147   Lefebvre, op cit, p102.

148   Bouloiseau, op cit, p144.

149   Ibid, p129, and Lefebvre, op cit, p96.

150   Bouloiseau, op cit, p163.

151   Ibid, p167.

152   See R Price, *An Economic History of Modern France 1730-1914*, (Macmillan, London, 1981), pp6-8.

153   Figures on the Terror from Lefebvre, op cit, pp119, 120, 136.

154   Despite the political problems with his whole approach Guérin's *Class Struggles...* is the best account of the details of this offensive against the popular movement.

155   The metric system of weights and measures we use today was introduced by the French Revolutionaries. They also planned to change the clock to a metric system— with the hours divided into 100 'minutes' and so on, but the revolutionary government did not survive long enough. Other measures were enacted in the autumn of 1793 to underline the end of the old order of privileges and deference. These included the compulsory use of the familiar 'tu' instead of the more formal 'vous' even in official documents.

156   Cowie, op cit, p98.

157   Lefebvre, op cit, p80.

158   Bouloiseau, op cit, p115.

159   Ibid, p192.

160   Soboul, *A Short History...* p111.

161   Ibid, p115.

162   Bouloiseau, op cit, p194.

163   Ibid, p150.

164   Guérin, *Class Struggles...* p241.

165   Bouloiseau, op cit, p188.

166   See Cowie, op cit, p111. The Great Terror was concentrated almost entirely in Paris. Elsewhere the period is not distinguishable from the rest of the Terror. And the targets in Paris are shown by the fact that the proportion of victims from the bourgeoisie doubled while that of nobles quadrupled in this period. See Bouloiseau, op cit, p211.

167   L Kelly, *Women of the French Revolution* (Hamish Hamilton, London, 1987), p145.

168   Robespierre seems to have recognised this and resigned himself to defeat. In his last speech to the Jacobins he said, 'The speech you have just heard is my last will and testament, I saw today that the league of the wicked is so powerful that I cannot hope to escape it. I submit without regret, I leave you my memory: it will be dear to you and you will defend it' (Guérin, *Class Struggles...*, p262). The argument that he was plotting to become a dictator and was directing the excesses of the Great Terror is, for instance, the view of some on the left such as Guérin and Belfort Bax as well as many right wing historians. It is an entirely unconvincing argument. Robespierre appears to have been the *only* person in the Convention to object to the excesses at the time (speech at Jacobin Club, 23 Messidor [11 July]). And he did not play any direct role in the government for almost six weeks before his downfall, and so on. This is not to paint a rosy picture of Robespierre—he was able to use the most ruthless methods when necessary—simply to reject the argument that the pre-Thermidor period can be understood in terms of a plot to set up a dictatorship by Robespierre (with St Just and Couthon). Equally ludicrous as an explanation is Guérin's 'Victory made him [Robespierre] bad tempered, afraid that somebody else might benefit from it'! (*Class Struggles...* p253.)

169   Text of Robespierre's last speech to the Convention, Wright, op cit, pp217-224.

170   Taylor, op cit, p107.

171   Ten sections rallied to the Robespierrists, 18 to the Convention, and the rest vacillated. But even in the pro-Jacobin sections only small numbers responded. See Soboul, *A Short History...* p118.

172   Bouloiseau, op cit, p224.

173   This period is one of amazing complexity, though usually, including here, it is treated as of only secondary importance, which is unfortunate. In particular it is in this period that the revolution had its greatest impact abroad through the war moving from the defensive to the offensive— ranging from Italy and Germany to an attempted invasion of Ireland. Though the Directory was internally reactionary, it was forced in its expansive wars to uproot aspects of the old order in a string of countries across Europe to achieve its goals. This process was continued under Bonaparte. Often this was done with the support of local 'patriots' (ie bourgeois revolutionaries) though they were strictly subordinated to the aims of the French and often suppressed when their national ambitions came into conflict with French plans. Republics were created such as the Cisalpine, Roman and Parthenopean in Italy or the Batavian Republic in Holland. I omit entirely any discussion of this. It is covered well in G Lefebvre's *The French Revolution* (Vol 2)—still the best account—and D Woronoff's *The Thermidorean Regime and the Directory*.

174   See, for instance, the account by A Hamilton Rowan in Cowie, op cit, pp111-112.

175   D Woronoff, op cit (Cambridge University Press, 1984), p1.

176   A Soboul, *A Short History...* p98.

177   Six former Montagnard deputies led by Soubrany spoke up in support of the demonstrators. They were later arrested and committed suicide or were executed.

178   D Woronoff, op cit, p18.

179   The term gradually acquired a wider political meaning during the revolution and came to denote all those who supported direct democracy and the utopian dream of a republic of small property owners regardless of whether they were actually petty bourgeois sans-culottes.

180   G Lefebvre, op cit (vol 2), p145.

181   D Woronoff, op cit, p23.

182   G Rudé, *The French Revolution*, p118.

183   A Soboul, *A Short History...* pp127-128.

184   Ibid, p132.

185   Ibid, p138.

186   Manifesto of the Plebians published in *Le Tribun du Peuple*, 9 Frimaire, Year IV

(30 November, 1795), quoted in ibid, p138.

187 Guérin, *Class Struggles...* p288.

188 This is clear from lists of subscribers to *Le Tribun du Peuple* and of 'patriots capable of taking command' discovered after the Conspiracy was smashed. See Woronoff, op cit, p49.

189 The question of private property was often fudged and the 'Constitution of 1793' elevated to major importance. See the documents in Wright, op cit, pp231-235.

190 The long delay was due to the fact that one of the leaders of the conspiracy was Drouet, a member of the Council of Five Hundred. This meant a lengthy constitutional procedure to allow the trial to proceed without raising the spectre of the purging of the Convention of the Year II. This Drouet was the village postmaster who had foiled the king's attempted flight at Varennes in 1791. He survived his trial and re-emerged as the leader of a Jacobin revival shortly before Bonaparte's coup in 1799. Buonarotti kept Babeuf's ideas alive and they would eventually be adapted by Blanqui in the 19th century.

191 Woronoff, op cit, p188.

192 The coup is usually referred to as taking place on 18 Brumaire, though in fact it took place on the 19th.

193 G Rudé, *The French Revolution*, p125.

194 Ibid, p126.

195 Lefebvre, *The French Revolution*, vol 2, p307.

196 Rudé, *The French Revolution*, p138. Similar concerns meant that he instructed his army not to interfere with Muslim religious practices in Egypt. He once said, 'If I were governing Jews I would restore the Temple of Solomon.' (Rudé, p139.)

197 Ibid, p139.

198 That this is possible—ie for a regime to be internally reactionary yet externally progressive—is a feature of the bourgeois revolution. It is an impossibility in the case of a socialist revolution.

199 See Trotsky, *Our political tasks* (New Park, London, nd), Appendix on 'Jacobinism and Social Democracy' pp121-128, for this and Trotsky's attack on Lenin's view.

200 Guérin, op cit, p287.

201 For the 'orthodox' tradition see the various works by Lefebvre, Soboul and Rudé referred to throughout. Rudé's *The French Revolution*, pp12-24, gives a useful summary of the changing views of historians.

202 See for these 'Revolution Denied' by John Rees in *Socialist Worker Review* (Issue 103, November 1987) and Brian Manning, 'Class and Revolution in Seventeenth Century England', in *International Socialism*, Issue 38. There are also important differences stemming essentially from the fact that France is a republic and most mainstream political currents in France derive their legitimacy from the revolution (though different phases of the revolution).

203 I am not accusing people like Lefebvre of being Stalinists! Rather the intellectual climate they operated in was permeated with ideas derived from Stalinist distortions of Marxism.

204 The work of recent French historians, in particular M Vovelle and M Bouloiseau, goes some way towards overcoming the weaknesses in the orthodox account. See works referred to throughout.

205 See A Cobban, *The Social Interpretation of the French Revolution* (Cambridge University Press, 1965), pp172, 173, for this conclusion.

206 W Doyle's *Origins of the French Revolution* (Oxford University Press, 1980) is probably the best summary of the revisionist case. G Comninel, *Rethinking the French Revolution: Marxism and the Revisionist Challenge* (Verso, London, 1987), despite his, in my opinion, badly mistaken conclusions provides a good summary of the various revisionist arguments and some of the attempts to reply. François Furet is easily the most important and influential of those attacking the Marxist view. See for instance his *Interpreting the French Revolution* (Cambridge University

Press, 1981). He has recently published two major new books which look set to dominate discussions during the bicentenary, but as yet I have not seen them.

207   Comninel, op cit. He ends up attacking Marx for being fooled by bourgeois liberal ideology and suggesting that the concept of a bourgeois revolution in France should either 'refer to 1871'(!) or 'it may be better simply to drop the idea of bourgeois revolution once and for all' (p205).

208   Ibid, p3.

209   Ibid, p23.

210   Miliband, 'Barnave...' p25.

211   The revisionists often tax Marxism with arguing that the French bourgeois revolution was an inevitable stage in the rise of capitalism. This is nonsense. It *was* an important part of that development, but history was, and is, made by human beings. Their scope for action, the possibilities, are circumscribed by objective circumstances but they *make* history by action within those limits. So Marxists will have no difficulty in agreeing with the revisionist William Doyle that the French Revolution 'was neither inevitable nor predictable. What was inevitable was the breakdown of the old order' (Doyle, op cit, p210). It is of course *possible* that this breakdown could have been resolved differently. But we are concerned with understanding *real* history with a view to making real history.

212   Whose general position is that what matters are long term changes—*'la longue durée'*—and not 'events'. Of course there is much of value in stressing the importance of long-term structural shifts in history, but not at the price of dismissing the importance of conscious human action, political battles, revolutions and so on.

213   He has the merit of writing well and has also made a serious study of Marx's writings on, and attitude to, the French Revolution (*Marx et La Révolution Française* [with Lucien Calvié] Flammarion, Paris, 1986). He has a particularly sharp understanding of the way Stalinism and the politics of the Popular Front influenced the 'orthodox account'.

214   Furet, *Interpreting...* p129.

215   Interview in the *International Herald Tribune*, 6 January 1989.

216   Ibid.

217   Which is why the conclusion of George Rudé's (otherwise quite good) new book, *The French Revolution*—'Has it not rather become a page from a history book, or a museum piece to be safely locked away or forgotten until the next National Day?'—(p183) is wrong.

218   quoted in Comninel, op cit, p43.

219   Ibid, p46.

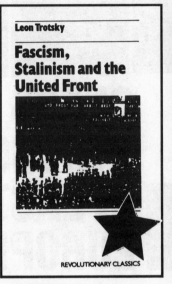

Bourgeois revolutions and historical materialism

ALEX CALLINICOS

'You never go so far as when you don't know where you are going.'
Oliver Cromwell

'The force of circumstances perhaps leads us to results we had not thought of.'
Louis de Saint-Just

Marxism and the French Revolution

The world historical significance of the French Revolution is beyond
dispute. As Alfred Cobban, one of its leading English historians, put
it: 'The revolution is the strategic centre of modern history. Its
interpretation is crucial both for the understanding of the age of social
change which preceded it and of the period—now nearly two centuries—
of revolution which has followed it.'[1] Of no form of social theory has
this been more true than for Marxism, which treats revolution not merely
as an object of scholarly study but as the goal of political activity. Marx
and Engels made clear the significance of the French Revolution in the
Communist Manifesto. Like the English Revolution of 1640 and the
German Revolution which they believed would break out that year, 1848,
it was a bourgeois revolution through which 'the bourgeoisie...conquered
for itself, in the modern representative state, exclusive political
sway.'[2]

Barely a year later, writing in the very thick of revolution, as editor
of the *Neue Rheinische Zeitung*, Marx elaborated on this judgement:

> *The revolution of 1789 (at least in Europe) had as its prototype only the
> [English] revolution of 1648; the revolution of 1648 only the revolt of the
> Netherlands against Spain. Both revolutions were a century in advance of
> their prototypes not only in time but also in content.*
>
> *In both revolutions the bourgeoisie was the class that **really** headed the
> movement. The **proletariat** and the **non-bourgeois strata of the middle class***

had either not yet any interests separate from those of the bourgeoisie or they did not constitute independent classes or class sub-divisions. Therefore, where they opposed the bourgeoisie, as they did in France in 1793 and 1794, they fought only for the attainment of the aims of the bourgeoisie, even if not in the manner of the bourgeoisie. All French terrorism was nothing but a plebeian way of dealing with the enemies of the bourgeoisie, absolutism, feudalism and philistinism.

The revolutions of 1648 and 1789 were not English and French revolutions, they were revolutions of a European type. They did not represent the victory of a particular class of society over the old political order; they proclaimed the political order of the new European society. The bourgeoisie was victorious in these revolutions, but the victory of the bourgeoisie was at the same time the victory of a new social order, the victory of bourgeois ownership over feudal ownership, of nationality over provincialism, of competition over the guild, of the division of land over primogeniture, of the rule of the landowner over the domination of the owner by the land, of enlightenment over superstition, of the family over the family name, of industry over heroic idleness, of bourgeois law over medieval privileges.[3]

Marx is unequivocal about both the nature of the class forces involved in the Revolution—above all, the bourgeoisie—and its results, the domination of the capitalist mode of production. His main interest, of course, lies in this outcome, since bourgeois domination for Marx ushers in the epoch of socialist revolution, in which the contradictions of capitalist society lead to the conquest of power by the working class. The significance of bourgeois revolutions for Marxists cannot, however, be restricted to their consequences. By mobilising popular violence to smash the structures of feudal society, these revolutions provided both an example and the beginnings of a tradition on which socialists could draw. Thus, in *The German Ideology* Marx defended Robespierre, Saint-Just and the other Jacobin leaders for their resort to methods of revolutionary terror, calling them 'the real representatives of revolutionary power, ie, of the class which *alone* was truly revolutionary, the "innumerable" masses.'[4]

Indeed during the 1848 Revolution, the victory of which he believed required Jacobin methods, Marx argued that 'there is only *one means* by which the murderous death agonies of the old society and the bloody birth throes of the new society can be *shortened*, simplified and concentrated—and that is by *revolutionary terror*'.[5] A similar attitude towards the great bourgeois revolutions was displayed by later Marxists. Thus Trotsky, in his polemic in *Where is Britain Going?* against the cult of gradual change practised by British Tories and social democrats alike, invoked the example of the English Revolution, even calling Lenin, 'The proletarian twentieth-century Cromwell.' Trotsky continued:

The French bourgeoisie, having falsified the revolution, adopted it and, changing it into small coinage, put it into daily circulation. The British bourgeoisie has erased the very memory of the seventeenth-century revolution by dissolving its past in gradualness. The advanced British workers will have to rediscover the English revolution and find within its ecclesiastical shell the mighty struggle of social forces. Cromwell was in no case a 'pioneer of labour'. But in the seventeenth-century drama, the British proletariat can find great precedents for revolutionary action. [6]

Marx was not the first thinker to have discovered at work within the French Revolution what Trotsky called 'the mighty struggle of social forces'. During the revolution itself, Barnave, a leader of the Feuillants (constitutional monarchists) in the Legislative Assembly who was guillotined under the Terror, wrote the first sketch of a materialist analysis which traced the fall of the monarchy to the expansion of trade and industry: 'Once the arts and commerce have succeeded in penetrating the people and creating a new means of wealth in support of the industrious class, a revolution in political laws is prepared: a new distribution of wealth involves a new distribution of power. Just as the possession of land gave rise to the aristocracy, industrial property increases the power of the people.' [7] Although Marx does not seem to have read Barnave, he acknowledged the influence of the great generation of bourgeois historians who studied the revolution under the restored monarchy of 1815-48—Thiers, Mignet, Guizot. [8]

Although it was thus bourgeois writers who pioneered the materialist analysis of the French Revolution, Marx's own influence inspired what Albert Soboul called 'the classical social interpretation' of the French Revolution. [9] Founded by Jean Jaurès at the beginning of the 20th century, when his celebrated *Histoire socialiste de la Révolution Française* was published, perhaps its greatest exponent was Georges Lefebvre. Lefebvre specialised in agrarian history, but also studied the major political events, for example in his immensely influential *The Coming of the French Revolution*, published during the 150th anniversary of the revolution in 1939. His view of its nature echoed Marx's: 'The Revolution is only the crown of a long economic and social evolution which has made the bourgeoisie the master of the world.' [10] Not the least of Lefebvre's achievements was to have encouraged a group of brilliant pupils to study the revolution 'from below': the results included Albert Soboul's *The Parisian Sans-Culottes and the French Revolution 1793-4* (1958), George Rudé's *The Crowd in the French Revolution* (1959) and Richard Cobb's *The People's Armies* (1961, 1963). [11]

Between Lefebvre's death in 1959 and his own in 1982, Soboul was the chief advocate of the 'classical social interpretation'. Soboul was a loyal member of the French Communist Party (PCF). The PCF had, since the days of the Popular Front in the 1930s, adopted the Revolution for its own as an anticipation of the 'national' road to socialism which they would open in alliance with the 'progressive', 'anti-monopoly' wing of capital. The Marxist interpretation of the revolution developed especially by Lefebvre and Soboul therefore became associated with the PCF. A somewhat similar process took place with respect to the English Revolution. Here the pioneering modern materialist studies of the revolution were made by the Christian socialist R H Tawney. In 1940 however, Christopher Hill, a young Communist historian, published an essay called *The English Revolution 1640*, in which he argued that 'the English Revolution of 1640-60 was a great social movement like the French Revolution of 1789. The state power protecting an old order that was essentially feudal was violently overthrown, power passed to the hands of a new class, and so the freer development of capitalism was made possible.'[12] Hill was one of a generation of highly talented CP historians—among the others were Edward Thompson, Eric Hobsbawm, Rodney Hilton and Victor Kiernan — who, after the Second World War under the influence of the economist Maurice Dobb, began to study the evolution of British society 'from below' just as Cobb, Rudé and Soboul were similarly investigating the French Revolution.[13] Hill left the CP in 1957, after the Hungarian Revolution, but continued his explorations of the class forces at work in the English Revolution, perhaps most successfully in *The World Turned Upside Down* (1972).

Today, almost a generation after the pioneering Marxist studies of Hill, Soboul and others, not simply is their work under attack, but a denial that the English and French Revolutions were bourgeois revolutions has become the orthodoxy among academic historians. More surprisingly, this orthodoxy has proved sufficiently powerful to persuade some Marxists that the concept of bourgeois revolution should itself be rejected.

This article is a defence of the Marxist theory of bourgeois revolutions. Its aim is to restate that theory in a form that is not vulnerable to the revisionist criticisms. I argue that, first, bourgeois revolutions are transformations which create the political conditions of capitalist domination. As such, they are not necessarily the work of the bourgeoisie itself, but can be achieved by a variety of different social forces. Secondly, there is no single pattern of bourgeois revolution. Looking at the historical record we can identify two main variants: the 'classical' bourgeois revolutions (Holland 1572, England 1640, America 1776, France 1789) in which broad coalitions of small producers were mobilised to smash the old order; and the bourgeois 'revolutions from above' (German and Italian unification, the American Civil War of 1861-5, the Meiji Restoration of 1868 in Japan)in which the existing state apparatus was used to remove the obstacles to bourgeois domination.

Which kind of revolution occurred depended to a large degree on the phase of capitalist development reached by the world economy; I therefore also discuss the transition from feudalism to capitalism which forms the objective context of these great political struggles. Finally, I briefly discuss a third variant of bourgeois revolution, which Tony Cliff calls 'deflected permanent revolution', the Third World revolutions of the 20th century whose main achievement has been the establishment of state capitalist regimes.

The revisionist onslaught

The most important single issue in the debates over the English and French Revolutions has concerned the nature of the class which led the revolution.

Marx believed that 'the bourgeoisie was the class that *really* headed the movement'. But where was the bourgeoisie to be found in the English Revolution? This was what was at stake in the famous 'storm over the gentry' which burst among historians at the end of the 1940s.[14] Tawney argued that the century before the revolution had seen the rise of the gentry, 'the landed proprietors, above the yeomanry, and below the peerage, together with a growing body of well-to-do farmers,' who, unlike the bulk of the aristocracy, responded to the great 16th century inflation by 'rationalizing the administration of their estates and improving their layout'.

More specifically, they consolidated their estates into large farms, began to enclose the commons, invested in land reclamation and engaged in other forms of enterprise such as mining and property speculation. 'The landowner living on the profits and rents of commercial farming and the merchant or banker who was also a landowner, represented not two classes, but one. Patrician and *parvenu* both owed their ascent to causes of the same order. Judged by the source of their incomes, both were equally bourgeois.'[15] This rising gentry, then, was the English bourgeoisie, by and for whom the Great Revolution of 1640 was made.

Tawney's thesis, and its elaboration by Lawrence Stone, was subjected to a demolition job by the Tory historian Hugh Trevor-Roper. The real division in 17th century England, he argued, was not that between a decadent feudal aristocracy and a progressive capitalist gentry. The gentry were hit as hard by the price revolution as the nobility. Those of either group who prospered did not so much because they adopted capitalist methods on their estates, but because they had access to 'the tenure of offices of the profits of trade'.

More particularly, the establishment of a centralised monarchy under the Tudors and early Stuarts led to an expansion of lucrative offices which were sold, generally becoming hereditary. The 'mere gentry' who could not afford to buy such offices found themselves under increasing economic pressure. Consequently, 'the significant distinction of Tudor and Stuart landed society' was that 'between "court" and "country", between the office-holders and the mere landlords'. The revolution was a consequence of the antagonism between court and country. The key force in the revolution was the Independents, whose chief leader was Cromwell, but they represented 'not "rising" gentry' but 'the declining gentry', long alienated from the court and at last given an opportunity to shape events by the crisis brought about by Charles I's attempt at personal rule.[16]

Trevor-Roper extended his argument in a second essay, where he took issue with Eric Hobsbawm's claim that the more general crisis of 17th century European society represented 'the last phase of the general transition from a feudal to a capitalist economy'.[17] The dislocation which provoked 'almost a general revolution' in the mid 17th century—not just the Civil War in England but the Thirty Years' War on the Continent—was not one, argued Trevor-Roper, between the forces and relations of production but 'a crisis in the relations between society and the state'.

Its outcome—the execution of Charles I—was, however, avoidable: the Stuarts suffered from 'a fatal lack of political skills'. Thus, had 'James I or Charles I had the intelligence of Queen Elizabeth or the docility of Louis XIII, the English *ancien régime* might have adapted itself to the new circumstances as peacefully in the seventeenth century as it would in the nineteenth.'[18]

This slide into the cock-up theory of history should not obscure the fact that Trevor-Roper, Tory and anti-Marxist though he is, remained committed to the social explanation of historical events: 'all revolutions, even though they may be occasioned by external causes, and expressed in intellectual form, are made real and formidable by defects of social structure'.[19] His chief difference lay in his conception of social structure, one in which the state enjoyed greater significance than it was given by Tawney or Hobsbawm.

Subsequent opponents of the Marxist interpretation of the English Revolution went much further. In the 1970s a much younger group of historians, generally known as the revisionists, emerged. They—their principal representative was Conrad (now Lord) Russell—were accurately, if disparagingly, described by Stone as 'young antiquarian empiricists. They write detailed political narratives which implicitly deny any deep seated meaning to history except the accidental whims of fortune and personality.'[20] In the revisionists' hands the English Revolution became little more than a scrimmage between provincial notables of no socio-economic or ideological significnance.[21]

Controversies concerning the French Revolution have followed, with some time lag, a similar course.[22] Here too the anti-Marxist onslaught was launched by a British historian, Alfred Cobban, in 1955. The central issue was, once again, the nature of the bourgeoisie. Cobban argued that by 1789 there was no clear dividing line between nobility and bourgeoisie. The bourgeoisie bought themselves into land on a large scale and were in many cases the owners of the seigneurial rights which were the target of the peasant risings in the summer of 1789.

The so called 'feudal reaction'—the systematic use of these rights by many of their owners to squeeze more out of the peasantry—which underlay these risings, far from being the last gasp of the aristocracy, represented an attempt by both noble and bourgeois landowners to apply modern business techniques in agriculture. The peasants were reacting *against* the penetration of capitalism into the countryside. Similarly, analysis of the composition of the revolutionary assemblies showed that 'the revolutionary bourgeoisie was primarily the declining class of *officiers* and lawyers and other professional men, and not the businessmen of commerce and industry'. Cobban concluded that 'the revolution was to an important extent one *against* and not *for* the rising forces of capitalism'.[23]

While Cobban dismissed the contribution of social theory in general, and Marxism in particular to historical understanding, like Trevor-Roper he remained committed to interpreting political events as consequences of more fundamental social forces.[24] Later revisionists, however, rejected any social interpretation of the French Revolution. Thus in 1965 François Furet and Denis Richet published a history of the revolution in which the most controversial thesis was that the radicalisation of 1791-2, from the flight to Varennes to the insurrection of 10 August 1792 which overthrew the monarchy and opened the door to the Jacobin dictatorship of 1793-4, represented 'the skidding off-course of the revolution' (*le dérapage de la révolution*). The collapse of the liberal compromise between the monarchy and the bourgeoisie embodied in the 1791 Constitution was not inevitable, Furet and Richet argued.[25]

The idea of *dérapage* was subjected to bitter criticism, not all of it from the left.[26] Furet responded in a series of polemical essays which did not reject the concept of bourgeois revolution, but insisted that the 'bourgeois revolution was made, and completed, without any sort of compromise with the old society, between 1789 and 1791'. Furet drew on Tocqueville's *The Ancien Régime and the Revolution*, which stressed the continuity between the monarchy and the post-Revolutionary state: the chief work of the Constituent Assembly, the Convention and the Napoleonic Empire alike was to complete the project of administrative centralisation begun by Philip Augustus in the 12th century. In contrast with this long term process operating through the revolution, there was the unfolding of political events from the storming of the Bastille, through the Terror and Thermidor, to Napoleon's *coup d'état*: 'for in what it involves of permanent *dérapage*, and in contradication with its social nature, [the revolutionary process] …is constituted by an autonomous political and ideological dynamic.' Central to this dynamic were the ideas of direct democracy motivating the revolutionary clubs and crowds: 'the Jacobin and Terrorist ideology functioned largely as an autonomous instance, independent of political and military circumstances'. It was this ideology rather than class interests or the threat of counter-revolution which explained the radicalisation after 1791.[27]

Furet's polemic reinforced the general drift among historians. Already by 1970, Cobb, whose *People's Armies* had painted a detailed collective portrait of the *sans-culottes*, and who, while never a Marxist, had earlier displayed a certain sympathy towards the Popular Front politics of the PCF, could dismiss the *sans-culotte* as 'a freak of nature, more a state of mind than a social, political or economic entity'.[28]

Historians' attention shifted away from the Year II, the focus of the great studies of the popular movement by Soboul and Rudé as well as by Cobb himself, towards the period before the revolution's *dérapage* into a mass mobilisation and Terror, of the Constituent and Legislative Assemblies, and indeed of the 'aristocratic revolution' of 1787 which forced Louis XVI to convene the Estates-General. By 1980 William Doyle could announce the appearance of a 'new international consensus' such that only 'isolated scholars now invoke the capitalist bourgeoisie as a revolutionary force'. Doyle's own attempt to provide a rival account of the revolution's origins to Lefebvre's presented developments between 1787 and 1789 as a succession of accidents in which much of the impetus for change had come from liberal nobles influenced by the Enlightenment.[29]

In his response to Cobban's first attack on the 'classic social interpretation' of the revolution, Lefebvre had commented:

> *I do not doubt that it reflects the ideological evolution of the ruling class under the influence of democratic pressure and above all of the Russian Revolution; feeling themselves threatened they repudiate the rebellion by their ancestors which assured them pre-eminence, because they discern in it a dangerous precedent.*[30]

This judgement applies even more strongly to Furet's interventions, and especially to his essay 'La Révolution Française est Terminée' (The French Revolution is Over). This was written in the spring of 1977 at a time when a group of disillusioned ex-Maoists, misnamed the *nouveaux philosophes* (new philosophers), had announced, to the great enthusiasm of the French media, that the Stalinist terror was a necessary consequence of Marxism. Furet explicitly aligned himself with this enterprise: 'Today, the Gulag leads to a rethinking of the Terror, in virtue of an identity of project.'[31]

The *nouveaux philosophes* were a symptom of the 'crisis of Marxism' which afflicted many of the generation of 1968 throughout Western capitalism in the late 1970s; but they also contributed to the bitter struggle between the French Communist Party (PCF) and the Socialist Party under François Mitterrand for dominance of the reformist left in France. Its success in identifying Marxism with Stalinism helped to draw much of the Parisian intelligentsia, Marxist influenced since the liberation in 1944, towards liberalism and social democracy.[32] But while the *nouveaux philosophes* helped secure Mitterand's hegemony, the Socialist Party regime installed after the 1981 presidential elections still needs the revolution as the traditional source of legitimacy for the French Republic. The rise of the extreme right—not simply Le Pen's *Front National* but sections of the Gaullist RPR—has led to an ideological assault on the revolution itself. Heading this offensive is Pierre Chaunu, a distinguished historian of the *ancien régime* who seems to have fallen in love with his object of study. Chaunu and his followers have focused on the bloodiest episode in the revolution, the suppression by the Jacobins of the risings by Catholic peasants in the Vendée and other western departments. According to Chaunu:

> *The Jacobin drift appears today as only the first act, the founding event of a long and bloody series, which goes from 1792 to our days, from the Franco-French genocide of the Catholic West to the Soviet Gulag, to the destructions of the Chinese Cultural Revolution and to the Khmer Rouge self-genocide in Cambodia.*[33]

Mitterand supporters such as Régis Debray and Max Gallo have responded by defending the revolution and even (in Debray's case) the Terror. The result is that the revolution's bicentenary—officially celebrated with great pomp and circumstance and culminating in a meeting in Paris on 14 July 1989 of the Group of Seven, among whom are to be numbered such revolutionaries as George Bush and Margaret Thatcher—is taking place amid intense ideological controversy.

Against this political background it might seem a little surprising that the lead up to the bicentenary should also have seen a Marxist attempt not simply to reject the 'classical social interpretation' of the French Revolution, but the very concept of bourgeois revolution itself. Nevertheless this is precisely what a book by the Canadian Marxist George Comninel, *Rethinking the French Revolution*, sets out to do. Comninel begins by asserting: 'It must now be accepted that the long-standing claims to historical validity of the Marxist interpretation of the French Revolution have been exploded.' He largely accepts the revisionist critique: 'The French Revolution was an *intra-class* conflict over basic political relations that at the same time directly touched on relations of surplus-extraction. It was a civil war within the ruling class over the essential issues of surplus-extraction.' Moreover, the pre-revolutionary 'bourgeoisie certainly was not a capitalist class', and capitalist relations of production existed nowhere in French society, least of all in agriculture, 'the overwhelmingly predominant sector of social production', but not even in the rapidly growing manufacturing sector, the profit from which 'was no more capitalist in character than the surplus produced in Roman manufacture'. Long after the revolution the French state continued to rest on 'the "extra-economic" modes of surplus extraction that Marx associated with *non*-capitalist societies in Volume III of *Capital*'. Only with the Third Republic (1871-1940) was a genuinely bourgeois regime installed, 'by which time capitalism can at last also be said to have existed'.[34] Comninel's acceptance of the revisionist critique of the Marxist theory of bourgeois revolution is part of a wider attempt to 'rethink' historical materialism (see Appendix).

The self emancipation of the bourgeoisie

The main thrust of the revisionist critique challenges the idea that the bourgeoisie as a class led either the English or the French Revolutions. The difficulty in the English case was well expressed by Tawney himself: 'Bourgeois revolution? Of course it was a bourgeois revolution. The trouble is that the bourgeoisie was on both sides.'[35] Comninel summarises the revisionist consensus with respect to France:

> *The essential proposition is that, since both the nobility and the bourgeoisie had marked **internal** differentiation, and no impermeable boundary existed between them, and the two statuses had a good deal in common in terms of their forms of wealth, professions, and general ideology, it therefore would be more accurate to recognize a **single** 'elite' in the **ancien régime** or, more precisely, a dominant social stratum comprising different, but sometimes overlapping 'elites'.[36]*

The revisionist claim is, however, damaging to classical Marxism only on condition that we conceive bourgeois revolutions as necessarily the result of the self conscious action of the capitalist class. Such a view has often been defended by Marxists—indeed by Marx himself, for example in the passage cited above where he says that in the English and French Revolutions 'the bourgeoisie was the class that *really* headed the movement.' There is indeed a tendency in the Marxist tradition to treat these as the 'classical' bourgeois revolutions, in which the capitalist class consciously appropriated political power. As such, these revolutions—but above all the French—then constitute a norm by which other, later candidates for the status of bourgeois revolutions, are judged.

But what happens when these candidates deviate from the norm? Lukács argued that the irrationalist and anti-democratic traditions exploited by the Nazis stemmed from Germany's failure to follow 'the normal road of bourgeois-democratic development'.[37] The idea that Germany's disastrous history in the first half of the 20th century was a consequence of its 'failed bourgeois revolution' in the 19th became part of the orthodoxy among liberal and social democratic historians and social scientists in post-war West Germany. Explaining Nazism in terms of Germany's *Sonderweg* (special path) had political implications: the triumph of fascism could be seen as a peculiarly German aberration rather than as one instance of a general capitalist crisis.[38]

David Blackbourn and Geoff Eley observe in their outstanding critique of the idea of the German *Sonderweg*:

> *In order to have an aberration it is clearly necessary to have a norm...here, sometimes explicitly, and often implicitly, it was 'Western' and most particularly Anglo-Saxon and French developments that were taken as a yardstick against which German history was measured and found wanting.*[39]

The trouble is that the cases which constitute the yardstick may themselves not conform to it. Perry Anderson's essay 'Origins of the Present Crisis' (1962) is an example of what happens when this is recognised but the use in particular of the French Revolution as a norm is not abandoned. Anderson sought to explain Britain's post-war decline by what he called the 'symbiosis' of the landed aristocracy and the industrial bourgeoisie. This process could be traced back to the English Revolution, *'the first, most mediated, and least pure bourgeois revolution of any major European country'*, 'a "bourgeois revolution" by proxy', made by a section of the gentry which could not be identified with 'a rising bourgeoisie'. 'Thus the three crucial idiosyncrasies of the English Revolution, which have determined the whole of our subsequent history': first, the effect of the Revolutions of 1640 and 1688 in stimulating the development of capitalism; secondly, the *'permanent partial interpenetration'* of aristocracy and bourgeoisie on terms favouring the former's continued hegemony; thirdly, the limits of Puritanism as a revolutionary ideology, which 'because of its "primitive", pre-Enlightenment character,...founded no universal tradition in Britain.'[40]

His interpretation of English history implies that Britain's economic decline relative to other developed capitalist societies could be reversed by a bourgeois 'modernisation' which eliminated those features—the monarchy, House of Lords, electoral system, etc—which represent a deviation from the norm. Much of the most celebrated and powerful of the many critiques of Anderson was Edward Thompson's great essay 'The Peculiarities of the English', one of whose targets was 'a model which concentrates attention upon one dramatic episode—*the* Revolution—to which all that goes before must be related; and which insists upon an ideal type of this Revolution against which all these others may be judged.'[41]

It is the French Revolution which provides Anderson with the source of his ideal type by which its English counterpart is found wanting. But what happens if even the French case deviates from the norm? Eley argues:

> *The idea of Germany's failed bourgeois revolution contains one further*

assumption that is the most dubious of all, namely that the model of 'bourgeois revolution' attributed to Britain and France (ie that of a forcibly acquired liberal democracy seized by a triumphant bourgeoisie, acting politically as a class, in conscious struggle against a feudal aristocracy) actually occurred. This assumption is both basic and extremely questionable. For the thesis of the abortive bourgeois revolution...presupposes a reading of the English and French experiences which is effectively discredited.[42]

Where are we left if even the French Revolution cannot be seen unproblematically as the self conscious action of the bourgeoisie?

The structure of bourgeois revolution

Responding to the revisionist attacks requires a shift in focus. Bourgeois revolutions must be understood, not as revolutions consciously made by capitalists, but as revolutions which promote capitalism. The emphasis should shift from the class which makes a bourgeois revolution to the effects of such a revolution—to the class which benefits from it. More specifically, a bourgeois revolution is a political transformation—a change in state power, which is the precondition for large scale capital accumulation and the establishment of the bourgeoisie as the dominant class. This definition requires, then, a political change with certain effects. It says nothing about the social forces which carry through the transformation.

Comninel would, I imagine, dismiss this formulation as a defensive manoeuvre designed to protect the theory of bourgeois revolutions from empirical refutation by the revisionists. But some such definition is required once we extend our gaze beyond the 'classical' bourgeois revolutions—the Netherlands, England, America, France—to consider other, more recent candidates, in particular, German and Italian unification, completed almost simultaneously at the end of the 1860s, and the Meiji Restoration of 1868 in Japan. Thus Gramsci, long before the revisionists had appeared, characterised the Italian Risorgimento, achieved by the monarchy of Sardinia Piedmont through the incorporation of both the northern bourgeoisie and the traditionally land owning classes, especially in the south, as a process of 'passive revolution', in which 'an ever more extensive ruling class' was formed through 'the gradual but continuous absorption, achieved by methods which varied in their effectiveness, of the active elements produced by allied groups—and even of those which came from antagonistic groups and seemed irreconcilably hostile.'[43]

It was on the basis of a comparison of the cases of England, France, and Germany that Nicos Poulantzas argued that:

no paradigm case of the bourgeois revolution can be found. However, one very striking point common to every case should perhaps be noted: namely

the bourgeoisie's lack of political capacity (because of its class constitution)
successfully to lead its own revolution in open action... The all-important
*factor here is the **non-typical** character...of the various bourgeois*
revolution.[44]

Although Poulantzas dismisses as *'mythical'* the idea that the French
Revolution is *'the example* of a "typically" successful bourgeois
revolution',[45] he does in fact think that bourgeois revolutions have a
'characteristic feature', namely that they are *not* the conscious work of
the bourgeoisie. What was supposed to be a problem for treating 1640
or 1789 as bourgeois revolutions now becomes (dare one say) typical.
Poulantzas's stress on the 'political incapacity' of the bourgeoisie stems
from his belief that the processes of economic competition so fragment
the capitalist class as to deprive them of cohesion. It seems to me that
he overstates his case: as Paul McGarr shows elsewhere in this journal
and as I argue below, the French Revolution was carried through under
bourgeois leadership. It is, however, exceptional for the capitalist class
to play the leading role in bourgeois revolutions.

But how can this be so? Lukács provides an important element of the
answer in his critique of Luxemburg's essay *The Russian Revolution.*
Luxemburg's objections to Bolshevik strategy reflect, according to
Lukács, an underlying misunderstanding: 'she imagines the proletarian
revolution as having the structural forms of bourgeois revolutions.'
Proletarian revolutions do not simply inherit an economic structure from
capitalism which is implicitly socialist. On the contrary, 'after the fall
of capitalism a *lengthy and painful process* sets in', involving the
'conscious transformation of the whole of society'.

> *It is this that constitutes the most profound difference between bourgeois and*
> *proletarian revolutions. The ability of bourgeois revolutions to storm ahead*
> *with such brilliant élan is grounded socially, in the fact that **they are drawing***
> ***the consequences of an almost completed economic and social process in***
> ***a society whose feudal and absolutist structure has been profoundly***
> ***undermined politically, governmentally, juridically, etc., by the vigorous***
> ***upsurge of capitalism.** The truly revolutionary element is the economic*
> *transformation of the feudal system of production into a capitalist one so that*
> *it would be possible in theory for **this** process to take place **without a bourgeois***
> ***revolution**, without political upheaval on the part of the revolutionary*
> *bourgeoisie. And in that case those parts of the feudal and absolutist*
> *superstructure that were not eliminated by 'revolutions from above' would*
> *collapse of their own accord when capitalism was already fully developed.*
> *(The German situation fits this pattern in certain respects.)*[46]

Capitalism, involving (though not, as we shall see in the next section,
reducible to) the spread of commodity circulation, necessarily develops

in a piecemeal and decentralised way within the framework of feudal political domination. It gradually subverts the old order through the infiltration of the whole network of social relationships and the accumulation of economic and political power by capitalists. The effect is both to tie many capitalists to the *ancien régime* but also to change the nature of that *régime*, so that old forms conceal new, bourgeois relationships.

Does this mean, as Lukács suggests, that at the limit this subtle process of socio-economic transformation can dispense with the political overthrow of the *ancien régime*? Gareth Stedman-Jones indeed seems to suggest that bourgeois revolution *is* this process: 'the triumph of the bourgeoisie should be seen as the global victory of a particular form of property relations and a particular form of control over the means of production, rather than as the conscious triumph of a class subject which possessed a distinct and coherent view of the world.'[47] This is, once again, to go too far. For as should become clearer below, the dominance of the capitalist mode of production requires a political transformation, a change in the nature of state power. Moreover, the term 'revolution' should not be dissolved into the long-term socio-processes involved in the development of capitalism. Anderson rightly insists that 'a revolution is an episode of convulsive political transformation, compressed in time and concentrated in target, that has a determinate beginning—when the old state apparatus is still intact—and a finite end when that apparatus is decisively broken and a new one erected in its stead.'[48] Bourgeois revolutions should be understood as revolutions in this sense.

Consequently, it is necessary to distinguish, as Eley puts it,

> *between two levels of determination and significance—between the revolution as a specific crisis of the state, involving widespread popular mobilization and a reconstitution of political relationships, and on the other hand the deeper processes of structural change, involving the increasing predominance of the capitalist mode of production, the potential obsolescence of many existing practices and institutions, and the uneven transformation of social relations.*[49]

Bourgeois revolutions exist at the intersection between objective historical processes and conscious human agency. As 'episodes of convulsive political transformation' they involve forms of collective action, including the intervention of political organisations of various kinds. But bourgeois revolutions also arise from and contribute to 'the increasing predominance of the capitalist mode of production'. As such, they tend to involve a gap between the intentions of the revolutionary actors and the objective consequences of their struggles.

Hill and Soboul, perhaps the most outstanding Marxist students of bourgeois revolution in the past generation, tended increasingly to stress this latter feature. Thus Soboul wrote in a book published in 1982 that even though the Jacobins

> had as their ideal a society of independent small producers, the results of the Revolution nonetheless remained quite different: they cannot be measured by the intentions of its artisans. The initiators of a social movement are not necessarily its beneficiaries: the fact that several of the leaders of the bourgeois revolution were not real bourgeois does not affect the argument. History, moreover, is not made only by the actors who occupy the front of the stage.[50]

Similarly, Hill has in recent years insisted that 'the Marxist conception of a bourgeois revolution, which I find the most helpful model for understanding the English Revolution, does not mean a revolution made by the bourgeoisie.'[51] Indeed, he has written of the English Revolution: 'Like the French Revolution, it took those who had to guide it completely by surprise', and even, 'It is of the essence of the situation that no one really understood what was happening.'[52]

Bourgeois revolutions are, then, political transformations which facilitate the dominance of the capitalist mode of production; it is in no sense a necessary condition of such revolutions that they are made by the bourgeoisie themselves. This definition allows us to distinguish between variants of bourgeois revolution. But before considering these we must first examine the objective processes of capitalist development with which they interact.

Paths to capitalism

The transition from feudalism to capitalism has been a subject of enormous controversy among Marxist historians and economists. The most celebrated debate on the question took place during the 1950s in the pages of the American journal *Science and Society* among members or sympathisers of the Communist Parties. It was provoked by Maurice Dobb's *Studies in the Development of Capitalism* (1946). Dobb defined feudalism as 'virtually identical with what we generally mean by serfdom: an obligation laid on the producer by force and independently of his own volition to fulfil certain economic demands of an overlord, whether these demands take the form of services to be performed or of dues paid in money or in kind.' Feudalism, he argued, was compatible with the relatively developed existence of markets. Consequently he rejected explanations of the decline of feudalism and rise of capitalism which gave primacy to the spread of trade and the growth of the towns as centres of commerce. Dobb argued that the merchant oligarchies of the early modern cities and the guild systems over which they presided acted as an obstacle to the development of capitalist production relations based on the exploitation of wage labour. The decisive change came with 'the birth of a capitalist class from the ranks of production itself', as the 'yeoman farmer of moderate means or handicraft small master' began 'to place greater reliance on the results of hired labour than on the work of himself and his family, and in his calculations to relate the gains of his enterprise to his capital rather than to his own exertions.'[53]

This interpretation was strongly challenged by the American Marxist Paul Sweezy, who insisted that the main causes of the decline of feudalism were the rise of the towns and the spread of the market. Nevertheless, the general drift of the subsequent debate—and perhaps particularly the major contribution by the Japanese historian Kohachiro Takahashi—was in Dobb's favour.[54] One reason for this outcome was the support apparently given to Dobb's position by Marx's own views in *Capital* Volume III. Chapter XX is devoted to 'Historical Facts about Merchant's Capital', merchant's capital being the form of capital predominant in the early modern era, in which profits are derived not from the direct extraction of surplus value from wage labour (the basis of what Marx calls productive capital) but from the purchase and sale of commodities. Marx calls merchant's capital 'historically the oldest free state of existence of capital': 'In all previous modes of production, and all the more wherever production ministers the immediate wants of the producer, merchant's capital appears to perform the function *par excellence* of capital.' Marx goes on to argue:

> *Money and commodity circulation can mediate between spheres of production of widely different organisation, whose internal structure is still chiefly adjusted to the output of use values...[Merchant's capital] in which spheres of production are connected by a third, has a two fold existence. On the one hand, that circulation has not yet established a hold on production, but is related to it as a given premiss. On the other hand, that the production process has not yet absorbed circulation as a mere phase of production. Both, however, are the case in capitalist production.*[55]

This does not mean, of course, that Marx denies any significance to the expansion of mercantile capitalism but he accords a decisive role to the prevailing relations of production. Their character would condition the impact of expanding trade upon the social formation in question, and thereby the nature of the subsequent transition to the capitalist mode of production, in which, as he shows in Part 8 of *Capital* Volume I, involved crucially the direct producers' separation from the means of production and subordination to capitals themselves subject to the pressures of competitive accumulation. Marx therefore goes on to distinguish two paths to capitalism:

> *The transition from the feudal mode of production is twofold. The producer becomes merchant and capitalist, in contrast to the natural agricultural*

economy and the guild bound handicrafts of the medieval urban industries. This is the really revolutionising path. Or else, the merchant establishes direct sway over production. However much this serves historically as a stepping stone...it cannot by itself contribute to the overthrow of the old mode of production, but tends rather to preserve and retain it as its precondition.[56]

This distinction came to be known as that between Way I, in which petty commodity producers develop into productive capitalists, and Way II, in which urban merchants progressively establish control over production, for example through the putting out system whereby they provided raw materials and sometimes money capital to rural cottage industries. Way I, Marx's 'really revolutionising path', certainly seemed to correspond to Dobb's idea of 'the birth of a capitalist class from the ranks of production itself'. It was Takahashi who most comprehensively drew the implications of the idea of the two paths for the understanding of bourgeois revolution:

*In both England and France that revolution had at its basis the class of free and independent peasants and the class of small and middle scale commodity producers. The revolution was a strenuous struggle for state power between a group of the middle class (the Independents in the English Revolution, the Montagnards in the French), and a group of the **haute bourgeoisie** originating in the feudal land aristocracy, the merchant and financial monopolists (in the English Revolution the Royalists and after them the Presbyterians, in the French Revolution the Monarchiens, then the Feuillants, finally the Girondins); in the process of both revolutions, the former routed the latter...*

However, in Prussia and Japan it was quite the contrary...the erection of capitalism under the control of the feudal absolute state was on the cards from the very first... Since capitalism had to be erected on this soil, on a basis of fusion rather than conflict with absolutism, the formation of capitalism took place in the opposite way to Western Europe, predominantly as a process of transformation of putting out merchant capital into industrial capital.[57]

Lenin had drawn a broadly similar distinction when discussing the development of capitalism in Russian agriculture. He argued that there are 'two paths of objectively bourgeois development'—the 'Prussian path' in which feudal lords gradually become capitalist landowners and the 'American path' in which small peasants evolve into commercial farmers.

For Lenin, a society's path of bourgeois development depends not simply on the prevailing relations of production but on political developments, and in particular on whether the small producers are able to sweep away the lords' estates by revolutionary means.[58] The fruitful implications of this approach for understanding the varieties of bourgeois revolution should be obvious. This focus on different historical trajectories has in recent years been challenged by a considerably developed version of the Sweezy thesis. Its main advocate is Immanuel Wallerstein who insists that 'the correct unit of analysis' in analysing the transition to capitalism is 'the world system', more specifically 'the European world economy' which emerged in the late 15th and early 16th centuries.[59]

The Sweezy-Wallerstein school has been subjected to the most thorough and forceful criticism by Robert Brenner.[60] Brenner's argument involves drawing a sharp distinction between capitalist and pre-capitalist modes of production. Capitalism is characterised by 'modern economic growth', in which the rapid development of the productive forces is made possible by investments which increase the productivity of labour; in Marx's terms these involve the extraction of relative, rather than absolute surplus value—higher productivity allows the rate of exploitation to be increased by reducing the share of labour time devoted to the reproduction of the worker, rather than by extending the working day. Such a mode of development is impossible in pre-capitalist formations. Consequently, pre-capitalist modes are subject to a long-term tendency towards stagnation: in the case of feudal Europe this took the form of 'Malthusian' crises in which the rate of population growth outstripping that of agricultural output.

Under capitalism, by contrast, both main classes have an incentive to develop the productive forces intensively: the capitalist is subject to the pressure of competitive accumulation; the worker, by contrast, separated from the means of production, can gain access to the means of subsistence only by selling his or her labour power on terms which subject him or her to pressure to increase output through a variety of mechanisms. There is then a qualitative difference between capitalist relations of production constituted by the exploitation of wage labour and those forms, even when involved in production for the market, which are based on coerced labour.[61]

This analysis underlay Brenner's celebrated interpretation of the role of agriculture in the development of capitalism. First put forward in 1976, it provoked a controversy which although involving primarily non-Marxist historians, was in many respects a continuation of the debate on Dobb's *Studies*. Brenner distinguished three outcomes of the late medieval crisis of feudalism. The first, east of the Elbe, involved the intensification of serfdom. The second, most importantly in France, saw, on the one hand, peasant communities securing effective possession of a large proportion of the land, and, on the other, the development of the 'centralised state' into 'a "class like phenomenon", that is "as an *independent* extractor of the surplus" in particular on the basis of its arbitrary power to tax the land.' The third was found only in England, where the lords were able to prevent the peasants from winning freehold title to the land; there emerged, consequently, the classical 'trinity' of commercial landowner, capitalist tenant, and wage labourer.

Brenner advanced three theses. The first was that the late medieval crisis reflected the way in which feudal property relations systematically prevented the intensive development of the productive forces. Secondly, the outcome of the crisis itself depended on the relative balance of forces between lords and peasants in the class struggles which shook Europe between the 14th and 16th centuries. The peasants were strong enough to win control of a significant proportion of the land in France, but were much weaker in England and eastern Europe where the results were, respectively, capitalist enclosures and the second serfdom. Thirdly, the emergence of capitalist property relations in rural England was an essential prerequisite of the Industrial Revolution. The increases in agricultural productivity which it made possible allowed England to escape from the Malthusian trap which sent continental Europe once again into general crisis in the 17th century; they also released a growing proportion of the working population into industrial pursuits; agricultural progress promoted the expansion of the home market as landlords, farmers and labourers bought increasing quantities of industrial goods.[62]

Brenner's account of the origins of capitalism has proved highly controversial. Two criticisms are directly relevant to the question of bourgeois revolutions. The first was that of voluntarism, of reducing the different trajectories taken by early modern societies to the contingent outcome of conflicts between lord and peasant. This criticism was perhaps most eloquently stated by the French Marxist historian Guy Bois, himself the author of a monumental study of late medieval Normandy:

> Brenner's Marxism is 'political Marxism'... It amounts to a voluntarist vision of history in which the class struggle is divorced from all other objective contingencies and, in the first place, from such laws of development as may be peculiar to a specific mode of production.[63]

In fact Brenner did put forward an account of the laws of motion of the feudal mode of production. This centred on the way in which the structural limits on the expansion of the productive forces promoted the drive to what he called 'political accumulation', the formation and expansion of centralised states:

> In view of the difficulty, in the presence of pre-capitalist property relations, of raising returns from investment in the means of production (via increases in productive efficiency), the lords found that if they wished to increase their income, they had little choice but to do so by **redistributing** wealth and income away from their peasants or from other members of the exploiting class. This meant that they had to deploy their resources toward building up their **means of coercion**—by investment in military men and equipment. Speaking broadly, they were obliged to invest in their politico-military apparatuses. To the extent

*that they had to do this effectively enough to compete with other lords who
were doing the same thing, they would have had to maximise both their military
investments and the efficiency of these investments. They would have had,
in fact, to attempt, continually and systematically to improve their methods
of war. Indeed, we may say that the drive to **political accumulation**, to **state-
building** is the **pre-capitalist** analogue to the capitalist drive to **accumulate
capital**.*[64]

There is, therefore, a tendency inherent in feudalism towards political
centralisation which arises from the military struggles between lords.
Or, as Brenner himself succinctly puts it, 'throughout the feudal
epoch...warfare was the great engine of feudal centralisation.' Moreover,
he argues that the relative strength of feudal states helps to explain the
abilities of the respective aristocracies to resist peasant encroachments
on the land.

Thus the fact that the English monarchy was from the early Middle
Ages 'unusually strong', indeed 'the most highly developed feudal state
in Europe', allowed the lords to highly effectively exploit the
peasants.[65]

Some indication of the relative strength of the ruling classes of France
and England is given by the fact that at the end of the 13th century the
English lords held outright in demesne (ie subject to their direct control)
one third of the cultivated land, compared to between one eighth to one
tenth so held by the French lords. The relative power and centralisation
of the French and English aristocracies led to the emergence of markedly
different state forms in the later Middle Ages.

The relative weakness of the lords and strength of the peasants in
France contributed to the gradual development of absolute monarchy in
which surplus extraction became increasingly the task of a state heavily
staffed by lords. Brenner, in conceiving the absolute state as an essentially
feudal regime, followed Engels who wrote of early modern absolutism:
'The political order remained feudal, while society became more and
more bourgeois.'[66] By tracing the roots of 'political accumulation' to
structural features of the feudal mode of production, he provides a
refutation of the attempt by Theda Skocpol, Anthony Giddens, Michael
Mann and other sociologists to treat the endemic warfare which played
so essential a role in the formation of the modern European states as
an autonomous tendency which cannot be explained in terms of the forces
and relations of production.[67] Brenner also emphasises that the
'absolute state was no mere guarantor of the old forms of feudal property
based on decentralised feudal reaction. Rather it came to express
transformed version of the old system', one in which the lords made
up for their limited power to extract rent from peasant communities by
participating in a state whose concentrated power allowed it to squeeze
the rural population by means of taxation.[68] The different forms of

state in England and France—respectively, precocious early medieval centralisation making possible continued lordly control of the land, and late feudal centralisation as compensation for seigneurial weakness—are crucial to understanding the specific character of each country's bourgeois revolution.

The second criticism involves an insistence on the central role of the cities and of the urban, mercantile bourgeoisie in the development of capitalism. This is expressed, for example, by Chris Harman.[69] Brenner's argument is defective, suffering from a 'rural economism', in neglecting what were after all the *urban* centres of the bourgeois revolutions. The decisive part played by the London crowd in 1640-2 and by the *sans-culottes* of Paris in 1789-94 cannot apparently be accomodated within a framework which focuses primarily on the rise of *agrarian* capitalism. The argument raises three issues.

The first concerns the actual contribution of urban merchants to the development of capitalism. The most detailed portrait of early modern mercantile capitalism confirms Marx's view of its conservative character. The great French historian Fernand Braudel writes 'Capitalism and the towns were basically the same thing in the West.' But for Braudel, capitalism necessarily involves the violation of the law of free competition on which the market supposedly rests, depending usually on the establishment of monopoly. It is 'an accumulation of power...a form of social parasitism.' As such, it tends to shun production:

> *Until the industrial revolution of the nineteenth century, when capital moved into industrial production, now newly promoted to the rank of large profit-maker, it was in the sphere of circulation, trade and marketing that capitalism was most at home; even if it sometimes made more than fleeting incursions into other territory; and even if it was not concerned with the whole of circulation, since it only controlled, or sought to control certain channels of trade.*[70]

Braudel shows in detail that capitalist involvement in either urban or rural production was very limited between the 15th and 18th centuries, for the fundamental reason that these activities were relatively unprofitable compared to long distance trade. The latter 'certainly made super profits: it was after all based on the price differences between two markets very far apart, with supply and demand in complete ignorance of each other and brought only into contact by the activities of the middle man.'[71]

Trade, not production, was thus the 'home ground' of early modern urban capitalism. It would, however, be ridiculous to conclude that the merchants and the global trade networks they spun were irrelevant to the development of capitalism—a point I emphasise below. Perhaps it is best to see the expansion of mercantile capitalism as a necessary but not sufficient condition for the dominance of bourgeois relations of production. As long as capitalism did not conquer production it was forced (and indeed largely content) to co-exist with feudalism.

The conquest of production by capitalists recruited largely from petty producers could only begin in agriculture—only the huge rises in agricultural productivity and output made possible by the establishment of rural capitalism offered a way out of the tendency towards demographic crisis which bedevilled Europe especially in the later Middle Ages and the 17th century. As Brenner puts it:

> *What, therefore, marks off the English economy from those of all its European neighbours in the seventeenth century was not only its capacity to maintain demographic increase beyond the old Malthusian limits, but also its ability to sustain continuing industrial and overall economic growth in the face of the crisis and stagnation of the traditionally predominant cloth industry. Although perhaps originally activated by cloth exports, the continuing English industrial expansion was founded upon a growing domestic market, rooted ultimately in the continuing transformation of agricultural production. It was, by contrast, the restricted and decaying home market—undermined by decaying agricultural productivity—which was at the root of the widespread drop off in manuyfacturing production throughout France, Western Germany and Eastern Europe.*[72]

The second issue raised is the relative weight of town and country in bourgeois revolutions. It is unquestionably true that the urban masses provided much of the radicalising impulse in some of the decisive stages of the English and French Revolutions. Nevertheless, this judgement requires qualification. The importance of the French peasantry, particularly in 1789-92 is something to which I shall return to below. And it is striking how often it was areas of *rural* industry, for example, cloth making around Cirencester and Colchester, which proved centres of mass mobilisation in support of Parliament at the beginning of the Civil War in 1642.[73] But thirdly, even if an exclusively urban focus were appropriate when analysing the bourgeois revolutions themselves, the same need not be true of the development of capitalism. There is no reason to believe—indeed it would be pretty reductionist to think— that the dynamics of these two forms of change would be the same. The fact that decisive events often occurred in the cities does not require that the main breakthrough to capitalism also took place there.

The existence of two distinct but related registers, those of socio-economic and of political transformation is worth insisting on because it seems that Brenner's influence has encouraged some to dissolve the process of bourgeois revolution into that of capitalist development. Comninel, for one, commits this error, reading the French Revolution through the lens of the rise of agrarian capitalism in England. The absence of agrarian revolution in 18th century France leads him to deny the very existence of capitalism there.[74] The argument seems to be that capitalists can only derive their profits from the extraction of surplus value from commodity producing wage labourers; if their income does not derive (at least indirectly?) from this source, then the group in question cannot be capitalists. Now whatever may be the merits of this claim, it does not correspond with Marx's views. As the passage cited above from *Capital* make clear, he regarded merchants as capitalists even though (by definition) their revenues came from 'commercial profit making'. Marx's refusal to equate capital with the exploiters of wage labour is important for any understanding of the transition from feudalism to capitalism. Thus Lenin argues that the emancipation of the Russian serfs undermined but did not destroy the *corvée* (labour service) economy on the feudal estates: 'The only possible system of economy was, accordingly, a transitional one, a system combining the features of both the *corvée* and the capitalist systems.'He analyses with great subtlety the variety of forms (depending on the extent to which wage labour becomes the substance if not the form of the relationship) in which the labour service and the capitalist systems were combined: 'Life creates forms that unite in themselves with remarkable gradualness, systems of economy whose basic features constitute opposites.'[75]

This is more than merely a methodological point, since the early modern period in fact saw the emergence of various 'transitional forms' through which mercantile capital began to establish control over production. One was the phenomenon of what has come to be called 'proto-industrialisation'—the spread of rural industry, usually producing textiles, often on the basis of the putting out system.

While some of the claims made for 'proto-industrialisation' are exaggerated, it was neither a necessary nor a sufficient condition for the later development of industrial capitalism, the spread of the cottage industry did represent the integration of peasant households into the market and their partial subordination to merchant capitalists seeking to escape the high wages and guild restrictions of the towns.[76]

Perhaps even more important was what Robin Blackburn calls the 'systematic slavery' of the British and French West Indies, later spreading to Cuba, Brazil, and the American South: the large scale exploitation of slave labour producing either mass consumption goods (sugar) or industrial inputs (cotton). The plantations were a perfect case of a 'transitional form', since the slaves largely met their own needs from subsistence cultivation, but worked in some of the largest industrial enterprises of the epoch and were integrated into the triangle of African slaves, colonial products and European manufactures underpinning the Atlantic economy.[77]

The significance of these 'transitional forms' for the case of the French Revolution in particular, is that they represent ways in which capitalism

was warrening into the feudal social and political order. The consolidation
of an absolute state based on the extraction of surplus labour in the form
of taxation from communities of peasant households meant, Brenner
contends, the long term stagnation of French agriculture.[78] Simply to
focus on this undoubtedly very important feature of *ancien régime* society
as Comninel does is, however, to ignore the complexity of the French
social formation. Thus Braudel distinguishes three Frances, 'France I',
'the Western seaboard', one of the main centres of the Atlantic enonomy,
'France II...the huge and varied interior', dominated by peasant
agriculture, and 'France III', the 'urban border zone to which Lyons
holds the key' oriented towards continental Europe.[79] The monarchy,
feudal in being based on coercive surplus extraction, presided over a
society undergoing substantial change—as is reflected by the fact that
during the 18th century French overseas trade grew faster than, and
industrial output as fast as, British trade and output.[80] Engels'
characterisation of absolutism can thus be applied to France on the eve
of the revolution: 'The political order remained feudal, while society
became more and more bourgeois.'

The classical bourgeois revolutions, I: England[81]

The 'classical' bourgeois revolutions are distinguished above all by the
way in which popular mobilisation from below interacts with a determined
but more conservative political leadership to transform the state. These
features were most fully present in France between 1789 and 1794. The
English case presents a similar but less developed pattern. Certain aspects
of its causes, course and consequences are, however, worth dwelling on.

   (i) *The crisis of the Stuart state.* The distinctiveness of England's
development explains the character of its revolution. Whereas the French
monarchy succumbed to the decay of absolutism, the Stuarts were a
casualty of an attempt to establish an absolutist regime. Brenner sums
up the decisive change of the century before 1640: 'the English greater
landed classes gradually gave up the magnate form of politico-military
organisation, commercialised their relationships with their tenants,
rationalised their estates, and made use of—but avoided dependance
upon—the court.' Thus, 'agrarian capitalism arose within the framework
of landlordism.'[82] From this perspective it becomes clear why it was a
mistake to identify the gentry with the bourgeoisie.

   As Hill put it, ' "the gentry" were not an economic class. They were
a social and legal class; economically they were divided.'[83] Some land
owners, in status terms nobles or gentry, became commercial landlords;
others did not. A portion, therefore, of what had once been the feudal
lordly class came to depend on agrarian capitalism for their income; they
should therefore be seen as part of the emergent bourgeoisie as much
as urban merchants.[84]

This transformation of the English aristocracy had implications for the kind of state consistent with their interests:

> *Able to profit from rising land rents, through presiding over a newly emerging tripartite capitalist hierarchy of commercial landlord, capitalist tenant and hired wage labourer, the English landed classes had no need to revert to direct, extra-economic compulsion to extract a surplus. Nor did they require the state to serve them indirectly as an engine of surplus-appropriation by political means (tax/office) and war.*
>
> *What they needed, at least on the domestic front, was a cheap state, which would secure order and protect private property, thus assuring the normal operation of contractually based economic processes.*[85]

What they got instead from the Stuarts were successive attempts to install a continental style absolute monarchy. The Tudors had never been able to build up the powerful standing army at the basis of royal power in France or Spain. Henry VIII's French war of 1543-6 proved of decisive importance, since to finance it he sold off the bulk of the lands seized from the Church in the Reformation, losing, as Anderson puts it, 'the one great chance of English Absolutism to build up a firm economic base independent of parliamentary taxation.'[86] James I and, more systematically his son Charles I, sought to remove the constraint imposed by the consequent need to gain the consent of the landed classes in Parliament to raise money. It was not only the bulk of the gentry who were antagonised: the royal policy of granting trading monopolies to City oligarchs especially alienated merchants involved in the burgeoning Atlantic trade.[87] Charles's policy of centralisation in Church, through Archbishop Laud's drive against Puritanism, as well as in state, threatened not only the gentry, responsible for local government as Justices of the Peace, but the more prosperous yeomen and artisans who had come to exercise some political power at the parish level as village constables and church wardens.[88] The collapse of Charles's attempt to rule alone, precipitated by rebellion in Scotland against Laud's attempt to impose episcopal rule on the Kirk, came at an unfavourable economic conjuncture, dominated by the collapse of cloth exports and a run of bad harvests. Thus the scene was set for the Long Parliament.

(ii) *The role of the 'middle sort'.* The work of Brian Manning has shown how the intervention of the London crowd was decisive in polarising the Long Parliament, driving much of the nobility and the gentry into the King's arms, but at the same time enabling the most determined leaders of the House of Commons, such as Pym, to gain their objectives; mass pressure also forced the parliamentary leaders to adopt a more radical, political and religious programme. Once the resulting confrontation between the 'popular party' and the 'party of order' developed into civil war, mass resistance to the royalists took the form of a series of risings, particularly in the industrial districts of Gloucestershire, Essex, Suffolk, Lancashire and Yorkshire.[89]

Manning argues that it was 'the middle sort of people' who played the main part in these struggles—'peasants and craftsmen', 'the independent small producers', in control of a household economy dependent primarily on family labour, distinct from landlords and merchants above, and wage labourers below. From within their ranks a layer of capitalists was emerging—yeoman farmers producing for the market and greater craftsmen, both of which groups employed wage labour. Despite the conflicting interests of this new capitalist class and the mass of peasants and artisans, 'the government of Charles I and the existing political, social and religious regime antagonised these bigger farmers and larger craftsmen, and led them to feel they had more in common with the main body of peasants and craftsmen than with the governing order and the ruling class. They assumed the leadership of "the middle sort of people" in opposition to the king, lords and bishops.'

The political tendency which articulated the interests of the 'middle sort' more than any other was the Levellers between 1646 and 1649. They developed a social critique of the old regime: at fault was not merely Charles I or even the monarchy itself, but a parasitic complex of interests embracing king, lords, clergy, lawyers and rich merchants. They sought to set in its place a decentralised democracy of small producers, in which all heads of household—but not women, servants or beggars—had the vote.[90]

Such a vision was profoundly at odds with the views and interests of the parliamentary leaders, their most radical wing, the Independent gentry represented by Cromwell and the other commanders of the New Model Army which defeated the king. The period after the end of the Civil War in 1646 saw Cromwell and the Independents engage in elaborate manoeuvres as they balanced between the conservative Presbyterian majority in Parliament, who wanted to disband the army and make a deal with Charles, and the Levellers, whose influence among rank and file soldiers was widespread. The decisive episodes unfolded in late 1648 and early 1649. The officers, with Leveller support, purged the House of Commons and then forced through the King's execution, the abolition of the House of Lords and the proclamation of a Commonwealth in the place of the monarchy; Cromwell then turned on the Levellers, crushing a series of mutinies and executing some of the ringleaders. The English republic provided the political carapace of a military government which completed the work of the Long Parliament by dismantling the remnants of Stuart absolutism. When its narrow social base sent the regime into crisis after Cromwell's death, Charles II was restored to the throne in 1660 on terms which required him to respect the changes made by the revolutionary governments. The attempt by James II to repeat his father's efforts to establish an absolutist regime led to his overthrow in the

Glorious Revolution of 1688, which replaced him by William of Orange and permanently limited the power of the Crown by that of a Parliament dominated, not by the 'middle sort', but by the landed classes.[91]

(iii) *The post-revolutionary state.* The mass of small producers certainly did not benefit from the revolution they had made. But who did? And can, indeed, the tumults of the 1640s and 1650s be described as a social revolution at all? The conservative historian J H Hexter and the radical sociologist Theda Skocpol are agreed that it cannot. According to Hexter, 'what makes the English Revolution suspect as a social revolution is the restoration of the peerage economically, socially, and ideologically after 1660.'[92] Skocpol offers a more theoretically elaborated argument, based on the claim that 'what is unique to social revolution is that basic changes in social structure and in political structure occur together in a mutually reinforcing fashion. And these changes occur through intense socio-political conflicts in which class struggle plays a key part.' Skocpol contends that the English Revolution meets neither of these conditions. 'It was accomplished not through class struggle but through a civil war between segments of the dominant landed class... And whereas the French Revolution markedly transformed class and social structures, the English Revolution did not. Instead it revolutionised the political structure of England...it reinforced and sealed the direct political control of a dominant class that already had many... members engaged in capitalist agriculture and commerce.' The English Revolution was thus 'a political, but not social, revolution.'[93]

Skocpol is clearly wrong about the first point: we have seen the role played by class struggle, by the intervention of the 'middle sort', of the small producers of town and country, in the revolution. But what of the apparent continuity of domination by the landed classes, which the final settlement of 1688 merely reinforced. Skocpol's argument, that what was involved was simply a political revolution is much too simplistic.

The capitalist class develops in a gradual and molecular fashion within the framework of feudal relations of production. But a point is eventually reached where its further development requires a change in the *form* of the state. It does not follow from the fact that such change is required that it will occur, but should it happen the resulting transformation cannot be seen as merely political. The new form of state has a different social content from the old, one which maximises capitalist development.

Hill summarises the changed nature of the English state as a result of 1640 and 1688:

Nobody, then, willed the English Revolution: it happened. But if we look at its outcome, when the idealists, the men of conscious will on either side had been defeated, what emerged was a state in which the administrative organs that most impeded capitalist development had been abolished: Star Chamber, High Commission, Court of Wards, and feudal tenures; in which the executive was subordinated to the men of property, deprived of control over the judiciary, and yet strengthened in external relations by a powerful navy and the Navigation Act; in which local government was safely and cheaply in the hands of the natural ruler, and discipline was imposed on the lower orders by a Church safely subordinated to Parliament.[94]

The significance of the new form of state—as Hill puts it, 'strong in external relations, weak at home'[95]—is best brought out in his critical discussion of Braudel's great study of early modern capitalism. Braudel strives unsuccessfully to explain why it was first the Netherlands and then England, rather than France, which dominated the world economy in the 17th and 18th centuries because, Hill argues, 'he underestimates the role of politics in the consolidation of Amsterdam's hegemony and its replacement by London.' More specifically: 'An absolute monarchy with a standing army and a permanent bureaucracy may intermittently favour trade and industry for its own military purposes, but it can control them. The looser, freer Dutch and English states allowed capitalist interest to preponderate.' The decisive factor in French failure and Dutch and English success in the global arena is thus 'the differences between the two types of state', between an absolute monarchy and early bourgeois states forged by revolution.[96]

The formidable character of the post-revolutionary English state is brought out in its capacity drastically to increase military expenditure to secure its dominant position in the world economy. The real spending of the British state rose fifteen fold between 1700 and 1815, with civil expenses never rising above 23 percent of total outlays.[97] Underlying this increase in military spending, which allowed the British ruling class to win their long series of wars with France between the 1690s and 1815, was formidable tax raising capacity. A recent study shows that the tax burden in Britain during the 18th century was not only higher than that in France but rose steadily, reaching a high point of 35 percent of physical output during the Napoleonic wars.[98] This reflected the English landed aristocracy's commitment to devoting the necessary resources to establishing global hegemony.

The British state's ability to find the resources for external expansion reflected its more advanced economic base as well as its class character. By contrast, the absolute monarchies suffered from endemic difficulties in financing their activities. Low productivity and high population growth limited the resources available. The nobility, integrated into the absolute state, generally enjoyed considerable tax immunities; the main burden therefore fell on the peasantry. The landed aristocracy provided the main obstacle to reform of the tax system: 'In all cases, it was difficult to do without the backing of the nobility which provided part of the administration and the greatest part of the military cadres, and which strung throughout every region a string of landlords, all interested in maintaining order.'⁹⁹ The ultimately feudal character of the absolute state, its roots in a land owning class dependent on the coercive extraction of surplus labour, set internal limits to its reform.

The classical bourgeois revolutions, II: France

It was, of course, one such attempt by an absolute monarchy to reform itself which precipitated the French Revolution. Ironically, the debt accumulated as a result of France's only significant victory over Britain during the 18th century, in the American War of Independence, finally broke the monarchy's back, pushing royal ministers to introduce reform packages, resistance to which by the aristocracy forced the convening of the Estates General, with consequences still resonating through the world.

(i) *Monarchy, nobles and bourgeois.* One of the most important general propositions about bourgeois revolutions is their cumulative impact. Each revolution alters the terms for its successors. Thus the English Revolution, by forging a formidable expansionist state, increased the burden on the French monarchy, which in any case was embroiled in military and diplomatic rivalries with the other Continental powers.

To the territorial and dynastic struggles of absolute monarchies such as Spain, France, and Austria formed by the competitive 'political accumulation' of feudal lords, were added the commercial rivalries generated by the formation of the world market, in which bourgeois states such as Holland and England increasingly had a marked advantage. But important though the international context of the French Revolution was, the *internal* contradictions of the *ancien régime* produced its collapse.

What were these contradictions? The revisionist case, supported strongly by Comninel, is that nobles and bourgeois overlapped with each other and were internally divided. He concludes that 'the French Revolution was essentially an *intra-class* conflict'. Now in the first place it is hard to imagine a revolution which did not involve a crisis within the ruling class. Lenin famously defined a revolutionary situation as occurring 'when the *"lower classes"* do not want to live in the old way and the *"upper classes" cannot carry on in the old way*'.¹⁰⁰ But Comninel seems to be saying that the French Revolution is *reducible* to a crisis within the ruling class. This view has implications for how one accounts for the role of the masses in the revolution. But it is worth first making a couple of points.

It is hard to see how else the bourgeoisie could have developed within the framework of an absolute state based on the social and political predominance of a still feudal landed aristocracy except by forming all sorts of ties with the nobility. The purchase, not simply of land, but of seigneurial rights over land and of patents of nobility conveyed significant economic advantages on the aspirant bourgeois. The attractions of state office and of nobility were especially great given the role of the state as the great engine of surplus extraction.

It does not, however, follow from the links between lords and bourgeois that there were no conflicts. Furet suggests that it was probably becoming more difficult for commoners to become nobles during the 18th century.[101]

He argues that the limits on commoners reflected the nature of 'the "absolute" monarchy', 'an unstable compromise between the construction of a modern state and the maintenance of principles of social organisation inherited from feudal times.' Royal power had developed at the expense of the aristocracy, but the 'ruling class' in control of the state consisted of 'the "court nobility" which attracted the global hostility of the rest of the order'. The divisions within the nobility reflected their attitudes towards 'the modernisation of the state'. Some—*á la polonaise*—were 'hostile to the state, nostalgic for their old local predominance', others—*á la prussienne*—'desired on the contrary to seize the modernisation of the state for their own advantage' especially by controlling the military, while yet others—*a l'anglaise*—advocated a 'constitutional monarchy, parliamentary aristocracy'.[102]

The absolutist state thus at the same time divided the aristocracy and set limits to the extent and nature of bourgeois advancement. On this basis, the kind of line up which emerged in the Estates General—with the bourgeois Third Estate overwhelmingly in favour of a single chamber which it would dominate, the clergy more or less evenly divided, and two thirds of the nobles opposed—was entirely predictable.

Even Doyle, generally hostile to interpretations of the revolution as bourgeois, concedes that the struggles following the meeting of the Estates General in May and June 1789 reflected the nobles' refusal 'to share political power':

> By the time the Estates actually met, nobility and bourgeoisie, who basically agreed on so much, had become competitors for power rather than partners in its exercise. Only when the right of nobles to separate treatment in anything had been destroyed could the new political elite of propertied 'notables' an amalgam of former notables and bourgeois, get down to the exercise of power.[103]

The outcome of the first phase of the revolution, concluded with the consolidation of the National Assembly's position, if not with the fall of the Bastille certainly after the march on Versailles in October 1789, was, in Doyle's words, a situation in which 'power in France now lay unchallengeably with a propertied elite recognising no special place for nobles, either at national or at local level.'[104] How different is this from Soboul's description of the Assembly 'building the new nation on the narrow social base of the property owning bourgeoisie'?[105] More generally, the French Revolution was, throughout its different phases, exceptional among bourgeois revolutions in that its leadership was overwhelmingly bourgeois. Lynn Hunt summarises in a recent study the conclusions of her research into the social background of those who held office during the revolution:

> *The revolutionary political class can be termed 'bourgeois' both in terms of social position and of class consciousness. The revolutionary officials were owners of the means of production; they were either merchants with capital, professionals with skills, artisans with their own shops, or more rarely, peasants with their land. The unskilled, the wage workers and the landless peasants were not found in positions of leadership or even in large numbers among the rank and file. The 'consciousness' of the revolutionary elite can be labelled as bourgeois insofar as it was distinctly anti-feudal, anti-aristocratic, and anti-absolutist. In their language and imagery, revolutionaries rejected all reminders of the past, and they included in their ranks very few nobles or Old Regime officials. The revolutionary elite was made up of new men dedicated to fashioning a new France.*[106]

Hunt goes on to argue that 'the Marxist version of the social interpretation' of the revolution 'is not so much wrong in its particulars' as 'insufficiently discriminating. It cannot explain the difference in regional responses, the divisions within the bourgeoisie, or the failure of the revolution to stop in 1791, when the capitalist and commercial sectors had made their greatest gains.'[107] These objections are best considered together with the question of the role of the masses in the revolution.

(ii) *The revolutionary dynamic.* Comninel observes: 'From the revisionist perspective, the revolution is properly bracketed by the Assembly of Notables [which met in the spring of 1787] and the society of *notables* [under Napoleon], and the revolutionary years of 1791-4 stand out as a more or less lamentable aberration along the way.'[108] But, since Comninel himself believes the revolution to have been 'an *intra-class* conflict' how does this view differ from his own, apart from the fact that he doesn't seem to think of 1791-4 as 'lamentable'? Involved here is the question of *dérapage*, of Furet and Richet's claim that the period from the royal flight to Varennes onwards represents the liberal, bourgeois revolution made by the Constituent Assembly in 1789-91 'skidding off course'. For them 1790 is the 'happy year', in which the Assembly laid the foundations of a new France from which privilege was gone, and in which free enterprise was born.[109]

Such a view presupposes that the regime established by the Constituent Assembly was inherently stable so that its fall was sheer bad luck. This assumption is quite untenable. In the first place, the general economic situation was unfavourable: rising food prices, reflecting a catastrophically bad harvest in 1788, were the driving force behind the great mobilisations of the Parisian crowd in July and October 1789. Another poor harvest in 1791 contributed to the inflationary surge which lay behind the popular *journées* of 1792. Secondly, the famous decrees of 4-11 August 1789 left in place many seigneurial rights on the spurious grounds that they involved claims over land rather than over persons; the peasants over whom these rights were exercised would have to buy them out through a series of redemption payments. The result was a chain of peasant risings and other forms of resistance throughout 1790-2. The Assembly only finally abolished surviving feudal rights after the insurrection of 10 August 1792 which overthrew the monarchy, and forced the election of the Convention.[110] The Assembly settled very little as far as the peasants were concerned.

Thirdly, there was the growing danger of counter-revolution. Furet dismisses the idea of an 'aristocratic plot' as an artefact of revolutionary ideology, but counter-revolutionary networks spread rapidly throughout 1790, which Michel Vovelle describes as a year when 'the counter-revolution was everywhere'—among the aristocratic emigrés in cities such as Metz, in local agitations in Montauban and Nîmes, in Burke's *Reflections on the Revolution in France*, and not least of all in the Tuileries, where Louis XVI wrote: 'I would rather be king of Metz than remain king of France in such a position, but that will soon come to an end.'[111]

Far from there being a profound discontinuity between 1789-91 and 1791-4 the entire period between the fall of the Bastille and Thermidor involves an increasingly radicalised version of the same pattern, in which popular movements, in the cities at least under the leadership of a section of the bourgeoisie, force through and defend changes against the opposition of counter-revolutionary forces whose strength is variable but which are always present. There were two main components of the mass movements of the Revolution. The first was provided by the peasantry, of which I have more to say below. It is, however, worth noting here Soboul's remark that 'from 1789 to 1793 and the definitive abolition of feudalism, the peasant revolt preceded the bourgeois revolution and pushed it forward.'[112]

The decisive political struggles generally occurred, however, in the towns, and above all in Paris. This is true even, P M Jones argues, in the case of issues affecting the peasantry: 'In the years that followed [4 August 1789] country dwellers tried *repeatedly* to abolish feudalism from below, but with negligible success. If any single event can be credited with accomplishing this feat, it was the Parisian and *fédéré* insurrection of 10 August 1792.'[113] Thanks to Rudé and Soboul, we know a fair amount about the urban popular movement that was the main driving force of the revolution. It was not a proletarian movement. While there may have been as many as 300,000 wage earners in Paris in 1791, Rudé points out that 'the wage earner had as yet no defined status as a producer and there were often numerous intermediate stages between workman and employer. The typical unit of production was still the small workshop, which generally employed but a small number of journeymen and apprentices.'[114] The mentality of the independent small producer dominated master and *compagnon* (journeyman) alike. As Soboul puts it,

> *The **sans-culotterie** did not constitute a class, nor was the **sans-culotte** movement based on class differences. Craftsmen, shopkeepers, and merchants, **compagnons** and day labourers joined with a bourgeois minority to form a coalition but there was still an underlying conflict between craftsmen and merchants, enjoying a profit derived from a private ownership of the means of production, and **compagnons** and day-labourers, entirely dependent upon wages.*[115]

Underlying this fragile unity was a common motivating factor: the scarcity and dearness of food. 'Hunger', Soboul observes, 'was the cement which held together the artisan, the shopkeeper, and the workman, just as a common interest united them against the wealthy merchant, the noble, and the bourgeois monopolist.' Indeed, he goes further and contends that 'the economic fluctuations provided the rhythm of the revolutionary movement.' It was economic pressure—and not the 'autonomous political and ideological dynamic' invoked by Furet—which provided the continuity underlying the revolutionary mobilisations from July 1789 to the unsuccessful risings against the Thermidorean regime in Germinal and Prairial III (April/May 1795). The *sans-culottes'* campaign for price controls, which triumphed when they forced the Convention to pass the Law of the General Maximum of 29 September 1793, did not, according to Soboul, 'reflect their concern for national defence as much as their interest in providing themselves and their families with sufficient food.' More generally the link the *sans-culottes* saw between their own economic situation and the Terror was summed up in remarks the cabinet maker Richet was accused of having made on 1 Prairial III (20 May 1795): 'Under Robespierre, blood flowed and there was enough bread. Today, blood no longer flows and there is a shortage. It seems, therefore, that we must spill a little blood before we can get bread.'[116]

The leadership of the popular moverment, above all in the decisive Year II, was provided by only a section of the bourgeoisie. Soboul presents the following alignment of class forces:

> *The most active wing of this revolution was not so much the commercial bourgeoisie (insofar as it continued to consist solely of traders and middlemen it managed to get on well with the old order—from 1789 to 1793, from the Monarchiens to the Feuillants and to the Girondins, it usually tended towards compromise), but the mass of the small direct producers whose surplus was*

> seized by the feudal aristocracy with the full support of the judiciary and the
> means of constraint available to the state under the Ancien Régime. The
> political instrument of change was the Jacobin dictatorship of the lower and
> middle sections of the bourgeoisie, supported by the popular masses—social
> categories whose ideal was a democracy of small, autonomous producers,
> working together and operating a system of free exchange.[117]

Jacobinism thus represented ' "the truly revolutionary way" from
feudalism to capitalism' in which a coalition of small producers under
bourgeois leadership sweeps away the remnants of feudalism. Broadly
to accept this analysis need not imply insisting on a strict correlation
between membership of a particular fraction of capital and political
alignment. The crucial point is that the bourgeoisie, itself a complex
formation shaped by its development within the framework of absolutism
and involvement in landowning, state offices, and mercantile capitalism,
was divided over whether to compromise with, or to smash, the old order.
On which side particular individuals or groups stood of this shifting line
was not determined by purely economic factors. Thus Hunt argues that
'the members of the new political class shared certain values that were
shaped in large measure by common cultural positions.'[117a] The point is
a perfectly valid one: not simply the formal system of political beliefs
which evolved during the revolution, drawing on Enlightenment
sources—above all, Rousseau, but also the complex set of revolutionary
rituals and visual and verbal symbols, to the study of which historians
have in recent years devoted much attention, played a crucial part in
forming a particular collective subject, the Montagnard wing of the
bourgeoisie and their *sans-culotte* allies. Hunt's error consists in
supposing that the complexity of the process through which this
collectivity was formed counts against the Marxist case.[117b]

It was the pressure of events which drove the Jacobins towards the
revolutionary destruction of the *ancien régime*, pressure produced by
two forces—the counter-revolution and the popular movement. The
danger that the Montagnards ran of being outflanked from the left as
well as from the right was very real. The *sans-culottes* were capable
of taking independent action to force the Jacobin government to go further
than it otherwise would have: the best example is provided by the *journées*
of 4 to 5 September 1793, when the Sections mobilised successfully to
push the Convention to pass decrees ordering the arrest of suspects,
forming a revolutionary army to ensure grain requisitions, and (towards
the end of the month) to impose general controls on prices and wages.
Soboul describes the Jacobin response: 'Themselves supporters of a
liberal economic policy, they nevertheless accepted regulation and price
fixing as a war measure and as a concession to the demands of the
people.'[118] Popular pressure sometimes pushed the Jacobins very far—
for example on the land question. The Convention finally abolished all

seigneurial dues on 17 July 1793. On 8 Ventôse II (26 February 1794) Saint Just went much further, proposing to the Convention that the property of suspects be seized and used to indemnify 'poor patriots'. The resulting decree was never implemented, but it is an indication of the extent to which the Jacobin regime was willing to make inroads into private property in order to preserve popular support.

To say that the Jacobins sought to accommodate pressure from below is not to say that they were confronted with a rival system of government, that a state of dual power existed in Paris.

However, the subordinate but indispensable role played by the popular movement underlines the significance of the Jacobins themselves in containing but also channelling pressures from below. To suppose, as Daniel Guérin and his followers do, that Robespierre and the Committee of Public Safety had become a reactionary force by November 1793 is an absurdity; it is to suppose that the Sectional movement, a coalition of small masters and artisans, could have provided the centralised political direction necessary to raise and command great armies, to construct and manage a war economy, to engage in the manoeuvres necessary to preserve a relatively wide political base for the revolutionary government. The radicalising impulses of the popular movement would have been dissipated without the leadership of the Jacobins. This leadership—like that of Cromwell and the Independents during the decisive phase of the English Revolution—was forced to balance between the masses and the bourgeoisie. The delicate nature of the operation involved was most obvious during the crisis of Ventôse-Germinal II (March 1794) when the Committee of Public Safety struck against the left and then the right, sending respectively Hébert and the other leaders of the Cordeliers and Danton and the Indulgents to the guillotine.

Underlying these manoeuveres was the consolidation of the Jacobin regime and the concentration of power in its hands. Progressively tighter restrictions were imposed on the Sections and on the popular societies which developed to evade these controls. The state bureaucracy ramified, incorporating within it many *sans-culotte* activists. At the same time large sections of the peasantry withdrew into political apathy, the better off having seen their main demands realised, the poorer disillusioned by the revolution's failure to deliver, most antagonised by the regime's efforts to requisition grain for the towns. Paradoxically, the centralisation of power weakened the Jacobin dictatorship since it dispersed the popular base without whose support it could not repel the offensive of a bourgeoisie which now felt that its services could be dispensed with.

In Soboul's words, 'the revolutionary government found itself caught as if suspended mid air, between the Convention which was impatient to throw off its yoke and the popular movement of Paris now irrevocably hostile to it.'[119] The final straw as far as the latter was concerned seems to have been the publication on 5 Thermidor II (23 July 1794) of a tariff of maximum wage rates for Paris implying significant pay reductions. This measure seems to have been an effort by the Jacobins, having suppressed the Hébertist left in Ventôse, to favour employers at the expense of workers and consumers at a time when the failure of the general maximum to prevent price rises had caused a considerable agitation among workers for higher wages (to which the government responded with repression). The effect was to antagonise the *sans-culottes* yet further when Robespierre's enemies were about to move against him. Stone masons were demonstrating against the new wage maximum on 9 Thermidor, the day of his fall. As Rudé and Soboul observe, 'the Robespierrists paid with their execution for the ineluctable contradictions of their policy.'[120]

(iii) *The 'peasant road' and French capitalism.* Bourgeois revolutions, I argue throughout this article, are to be understood primarily in terms of their consequences. But in the case of this, the greatest of bourgeois revolutions, we must confront what Hobsbawm calls 'one gigantic paradox', namely that French economic growth in the century after the revolution was, at best, sluggish.[121] A majority of commentators argue that the main factor underlying this outcome is the revolutionary agrarian settlement, which consolidated and extended the economic power of the peasant smallholders, who in 1789 represented two thirds of the population and already owned a third of the land.[122] The domination of rural France by petty proprietors limited the development of industrial capitalism:

> *The diseconomies of scale involved in small plot agriculture produced very low levels of profitability, and in consequence, very little capital surplus was surrendered by the land... Low profits also turned agriculturalists towards self-sufficiency, denying the urban-industrial sector a valuable measure of internal demand. And, in turn, the guarantees of equal inheritance worked against mobility of labour, imposing upon industrialists severe constrictions in the supply of factory workers.*[122a]

It is argued that, judged by its economic consequences, the French Revolution cannot be regarded as bourgeois. Skocpol's judgement, reaffirmed by Comninel, is that its 'overall outcome' was 'the symbiotic co-existence of a centralised, professional bureaucratic state with a society dominated by some moderately large and many medium and small owners of private property.[123] There is, however, considerable controversy about the peasants in the French Revolution. Lefebvre argued that 'there was not one revolution, but several'—aristocratic, bourgeois, popular and peasant. The peasant revolution in particular 'possessed an autonomy proper to its origin, its procedures, its crises and its tendencies': it was 'autonomous above all in its anti-capitalist tendencies'. The 'mass of small proprietors...were profoundly attached to collective rights of regulation, that is to a pre-capitlaist economic and social world, not only by habit, but also because of the capitalist transformation of agriculture aggravated their conditions of existence.'

The peasant risings which began with the Great Fear of July 1789 were therefore anti-capitalist as well as anti-feudal: 'despite appearances, their influence was as much conservative as revolutionary: they overturned the feudal regime, but they consolidated the agrarian structure of France.' The result was thus a compromise, in which the poor peasants preserved their collective rights but gained little otherwise, the larger peasants obtained some of the church lands sold off by the revolutionary governments, and the rural communities retained much of their cohesion.[124]

Soboul initially accepted this but came later to revise his views under the impact of the research of the Russian historian Anatoli Ado, published in 1971. Ado, and following him Soboul, distinguished two main phases in the peasant movements during the revolution: that between 1789 and 1792, which saw risings whose main objective was the abolition of seigneurial rights and that of 1792-3, in which struggles were aimed at dividing common land and securing adequate food supplies. The Year II saw the better off peasants concentrate on protecting the gains they had already made. The poorer peasants, by contrast, launched a series of movements demanding the implementation of the decree of 10 June 1793 authorising the division of the commons among individual proprietors. Lefebvre had thought that it was the larger peasants who had favoured breaking up the common land. Not only did Ado and Soboul deny this, but they contended that:

> despite its anti-capitalist tendencies, the programme of the small peasantry did not enter objectively into contradiction with the capitalist development of the countryside. In demanding the extension of free small property and small cultivation, and thus of commodity production, the peasants were fighting also for the enlargement of the base necessary for the development of capitalism.[125]

The slow growth of capitalist agriculture in 19th century France reflected not so much the extension of petty production but 'a considerable persistence of large property', involving such backward forms of cultivation such as share cropping. This state of affairs represented the relative failure rather than the success of the struggles of the small peasants. This new perspective on the peasants' contribution led Soboul to reappraise the traditional Marxist view of the French Revolution as the model bourgeois revolution and rather to stress its uniqueness.[126]

Soboul's abandonment of a general model of bourgeois revolution did represent a response to real difficulties. It did not, however, dispose of these difficulties. There is evidence that small peasants did press for the division of the commons, but there is much less of their success.[127] Moreover, if there had been a more extensive redistribution of land to the benefit of the petty producers, it does not follow that the result would have been the more rapid development of agrarian capitalism. As the English case shows, large scale property is not an obstacle to this development provided that it involves, rather than such *rentier* forms as share cropping, the trinity of commercial landlord, capitalist tenant, and wage labourer. It is hard not to see the revolution in the countryside as yet another phase in the French peasantry's struggle to maintain and to extend its control of the land, under conditions which meant the relatively slow commercialisation of agriculture at a time when other powers—first Britain, later Germany—were making the transition to industrial capitalism.

What about the other side of Skocpol's equation, the 'centralised, professional bureaucratic state' which emerged from the revolution? Marx, on numerous occasions, stressed how the revolutionary and Napoleonic regimes completed the process of forming this state initiated by the monarchy. Consider, for example, this passage from the *The Eighteenth Brumaire of Louis Bonaparte*:

> *This executive power with its enormous bureaucratic and military organisation, with its extensive and artificial state machinery, with a host of officials numbering half a million, besides an army of another half million, this appalling parasitic body, which enmeshes the body of French society like a net and chokes all its pores, sprang up in the days of the absolute monarchy, with the decay of the feudal system, which it helped to hasten…The first French Revolution, with its task of breaking all separate, local, territorial, urban and provincial powers in order to create the civil unity of the nation, was bound to develop what the absolute monarchy had begun: the centralisation, but at the same time the extent, the attributes and the agents of governmental power. Napoleon [I] perfected this state machinery.[128]*

Comninel concludes that Marx is describing a state based on a '*non*-capitalist' form of surplus extraction, 'centralised rent extracted directly from the peasantry'.[129] But while Marx does lay great stress on the French peasantry as the basis of the French state he argues that they had become subordinated to capital. Thus: 'The bourgeois order, which at the beginning of the century set the state to stand guard over the newly arisen smallholding and manured it with laurels, has become a vampire that sucks out its blood and brains and throws them into the alchemists' cauldron of capital.' Moreover, Louis Bonaparte, after his 1851 coup 'the executive authority which has made itself an independent power', would, Marx predicted, favour the economic interests of the bourgeoisie, while restricting its political influence.[130]

Nineteenth century France's most important phase of industrial and agricultural growth came under the Second Empire. Napoleon III's government promoted the rapid growth in railway construction and the activities of the Crédit Mobilier, the first major European investment bank, which concentrated savings to lend to entrepreneurs. The autonomy of the Bonapartist regime helped to promote this orientation. The state forged by the revolution, regarded by Comninel as '*non*-capitalist', proved, under certain conditions, a formidable instrument of capitalist industrialisation.[131]

The fact that the French Revolution completed the formation of a centralised state capable of promoting capitalist development does not entirely remove Hobsbawm's 'gigantic paradox'. The advanced character of the revolution, the intense mobilisation of the small producers of town and country under radical bourgeois leadership to destroy the remnants of the *ancien régime*, set limits to the subsequent development of capitalism. Having leaned on the peasantry to extirpate feudalism, the bourgeoisie was forced to compromise with them—a compromise indeed which most did not find onerous, since they too were small scale captitalists. This outcome does not invalidate the view of the revolution as bourgeois, since it undoubtedly benefitted the 'really existing' capitalist class in France as opposed to some ideal construct derived from comparison with England. The fact that the revolution's consequences were contradictory, both promoting and limiting capitalist development, is damaging only to a vulgar Marxist view of history in which the 'rising class' always and necessarily triumphs.

Bourgeois revolutions from above: Germany, the United States, Japan

The English and French Revolutions thus represented a form of bourgeois revolution based on the 'truly revolutionising path' and involving the intervention of broad coalitions of small producers. But there is another variant of bourgeois revolution whose understanding is vital since it produced three of the four most powerful contemporary states—Germany, the United States and Japan. These are cases of 'revolutions from above', in which the existing state apparatus was used violently to remove the obstacles to the construction of unified capitalist economies. It is essential, therefore, to consider some of the main features of these revolutions.

(i) *The Prussian path and German unification.* The unification of Germany under Bismarck is generally regarded as the paradigm case of 'revolution from above', achieved through the fusion of the old Prussian *Junker* landed class and the modern industrial bourgeoisie. But what are the conditions of such a form of development? Soboul stresses the importance of agrarian class relations: 'the structure of modern capitalism has been determined by what were, in each country, in the course of the transition, the internal relations between the decomposition of feudal landed property and the formation of productive capital.'[132] And of course this is true: the existence of the *Junker* estates producing for the market provided the framework, after the Prussian Reforms of Stein and Hardenberg during the Napoleonic Wars, for an evolution from serfdom to wage labour on a 'labour repressive' basis which left landlord political power intact.[133] But there were other conditions as well, involving the changed forms taken by the class struggle and the development of the world economy.

Analysing the failure of any section of the German bourgeoisie to play during the 1848 Revolution the kind of part performed by the Jacobins in France, Marx stressed the belated development of German capitalism: 'The German bourgeoisie developed so sluggishly, timidly and slowly that at the moment when it menacingly confronted feudalism and absolutism, it saw menacingly confronting it the proletariat and all sections of the middle class whose interests and ideas were related to those of the proletariat.'[134] Fearing the working class more than the *ancien régime*, the bourgeoisie sought a compromise with the Prussian monarchy. The revolutionary coalitions of the 1640s and 1790s failed to emerge in 1848 because the onset of industrialisation had widened the gap between labour and capital. As Stedman Jones observed:

> In general the more industrial capitalism developed, the stronger was the economic power of the **grande bourgeoisie** in relation to the masses of small producers and dealers from which it had sprung, and the greater the distance between their respective aims. Conversely, the less developed the bourgeoisie, the smaller the gulf between 'bourgeois' and 'petty bourgeois', and the greater the preponderance and cohesion of the popular movement.[135]

The *débacle* of 1848 provided the context in Italy as well as Germany, for Gramsci's 'passive revolution', in which the bourgeoisie secured one of its most basic objectives—political unification—by means of an alliance with sections of the landed aristocracy. The basis of this accomodation was a more subaltern political role for the bourgeoisie—the upper echelons of the old state apparatus continued to be staffed by the old landed classes, even though it increasingly operated in the interests of capital. Eley argues of German and Italian unification, as well as of the Meiji Restoration in Japan:

> Each might be described as a 'bourgeois revolution from above', in the specific sense that in a concentrated space of time and through a radical process of political innovation it delivered the legal and political conditions for a society in which the capitalist mode of production could be dominant. This was achieved by quite far sighted and visionary interventions by the existing states (or at least by the political pragmatism of 'modernising' tendencies within them), but without the social turbulence and insurrectionary extravagance

which marked the earlier Franco-British patterns.[136]

Once again the effects of previous bourgeois revolutions provided the context for these new transformations, in this case what Hobsbawm calls 'the "dual revolution"—the French Revolution of 1789 and the contemporaneous (British) Industrial Revolution.'[137]

Two questions are raised by viewing German unification in this way. First, can the changes involved be described as a *revolution*? If we recall Anderson's definition of revolution as 'an episode of convulsive political transformation, compressed in time and concentrated in target', German unification meets these conditions. Its achievement depended in Prussia's victory in two major wars, with Austria in 1866 and France in 1870. The fragility of Bismarck's postition and indeed of that of the Prussian monarchy is shown by the fact that a hostile bourgeois opposition could only be split and largely incorporated by one of the most reactionary *ultras* of 1848 pursuing a main objective of the revolution he had so detested—the destruction of the post-1815 German political order and its replacement by a unified state. That state, while based on a *Junker* dominated bureaucracy, included the institutional means for incorporating both bourgeoisie and labour movement alike in the *Reichstag* elected by manhood suffrage, and presided over Germany's replacement of Britain as the chief European industrial power.

Secondly, was the bourgeois revolution in Germany completed as a result of this transformation?[138] Or did the post-1871 German state only imperfectly represent capitalist interests? This is precisely the target of Blackbourn and Eley's critique of the idea of Germany's *Sonderweg* (special path). They argue that 'by comparison with Britain it was precisely the most "modern" and "progressive" aspects of Imperial Germany's capitalist development—namely, the higher levels of concentration, the rapid investment in new plants and technology, the experimentation with more sophisticated divisions of labour—that first permitted...repressive labour relations...to develop.' Furthermore, 'the massive growth of the SPD after 1895-6...forced many of the largest employers to continue a close political relationship with the big landlords', not as 'an ideological rejection of "modernity"' but as 'a rational calculation of political interest in a situation where greater levels of parliamentary democracy necessarily worked to the advantage of the socialist left'. Thus 'the *Kaiserreich* was not an irredeemably backward and archaic state indelibly dominated by "pre-industrial", "traditional" or "aristocratic" values and interests, but was powerfully constituted between 1862 and 1879 by (amongst other things) the need to accommodate bourgeois capitalist forces.'[139]

(ii) *The American Civil War and Reconstruction.* There is, however, one very important case of what Anderson calls a 'revolution after the revolution'—the United States. The revolution of 1776 was a 'classical' bourgeois revolution on the English and French pattern: a coalition of New England merchants and Southern planters was driven into the struggle for the independence of the American colonies by the intransigence of the British imperial government and pressure from below from a plebeian movement of small producers in the great ports such as Boston and Charleston.[140] But in the mid 19th century the state created by that revolution was convulsed by a titanic conflict—the American Civil War of 1861-5, the greatest armed struggle involving a developed country between 1815 and 1914. The war was more than a merely military affair, ending as it did in the emancipation of four million black slaves. For the American Marxist, George Novack, 'the first American Revolution and the Civil War form two parts of an indivisible whole. They comprised distinct but interlinked stages in the development of the bourgeois democratic revolution in the United States.'[141]

Why did the US need a second bourgeois revolution? American society in the mid 19th century involved three main elements. The north eastern seaboard was experiencing an industrial revolution, as mass consumer industries—textiles, boots and shoes, brewing—developed on the basis of factory labour. The western frontier was pushed steadily towards the Pacific by small holding farmers involved in petty commodity production. And the South was dominated by plantations worked by chattel slaves producing cash crops—above all raw cotton for the Lancashire factories at the hub of the industrial revolution.[142] At the heart of the Civil War lay the conflict between the emergent industrial capitalism of the North and the slave power of the South. Marx called it 'nothing but a struggle between two social systems, between the system of slavery and the system of free labour.'[143]

This conflict did not, however, spring from some necessary incompatability between capitalism and slavery. As Robin Blackburn argues, the three great 19th century slave powers—the US, Cuba and Brazil—flourished thanks to the demand for their cotton, sugar, and coffee in the key industrial capitalist society, Britain:

> Around mid-century, the prospects for marketing the slave produce of the Americas had never been better. Capitalism as an economic system. . .thoroughly permeated and integrated the expanding slave systems in the Americas in the 1850s. British capital found advantageous outlets in each of the expanding slave states of the Americas, helping to build railways, equip plantations and finance trade.[144]

That precisely was the problem for the Northern capitalists, who, along with the western farmers, put the free labour Republican candidate Abraham Lincoln into the White House in 1860, thus precipitating Southern secession from the US. The South, its plantations producing cotton for the Lancashire mills, was effectively an extension of the British economy. Michel Aglietta is only slightly overstating the case when he declares that:

> The American Civil War was the final act of the struggle against colonial domination... The slave form of production in the South owed its existence and its prosperity to an English dominated international trade. It blocked the unification of the American nation at every level, and threatened to put an end to the frontier expansion. The long phase of industrial growth in England after 1849 with its strong demand for agricultural raw materials, including cotton, incited the slave owners to expand their territory. Hence slavery gained new footholds in the lands conquered in the south west. In this way slavery braked the expansion of the textile industry and other industries using sub-tropical raw materials, and prevented the exploitation of immense mineral resources. The slave owners also exercised a preponderant influence in Congress, sufficient to thwart any protectionist policy. Industrial capitalism thus suffered as a whole, for the pilot industries of the economic division of labour were unable to withstand English competition. What was at stake in the Northern war effort was thus simultaneously the direct penetration of capitalism to the entire territory of the Union, the establishment of tariff protection, and the political and ideological unification of the nation under the leadership of the industrial and financial bourgeoisie. The reasons for the political alliance between the capitalists and the small agricultural producers are clear enough. The latter feared above all else the extension of the slave system to the free lands of the west, and the blocking of the sale of public land by a Congress dominated by the slave owners' representatives. Finally, these fiercely individualistic petty producers were also very strongly attached to the ideology and institutions of bourgeois democracy. Yet they were soon to find out to their cost that this was an alliance with the devil himself.[145]

Lincoln in his conduct of the war made it clear that the central issue was preserving and strengthening the American state, not freeing the slaves. Not simply Lincoln's own often highly authoritarian methods of government but the mobilisation of resources required to defeat the South transformed the American state. As James McPherson puts it in his outstanding recent history of the Civil War:

> The old federal republic in which the national government had rarely touched the average citizen except through the post office gave way to a more centralised polity that taxed the people directly and created an internal revenue bureau to collect the taxes, drafted men into the army, expanded the jurisdiction of the federal courts, created a national currency and a national banking system, and established the first national agency for social welfare—the Freedman's Bureau.[146]

The Civil War was very much a revolution from above, waged by conventional armies and won by a federal government concentrating considerable powers in its hands. Nevertheless there were considerable pressure from below. The toilers who backed Lincoln were profoundly influenced by the 'free soil, free labour' ideology, projecting the image of a community of small producers in which all had the opportunity to rise, which he was so effective at articulating. And the Northern Abolitionists were prepared, in the period before the outbreak of war, to resort to illegal methods to destroy slavery—not simply to harbour fugitive slaves, but, in John Brown's case, to take up arms.[147] Thirdly, and above all, the slaves themselves played an indispensable part in the Northern victory. As the Union armies penetrated the South many slaves abandoned their plantations. By the end of the war there were perhaps half a million black refugees behind the Northern lines. Even more important, 200,000 blacks served in the Union armies, providing a crucial source of manpower given the growing opposition in the North to the draft, which precipitated the terrible New York race riot of July 1863.[148]

Slave and free blacks rallied to the Union cause as a result of Lincoln's decision to issue 'as a just and necessary war measure for suppressing...rebellion' the Emancipation Proclamation of 1 January 1863 freeing all slaves in the secessionist states.[149] Lincoln's reasons for taking this step were pragmatic—both to isolate the Confederacy internationally by appealing to anti-slavery opinion, above all in the British working class movement, and to undermine the slave power internally. The consequences were enormous. In Eric Foner's words: 'The Emancipation Proclamation and the presence of black troops ensured that, in the last two years of the war, Union soldiers acted as an army of liberation.'[150] Like Cromwell and Robespierre before him, Lincoln gradually adopted increasingly radical policies under the pressure of events rather than by design. McPherson argues: 'He had moved steadily leftward during the war, from no emancipation to limited emancipation, with colonization and then universal emancipation with limited suffrage [for blacks]. This trajectory might well carry him to a broader platform of equal suffrage by the time the war ended.'[151] Lincoln's assassination in the very hour of victory, on 14 April 1865, cut short his leftward evolution, but there is no doubt that he belongs , along with Cromwell and Robespierre, in the pantheon of great bourgeois revolutionary leaders.

Northern victory freed the slaves, but left open the nature of the social and political regime that would succeed the Southern slavocracy. A conflict rapidly developed between Lincoln's successor, Andrew Johnson, and the Radical Repulicans led by Thaddeus Stevens in the Congress. The Radicals represented the wing of Northern capital which wished to use the power of the federal government, under whose military rule the rebel states now found themselves, to reconstruct Southern society by breaking planter power, enfranchising the freedmen, and even redistributing land so as to provide the basis of a small producers' democracy. During the phase of Radical Reconstruction at the end of the 1860s, Republican governments were installed in the South on the basis of an alliance of Northern immigrants, a section of Southern whites, many of them poor whites who had suffered under planter rule, and the freed slaves.

Had this experiment succeeded, conditions of bourgeois democracy would have been established in the South as well as the North. That it failed was a consequence not simply of ferocious resistance by the planters and their allies, leading to the formation of terrorist organisations such as the Ku Klux Klan, but of the waning enthusiasm of the Republican dominated federal government. Confronted by the economic depression which struck in 1873 and by escalating class struggle which led, for example, to the Great Strike of 1877, Northern capital lacked the stomach to break Southern racist resistance to Reconstruction.

The final step in the retreat from Reconstruction came when, as part of the deal under which the Republicans got the White House after the hung presidential election of 1876, federal troops were withdrawn from the South, which was restored to 'home rule'. The South, under the 'Redeemer' Democratic regimes thereby installed, saw the political disenfranchisement of blacks, their subjection to a system of racist Jim Crow laws, and the establishment in place of slavery of other forms of coerced labour such as sharecropping . Even the formal political equality of bourgeois democracy was only won by Southern blacks as a result of the Civil Rights Movement of the 1960s.[152]

The Civil War established the political hegemony of the Northern industrial and financial bourgeoisie. The power of the strengthened federal government could be—and was systematically—used to promote their interests. On this basis, the United States began its ascent to the status it achieved at the beginning of the 20th century, of the world's greatest industrial power.

(iii) *The Meiji Restoration in Japan.* The Meiji Restoration of 1868—the overthrow of the Togukawa family who had ruled as *shoguns* since the end of the 16th century, carried out by a group of *samurai* (warrior nobles) in the name of the hitherto purely titular Emperor (who took the name of Meiji)—was to a significant degree a response to the global dominance of Western industrial capitalism. The revolutionaries proceeded radically to modernise Japanese society, abolishing with the local governments of the *daiymo* (great lords), introducing civil equality and a uniform taxation system, imposing individual land ownership, replacing the military power of the *samurai* with a conscripted army, and providing a limited measure of parliamentary representation.

The nature of this transformation was a subject of great controversy among Japanese Marxists between the wars. One school, the *Kôza-ha*, linked to the Japanese Communist Party, argued, in line with Stalinist orthodoxy, that Japan remained a semi-feudal society reflected in the military, bureaucratic nature of the state and its basis among the large land owners; the bourgeois revolution had still to be completed in Japan. The other school, the *Rônô-ha*, argued that the industrial and financial bourgeoisie were politically dominant and that socialist revolution was on the agenda in Japan.[153] The issues involved are complex.[154]

First the Meiji Restoration differs from other bourgeois revolutions in that it did not occur against the background of the transition from feudalism to capitalism. The dominant mode of production in Tokugawa Japan was not feudalism but the tributary mode of production. Both modes involve the coercive extraction of surplus labour from a smallholding peasantry, but whereas under feudalism it is the landlord who is the main agent of exploitation, in the tributary mode it is the state bureaucracy which taxes the peasantry of their surplus product. The *daimyo* held their land at the will of the *shogun*, rather than by hereditary right, and the *samurai* were rewarded for their services to their lords not with land but with stipends of rice.[155] One consequence of this pattern was that the *daimyo* and the *samurai* tended to be concentrated in the towns, unlike feudal lords, the basis of whose power is rural. The consumption needs of the urban based nobles contributed to the commercialisation of agricuture. By the 18th century a layer of peasant landlords had emerged, amassing holdings, employing wage labour and producing cash crops. Some branched out into rural industry (*saki* brewing, silk weaving etc.), as did some provincial merchants, although the *chonin* (merchants) of the cities were firmly subordinated to the *daimyo*.

It was not, however, the merchants or the peasant landlords who made the 1868 revolution. Ellen Trimberger argues that 'autonomous military bureaucrats' played the decisive part in the Meiji Restoration. The tributary relations of production dominant in Tokugawa Japan 'bureaucratized the aristocracy and removed from control over the land.' This created the possibility that a section of the ruling class, detached from production and located in the state apparatus, might contemplate a radical transformation of economic relations. The incentive to achieve such a transformation was provided by the intrusion of the West from 1853. Contact with the outside world convinced a number of young *samurai* that Japan could avoid the colonial or semi-colonial status to which the rest of Asia was being reduced, only if they adopted political and social structures analogous to those which had allowed Western capitalism its stunning technological and therefore military superiority over the rest of the world. These radical *samurai* first overturned the *shogunate* and then dealt with conservative resistance with a combination of methods ranging from bribery to civil war.[156]

Takashi Toyoda argues that the leading role of *samurai* in the Meiji

Restoration means that it cannot be regarded as a bourgeois revolution:

> *Neither politically not economically were the bourgeois promoters of the Meiji Revolution. The bourgeoisie of the time, parasitically attached to the seigneurial nobility, adapted passively to the political upheaval, without preserving the slightest spirit of enterprise. The first task of the revolutionaries was to preserve the independence of Japan amidst the Powers by building a modern industry oriented towards military needs; but the bourgeois, without understanding these government imperatives at all, remained disoriented faced with the demands of the conjuncture. It was the **samurai**, linked to the government . . . who took direction of the economy and became capitalists, a phenomenon which characterised the Meiji Revolution.*[157]

The supine role of the bourgeoisie counts for nothing, however, unless it can be shown that the Meiji Restoration did not promote the development of capitalism. Here Takashi undermines his own case when he challenges the *Kôza-ha* characterisation of the Meiji state as semi-feudal and absolutist : 'The French Revolution, after having broken absolutism, had abolished all feudal survivals and centralization all the expressions of sovereignity in the democratic state . . . But the Meiji Revolution had from its beginning essentially realized this immense world of the French Revolution.'[158] There is, in fact, not the slightest doubt that the Meiji régime promoted the rapid development of industrial capitalism, building on the commercialisation of economic life under the *shogun*. The fact that the state bureaucracy which presided over this process was recruited from the *samurai* and autonomous of merchants and peasant landlords alike in no way alters the consequences of their policies, any more than does the fact that their reasons for seizing power and modernising Japan involved above the need to acquire the military power necessary to match the Western 'barbarians'. The central feature of bourgeois revolutions is, as we have seen, the changes they bring about in the character of the state. The fact that this transformed state so directly involved itself in the promotion of capitalist industrialisation in Japan reflects the processes of uneven and combined development at work on the world stage—the global dominance of industrial capitalist powers to avoid succumbing, to which backward countries had to transform themselves. The state stepped in to fill the gap left by a weak and conservative local bourgeoisie. In thus adopting state capitalist policies the Meiji revolutionaries blazed a trail which others were to follow in the 20th century.

Conclusion

In its effects at least, the Meiji Restoration occupies a borderline between the 'revolutions from above' of the mid 19th century and a third variant of bourgeois revolution prevalent in the present century. This Tony Cliff has named 'deflected permanent revolution'. Trotsky argued that the process of permanent revolution arose as a result of uneven and combined development: the global integration of capital created pockets of advanced industry amid backward peasant societies. The Russian Revolutions of 1905 and 1917 revealed what this made possible . The bourgeoisie, even more terrified than its German counterpart in 1848 of the new industrial proletariat, sought an accommodation with the absolutist state; workers and peasants united in an alliance in whose programme the objects of bourgeois and socialist revolutions merged. The triumph of soviet power in October 1917 sanctioned both the break up of the gentry's estates by the peasants and the establishment of workers' control of factories. In Lenin's phrase, bourgeois 'passed over' into socialist revolution; the essentially bourgeois democratic objectives of republican government and land redistribrution were achieved by the dictatorship of the proletariat.

But what happened if the proletariat lacked the political organisation needed to provide revolutionary leadership to the peasantry? A succession of revoltuions in the Third World—China, Cuba, Vietnam, Mozambique, Nicaragua—showed how things could then turn out. Nationalist movements, often marching under 'Marxist-Leninist' colours but dominated by the urban petty bourgeoisie, were able to lead and organise successful peasant wars against imperialism and its allies. The regimes brought to power by these revolutions proceeded to construct state capitalist social orders, in which the task of capital accumulation was assumed by a state bureaucracy recruited from the victorious movement and collectively exploiting workers and peasants alike.[159]

The historical irony that movements claiming the inspiration of Marxism should do the work of capitalism, merely underlines the fundamental difference between bourgeois and socialist revolutions. Bourgeois revolutions are characterised by a disjunction of agency and outcome. A variety of different social and political forces—Independent gentry, Jacobin lawyers, *Junker* and *samurai* bureaucrats, even 'Marxist-Leninists'—can carry through political transformations which radically improve the prospects for capitalist development. No such disjunction characterises socialist revolutions.'All previous historical movements were movements of minorities,' writes Marx in words I have already quoted from the *Manifesto*. 'The proletarian movement is the self conscious, independent movement of the immense majority, in the interest of the immense majority.' Socialist revolutions involve the working class taking power for itself, rather than, as in both the 'classic' bourgeois revolutions and recent Third World revolutions, the masses being mobilised to secure the political dominance of capital.

Bourgeois revolutions thus tend to be minority affairs. This is true even of those which did involve a significant degree of popular mobilisation. Christopher Hill has explored in various recent works the dilemma of the English revolutionaries, confronted by the fact that the majority of the population were indifferent or hostile to their cause.[160] Richard Cobb's brilliant study of the *armée révolutionaries* dispatched into the French countryside during the Year II dramatises the conflict this involved between a primarily urban based movement and the mass of the peasantry resentful of these intrusions.[161] This state of affairs reflects the relatively low level of development of the productive forces: England in the 1640s and France in the 1790s were still primarily rural societies, in which most people lived in peasant communities isolated by poor communications whose horizons, even when their mood was radical, were primarily local. Hence the significance of the cities and the armies, both of which involved the concentration of relatively large numbers under conditions often encouraging political militancy.

The dominance of the capitalist mode of production made possible by these revolutions radically changes both the social and material conditions of further transformation. The progressive proletarianisation of the mass of the population creates a class whose interest lies in the common ownership of the means of production rather than some new form of exploitation, and whose mode of life encourages it to act collectively. The development of the productive forces, involving huge urban concentrations, vastly improved communications, and a radical increase in labour productivity, promotes the collective action of the working class and makes the goal of communism, the rule of the associated producers, feasible. But if in all these respects the nature of socialist revolution is radically different from that of bourgeois revolutions, there are continuities as well. Hill observes: 'The idea of consciously making a revolution arrives late in human history, is perhaps not fully formulated till the *Communist Manifesto*.[162] But, as his own work has shown, Marx and Engels could build on earlier efforts to articulate and fight for the idea of the masses taking control of their own destiny, efforts which have flourished above all during the great bourgeois revolutions among the Levellers and Diggers of the 1640s and 1650s, among the Parisian *sans-culottes* of the 1790s. In these movements, aspirations to a far more radical social revolution than any dreamt of by Cromwell or Robespierre were expressed, for example by Winstanley and Babeuf. It is as much because of these intimations of the future as of the examples of revolutionary change they offer that Marxists regard 1640 and 1789 as part of the tradition whose high point—so far—came on 25 October 1917.

Appendix:

Comninel and historical materialism

Comninel devotes little space to developing or justifying his interpretation of the French Revolution, though we are promised a second volume which will apparently fill this gap. He is rather concerned to show that 'the theory of bourgeois revolution did not develop with Marx, and in fact is not even consistent with the original social thought which Marx did develop.' Comninel devotes much space to elaborating this claim by tracing the concept of bourgeois revolution to what he calls the 'liberal materialism' of the Enlightenment.

Marx's own early writings, and especially *The German Ideology*, apparently suffer from a 're-infusion of liberal materialist ideology, the effects of which continue to bedevil Marxist thought' by encouraging 'an uncritical focus on production as such, and an attendant precedence of productive technique over property relations.' It was within this theoretical framework, still marked by bourgeois thought, that Marx identified the French Revolution with the triumph of the bourgeoisie. But later, in *Capital*, Marx's 'point of departure and continual focus was...*class exploitation*.' This approach, however, is inconsistent with the concept of bourgeois revolution:

> It is hard to see how any sense can be made of bourgeois revolution, in its usual form, from the perspective of class exploitation. For the peasantry, who might be expected to be opposed to the feudal aristocracy, are not usually included at all...The enduring struggle is that of the bourgeoisie and the urban people against the aristocracy. Where do relations of **exploitation** figure among those classes..? And if the bourgeoisie **were** to be taken as capitalists, **whom** do they exploit?[163]

Comninel's argument bears some resemblance to that of an essay by Brenner on the English Revolution.[164] Several commentators have noted in *The German Ideology* the absence of the concept of the relations of production; instead Marx tends to use the vaguer expression 'form of intercourse' *Verkerhrsform*; the meanings of '*Verkehr*' include 'communication', 'commerce', and 'trade'[165]. I have argued elsewhere that Marx's reliance on the division of labour in *The German Ideology* involves 'a persistent confusion of technical and social relations', and that 'the first version of historical materialism bears some resemblance to the views of the 18th century Scottish historical school'—Adam Ferguson, Adam Smith, John Millar *et al*, the wing of the Enlightenment which sought most systematically to develop the idea of society progressing through distinct stages based on different modes of subsistence.[166] But these reservations about *The German Ideology* do not entail the rejection of the concept of bourgeois revolution.

The main theoretical influence on Comninel's work appears to be that of the Canadian Marxist, Ellen Wood, who supervised the doctoral dissertation that forms the basis of his book. Wood has sought to develop a version of Marxism which avoids the pitfalls of both 'orthodox' historical materialism, as defended by G A Cohen, which explains social phenomena by their tendency to develop the productive forces, and Althusserian Marxism, which reduces human beings to the 'bearers' of social structures.[167] The trouble with Wood is that, while she is quite clear about what she is against, she is fairly vague about the content of her own theory, beyond the (hardly original) point that the relations of production are simultaneously economic and political and that the separation of state and market characteristic of capitalism is therefore fundamentally misleading.

Comninel takes over this vagueness and squares it. Thus he tells us that 'the central concept of historical materialism' is 'that the *realisation* of human social existence has corresponded to the *development of private property* and the fundamental social antithesis of the propertied and the propertyless', which is about as clear as mud. His 'Outline of the Method of Historical Materialism' is equally illuminating: '1...the key to social analysis is the specific relationship by which surplus extraction is effected'; '2...Class exploitation is intrinsically *political* as well as *economic*', '3...Each era of class society is marked off by a *specific*, but *dynamic*, continuity of exploitation within the larger continuum of class history', One thing is clear, though, namely that Comninel has no time at all for the productive forces. He wilfully and explicitly misreads one passage from *Capital* Volume III where Marx refers to 'the direct relationship of the owners of the conditions of production to the direct producers' as 'always naturally corresponding to a stage in the development of the methods of labour', arguing that 'the "direction" of this correspondence can be reversed from what is usually understood, and priority can instead be given to the *exploitative relationship*, as it relates to 'the development of the methods of labour'.[168]

Comninel is, of course, entitled to his own views, though it's a bit rich that he should present them as Marx's 'mature' theory. The effect of his excision of the development of the productive forces from historical materialism is that it ceases to be a theory of *change*, and becomes instead what Comninel at one point revealingly calls '*historical sociology*'.[169] Whatever its weaknesses, *The German Ideology* is a work of fundamental importance because it identifies as the source of historical change in the contradiction between the development of the productive forces and prevailing social realations (not yet specified as the relations of production) which have become fetters on this development. Comninel provides no alternative mechanism of historical change. It is not clear, therefore, in what respect he can claim to provide a theory of history as opposed to a sociology of forms of exploitation, since he has no account of what leads one such form to succeed another.

To insist on the necessary role of the productive forces in explaining historical change is not to collapse into technological determinism, but is rather to insist that there is what Erik Olin Wright calls a 'weak impulse' for the productive forces to develop without which the succession of more advanced modes of production would be impossible.[170] Comninel's views on the relations of production are hardly more satisfactory. He tends to identify them exclusively with the form of extraction of surplus labour, leaving out of account the particular mode of effective control of the means of production which this form presupposes. Moreover, he fails to observe that Marx first developed the concept of the relations of production in *The Poverty of Philosophy*. Marx wrote this book in 1847, *before* many of the important passages on bourgeois revolutions which I have cited above. This doesn't sit well with the idea that the concept of bourgeois revolution represents Marx's immature thought.

As befits one of Wood's desciples, Comninel parades his hostility to Althusser and all his works. But there is nothing of which his book is more reminiscent than of one of the lesser works of the Althusserian school in its heyday. This is partly a matter of its form—all methodological preliminary, no substantive content. One searches the book vainly for any elaborated analysis of the French Revolution which the book claims to 'rethink'. But there are many similarities of substance. Comninel postulates an absolute 'break' between Marx's 'early' and 'mature' work. He also, like the Althusserians, accords primacy to production relations over the productive forces, sliding into a voluntarism as bankrupt as the technological determinism of Second International Marxism. Finally, because of earlier generations of Marxists' failure to understand Marx, historical materialism must be recommenced: 'While Marxists have made seminal contributions to history—*as historians*—the historical process, and its class dynamics in pre-captitalist societies, have so far eluded the practice of Marxist history.'[171] There may be some who find this iconoclasm exhilarating, but to me (once bitten, twice shy perhaps) it seems like poor stuff indeed.

Notes

The ideas in this article have been floating around in my head for many years now, and were sketched out in the concluding section of *Making History* (Cambridge, 1987). I am grateful for the opportunities I have had to develop them in argument on various occasions: in a debate with Norah Carlin on bourgeois revolutions at Marxism 85, in the discussions of the transition from feudalism to capitalism in several meetings at Marxism 88, and in a stimulating exchange with Bob Brenner in a Chancery Lane cafe. Duncan Hallas has covered all the ground labouriously explored in this article with exemplary panache and brevity in 'The Bourgeois Revolution', *Socialist Worker Review* (hereinafter *SWR*), January 1988. I am grateful to Colin Barker, Lindsey German, Chris Harman, John Rees and Ann Rogers for their comments on this article in draft.

1   A Cobban, *The Social Interpretation of the French Revolution* (Cambridge, 1964), p7.
2   Marx and Engels, *Collected Works* (50 vols published or in publication, London, 1975; hereinafter *CW*), VI, p486; see also ibid, p519.
3   Ibid, VIII, p161.
4   Ibid, V, p178.
5   Ibid, VII, p506.
6   L Trotsky, *Collected Writings and Speeches on Britain* (3 vols, London, 1974), II, pp86-87.
7   A-P-J-M Barnave, *Introduction á la Révolution française*, quoted in A Soboul, *La Révolution française* (Paris, 1988), p589. Oddly, the crucial phrase 'a new distribution of wealth involves a new distribution of power' is omitted from the English translation of this passage: E Chill, *Power, Property and History* (New York, 1971), p82.
8   See for example, *CW*, XXXIX, pp62 and 65, and, on the Restoration historians, A Soboul, *La Civilisation et la Révolution française* (3 vols, Paris, 1970, 1982-3), II, pp23-6.
9   A Soboul, *La Civilisation*, pp27-34.
10 G Lefebvre, *Etudes sur la Révolution française* (2nd rev edn, Paris, 1963), p339. See Richard Cobb's brilliant portrait, 'Georges Lefebvre', in id., *A Second Identity* (London, 1969).
11 Rudé's preface to *The Crowd in the French Revolution* (Oxford, 1972), vii, stresses the collaborative nature of the work undertaken by Cobb, Soboul, and himself under Lefebvre's guidance.
12 C Hill, *The English Revolution 1640* (London, 1972), p6.
13 See, for example, E J Hobsbawm, 'The Historians' Group of the Communist Party', in M Cornforth, ed, *Rebels and their Causes* (London, 1978).
14 See J H Hexter, 'Storm over the Gentry', in *Reappraisals in History* (London, 1961), and L Stone, *The Causes of the English Revolution 1529-1642* (2nd edn, London, 1986), ch 2.
15 R H Tawney, 'The Rise of the Gentry, 1558-1640', *Economic History Review*, XI (1941), pp4, 14, 18.
16 H R Trevor-Roper, 'The Gentry 1540-1660', *Economic History Review Supp* No1 (1953), pp8, 18, 26, 34 and *passim*.
17 E J Hobsbawm, 'The Crisis of the Seventeenth Century', in T Ashton, ed, *Crisis in Europe 1560-1660* (London, 1965), p5.
18 H R Trevor-Roper, "The General Crisis of the Seventeenth Century", in Ashton, ed, *Crisis*, pp59, 67, 95, 93 and *passim*.
19 Ibid, p63.
20 L Stone, 'The Revival of Narrative', *Past & Present* (hereinafter *P&P*), 85 (1979), p20.
21 Critical surveys of revisionist historiography include Stone, *Causes*, ch 4, and B

Manning, 'Class and Revolution in Seventeenth Century England', *International Socialism* 2:38. There was, of course, a political undertow beneath all this. Trevor-Roper, appointed Regius Professor of Modern History at Oxford by Harold Macmillan in preference to the more left wing A J P Taylor, retired to Peterhouse, Cambridge, hatching ground of such pillars of the New Right as the philosopher Roger Scruton. In 1975 the Princeton historian J H Hexter, launched a savage and highly personal attack on Hill. 'The Historical Method of Christopher Hill' reprinted in *On Historians* (London, 1979).

More recently, a young Cambridge historian, Jonathan Clark, has developed a generalised critique of what he called 'the 1960s model', which he associated with such diverse figures as Hill and J H Plumb, and which 'placed capitalism at the centre of the picture' relying on 'an economic determinism' which, for example, explained 'social change in the eighteenth century' in terms of 'a fictitious entity called the Industrial Revolution.' Clark, whose skills at polemic and self advertisement earned him the just reward of a Fellowship of All Souls, made his Thatcherite loyalties explicit, invoking 'the change in mood of the late 1970s' to explain the decline of 'the characteristic historiography of the late 1960s', rooted as it was in 'Attlee's England and the world view on which it was premissed', J C D Clark, *English Society 1688-1832* (Cambridge 1985) pp1-7.

22   Probably the most comprehensive survey of these controversies is W Doyle, *Origins of the French Revolution* (Oxford, 1980), Part 1.
23   Cobban, *Social Interpretation*, pp67, 168, and *passim*.
24   See Cobban's attack on social theory, ibid, 12-14.
25   F Furet and D Richet, *La Révolution française* (rev, edn, Paris, 1972), p126.
26   See, for example, R Cobb, 'Nous des *Annales*', reprinted in *A Second Identity*, and C Mazauric, 'Réflexions sur une nouvelle conception de la Révolution française', *Annales historiques de la Revolution française* (hereinafter *AHRF*), *39* (1967).
27   F Furet, *Penser la Révolution française* (Paris, 1978), pp167, 122, 34, 28, 170, 168.
28   R Cobb, *The Police and the People* (Oxford, 1972), p200.
29   Doyle, *Origins*, p24. See also the exchange between A Soboul, W Doyle and J Leith in *AHRF*, *54* (1982), pp620-39.
30   G Lefebvre, 'La Mythe de la Révolution française', ibid, 28 (1956), p344.
31   Furet, *Penser*, p26; see also ibid, pp24-5.
32   See A Callinicos, *Is there a Future for Marxism?* (London, 1982), ch 1.
33   Quoted in H Gough, 'Genocide and the Bicentenary' *Historical Journal 30* (1987), p978.
34   G Comninel, *Rethinking the French Revolution* (London, 1987; hereinafter *RFR*), pp3, 200, 180, 195, 203, 205.
35   Quoted in C Hill, *Change and Continuity in Seventeenth Century England* (London, 1974), p279.
36   *RFR*, pp 19-20.
37   G Lukacs, *The Destruction of Reason* (London, 1980), p57; see generally ibid, ch 1.
38   See D Blackbourn and G Eley, *The Peculiarities of German History* (Oxford, 1984).
39   Ibid, p10.
40   P Anderson, 'Origins of the Present Crisis', in id and R Blackburn, eds, *Towards Socialism* (London, 1965), pp13-17.
41   E P Thompson, *The Poverty of Theory and Other Essays* (London, 1978), p47. See also the responses to Anderson's restatement of his case in 'The Figures of Descent', *New Left Review 161* (1987) (hereinafter *NLR*). M Barratt Brown, 'Away with All Great Arches', ibid, *167* (1988), A Callinicos, 'Exception or Symptom?', ibid, 169 (1988), and C Barker and D Nicholls, eds, *The Development of British Society* (Manchester, 1988).
42   Blackbourn and Eley, *Peculiarities*, p59.
43   A Gramsci, *Selections from the Prison Notebooks* (London, 1971), pp58-9; see also ibid, pp105-20.

44   Poulantzas, *Political Power and Social Classes* (London, 1973), p183; see generally ibid, pp168-84.
45   Ibid, p173.
46   G Lukacs, *History and Class Consciousness* (London, 1971), pp284, 283, 282.
47   Stedman-Jones, 'Society and Politics at the Beginning of the World Economy' *Cambridge Journal of Economics* I (1977).
48   P Anderson, 'Modernity and Revolution', *NLR*, *144* (1984), p112.
49   Blackbourn and Eley, *Peculiarities*, pp82-3.
50   A Soboul, *La Civilisation*, II, pp45-6.
51   C Hill, *Continuity*, p279.
52   Id, 'Parliament and People in Seventeenth Century England', *P&P*, 92 (1981), pp 104, 108.
53   M Dobb, *Studies in the Development of Capitalism* (London, 1946), pp35, 40, 126; see generally ibid, chs 2-4.
54   R H Hilton, ed, *The Transition from Feudalism to Capitalism* (London, 1976).
55   K Marx, *Capital*, III, pp325, 326-7, 328.
56   Ibid, p336.
57   K Takahaishi,"A Contribution to the Discussion', in Hilton, ed, *Transition*, pp94-6.
58   V I Lenin, *Collected Works* (Moscow, 1965), XIII, 239.
59   I Wallerstein, *The Modern World System*, I (New York, 1974), pp7, 127; see also ibid, pp91ff.
60   R Brenner, 'The Origins of Capitalist Development', *NLR 104* (1977), p37; see generally ibid, *passim*.
61   See especially id, 'The Social Basis of Economic Development', in J Roemer, ed, *Analytical Marxism* (Cambridge, 1986).
62   Id, 'Agrarian Class Structure and Economic Development in Pre-Industrial Europe', in T H Aston and C H E Philpin, eds, *The Brenner Debate* (Cambridge, 1985), p55 and *passim*.
63   G Bois, 'Against the Neo-Malthusian Orthodoxy', in Aston and Philpin, eds, *Brenner*, p115.
64   R Brenner, 'Social Basis', pp31-2. How close an analogy there is in fact between 'political accumulation' and capital accumulation is open to question, since the latter, but not the former, involves competition forcing on units of production the need to innovate technologically and to increase labour productivity.
65   Id, 'The Agrarian Roots of European Capitalism', in Aston and Philpin, eds, *Brenner*, pp239, 257, 258.
66   F Engels, *Anti-Dühring* (Moscow, 1969), p126. See also C Hill, 'A Comment', in Hilton, ed, *Transition*, and P Anderson, *Lineages of the Absolutist State* (London, 1974).
67   See Callinicos, *Making History*, pp157-72.
68   R Brenner, 'Agrarian Roots', op cit, p81.
69   At meetings on the transition from feudalism to capitalism at Marxism 87 and 88.
70   F Braudel, *Civilisation and Capitalism 15th-18th Century* (3 vols, London, 1981), I, p514, II, pp122, 231-2.
71   Ibid, II p405. See generally ibid, ch 4.
72   R Brenner, 'Agrarian Roots', op cit, p325.
73   B Manning, *The English People and the English Revolution 1640-1649* (London, 1976), pp163-83.
74   *RFR*, p180.
75   V I Lenin, *The Development of Capitalism in Russia* (Moscow, 1967), pp196, 199; see generally ibid, ch III.
76   The concept was coined by Franklin Mendels: see 'Proto-Industrialisation: The First Phase of the Industrialisation Process', *Journal of Economic History*, XXXII (1972). For a Marxist synthesis of early modern economic history laying great stress on proto-industrialisation see P Kriedte, *Peasants, Landlords and Merchant*

Capitalists (Leamington Spa, 1983), and for a critique, D C Coleman, 'Proto-Industrialisation: One Concept Too Many', *Economic History Review*, XXXVI (1983).

77   See R Blackburn, *The Overthrow of Colonial Slavery 1776-1848* (London, 1988), and S Mintz, *Sweetness and Power* (New York, 1985).

78   R Brenner, 'Agrarian Roots', pp299-323.

79   Braudel, *Capitalism*, III, pp342-3. The diversity of France is one of the main themes of Braudel's last book: see *The Identity of France*, I (London, 1988), Part 1.

80   See C Trebilcock, *The Industrialisation of the Continental Powers 1780-1914* (London, 1981), pp112,114.

81   I do not discuss in any detail what are generally described as the other two 'classical' bourgeois revolutions, the Dutch and American Revolutions (although mention of the latter is made is made below). The revolution of the Netherlands of 1572 brought into being the United Provinces, a merchant republic which dominated the world economy for much of the 17th century: see for example, G Parker, *The Dutch Revolt* (Harmondsworth, 1979) and I Wallerstein, *The Modern World System*, II (New York, 1980). Hobsbawm calls the Netherlands 'in many respects a "feudal business" economy; a Florence, Antwerp or Augsburg on a semi-national scale. It survived and flourished by cornering the world's supply of certain goods and much of the world's business as a commercial and financial intermediary. Dutch profits did not depend greatly on capitalist manufacture', *Crisis*, p42. For an excellent survey of the debate on the English Revolution, see J Rees, 'Revolution Denied', *SWR*, November 1987.

82   R Brenner, 'Bourgeois Revolution and the Transition to Capitalism', in A L Beier, ed, *The First Modern Society* (Cambridge, 1989), p302; he is here summarising Lawrence Stone's major study, *The Crisis of the Aristocracy 1558-1641* (Oxford, 1965). I am grateful to Bob Brenner for letting me see this article before publication.

83   C Hill, *Puritanism and Revolution* (London, 1968), p17.

84   Norah Carlin is therefore wrong to identify the bourgeoisie entirely with urban capital: see 'Marxism and the English Civil War', *IS* 2:10 (1980/1), pp110-12.

85   R Brenner, 'Agrarian Roots', p298.

86   Anderson, *Lineages*, p125.

87   R Brenner, 'The Civil War Politics of London's Merchant Community', *P&P*, 58 (1973), a study further developed in a forthcoming book.

88   C Hill, 'Parliament and People', pp119ff.

89   B Manning, *English People*, chs 1-5, 7.

90   Ibid, pp152-3, and chs 9-10.

91   For a lucid summary of the progression from 1640 to 1688, see D Hallas, '1688—the Decisive Settlement', *SWR*, October 1988.

92   Hexter, *On Historians*, p221.

93   T Skocpol, *States and Social Revolutions* (Cambridge, 1979), pp5, 141, 294.

94   C Hill, 'A Bourgeois Revolution?', in J G A Pocock, ed, *Three British Revolutions* (Princeton, 1980), pp134-5.

95   Ibid.

96   Id, *Collected Essays*, III, (Brighton, 1986), pp132, 137, 138, 140.

97   M Mann, *The Sources of Social Power*, I (Cambridge, 1986), pp483-5.

98   P Mathias and P O'Brien, 'Taxation in Britain and France, 1715-1810', *Journal of European Economic History 5* (1976).

99   G Ardant, 'Financial Policy and Economic Structure of Modern States and Nations', in C Tilly, ed, *The Formation of Nation States in Western Europe* (Princeton, 1975), pp205, 213, and *passim*.

100 V I Lenin, *Collected Works*, XXXI, p85.

101 Furet, *Penser*, pp144-5.

102 Ibid, pp147, 140, 150.

103 Doyle, *Origins*, pp211-12.

104 Ibid, p212.
105 A Soboul, *The French Revolution* (2 vols, London, 1974), I, p208.
106 L Hunt, *Politics, Culture, and Class in the French Revolution* (London, 1986), p177; see generally ibid, ch 5.
107 Ibid, p178.
108 *RFR*, p21.
109 Furet and Richet, *La Révolution*, ch 4.
110 P M Jones, *The Peasantry in the French Revolution* (Cambridge, 1988), ch 4.
111 M Vovelle, *La Chute de la monarchie 1787-1792* (Paris, 1972), pp139, 145, 153, 168; see generally ibid, chs 4 and 5, which are to some degree a running critique of the *dérapage* thesis.
112 A Soboul, 'A propos d'une thèse récente sur le mouvement paysan dans la Révolution francaise', *AHRF, 45* (1973), p89.
113 Jones, *Peasantry*, p122.
114 Rudé, *Crowd*, pp17-18.
115 Soboul, *Parisian Sans-Culottes*, p254.
116 Ibid, pp53, 54, 252, 54.
117 Id, *French Revolution*, I, p8.
117a Hunt, *Politics, Culture and Class, pp178-9.*
117b See more generally on the nature and formation of collectivities, see Callinicos, *Making History*, chs 4 and 5.
118 Soboul, *French Revolution*, II, p382.
119 Ibid, p408. See id, *Parisian Sans-Culottes*, 251ff, and M Bouloiseau, *La Republique jacobine* (Paris, 1972), ch 6.
120 G Rudé and A Soboul, 'Le Maximum des salaires parisiens et le 9 thermidor', *AHRF*, 26 (1954), p22 and *passim*.
121 E J Hobsbawm, *The Age of Revolution* (London, 1973), p217.
122 See Jones, *Peasantry*, esp chs 1 and 5.
122a Trebilcock, *Industrialisation*, p135. For a very similar judgement from a Marxist perspective, see T Kemp, *Industrialisation in Nineteenth Century Europe* (2nd ed, London, 1985), ch 3.
123 Skopcol, *States*, p204. Compare *RFR*, p202.
124 G Lefebvre, 'Les Paysans et la Révolution française', in id, *Etudes*, pp341, 342, 343-4, 352, 353, and *passim*.
125 Soboul, 'Mouvement paysan', p95.
126 Ibid, pp99, 100. Soboul's concentration towards the end of his life on agrarian questions—see especially *Problèmes paysans de la Révolution, 1789-1848* (Paris, 1976)—does make Comninel's claim that Marxist historians of the revolution have ignored the peasantry (*RFR*, p151) seem particularly silly.
127 Jones, *Peasantry*, pp137-54.
128 *CW*, XI, 185.
129 *RFR*, p203.
130 *CW*, XI, pp190-1, 194.
131 See Trebilcock, *Industrialisation*, pp150-5, 185-7. David Harvey offers an interesting Marxist analysis of Paris under the Second Empire which makes some of the same points in *Consciousness and the Urban Experience* (Oxford, 1985), ch 3. See also Blackburn's comment on Comninel in *Overthrow*, pp549-50 n 4. This book is, incidentally, a splendid vindication of the concept of bourgeois revolution as an essential instrument for understanding the modern world. Perhaps its central theme is that 'anti-slavery was linked to an over arching process of "bourgeois-democratic" revolution' (ibid, p538)—a link demonstrated above all by the decree of the Convention of 16 Plûviose II (4 February 1794), which abolished slavery in the colonies, thus allying the Jacobin republic with the insurgent slaves of St Domingue: see ibid, ch VI.
132 Soboul, *La Civilisation*, p63.

133 See Anderson, *Lineages*, Pt II, ch 3.
134 *CW*, VIII, p162.
135 Stedman Jones, 'Society and Politics', pp 86-7.
136 Blackbourn and Eley, *Peculiarities*, p84.
137 Hobsbawm, *Age*, p11.
138 In a recent article Anderson argues to the contrary, advancing the general thesis that capitalist states have generally undergone periods of radical change subsequent to the original revolutions which established them—Holland's 'Batavian Revolution' of the 1780s, the 19th century French Revolutions, the American Civil War, the German Revolution of 1918, and the upheavals experienced by continental Europe and Japan as a result of the Second World War:

The general significance of these 'revolutions after the revolution' was everywhere the same. They were essentially phases in the modernisation of the state, which thereby permitted a reinvigoration of the economy. The most conservative and or regressive social elements—Dutch regents, Southern slave owners, French legitimists, Japanese landlords, Prussian junkers, Italian latifundists—were eliminated. Something like a fresh historical start occured, at the summit of society. (Anderson, 'Figures' p48).

The function of this theory is to rehabilitate Anderson's normative conception of bourgeois revolution, according to which Britain's relative decline is explained by its failure to conform to this pattern, since it alone of the major capitalist states did not undergo such a 'revolution after the revolution'.

139 Blackbourn and Eley, *Peculiarities*, pp109, 123, 124-5, 146. Ironically, Eley draws in his analysis of the Wilhelmine state on Anderson's discussion of Prussian Absolutism: compare ibid, p133 and *Lineages*, pp277-8. Anderson's ideas about 'modernising' revolutions seem to be connected with Arno Mayer's claim that the European *ancien régimes* survived into the 20th century: see Mayer's *The Persistence of the Old Régime* (New York, 1981) and my critique in *Against Post-modernism* (Cambridge, 1989), ch 2.

140 See esp, H Frankel, 'Class Forces in the American Revolution' in G Novack, ed, *America's Revolutionary Heritage* (New York, 1976; hereinafter *ARH*).

141 G Novack, 'The Civil War—its Place in History', in *ARH*, pp249-50.

142 See, for an overview of American society in this period, J McPherson, *Battle Cry of Freedom* (New York, 1988), ch 1, and, on the nature of America's Industrial Revolution, D M Gordon *et al*, *Segmented Work, Divided Workers* (Cambridge, 1982), ch 2.

143 Marx and Engels, *The Civil War in the United States* (New York, 1961), p81.

144 Blackburn, *Overthrow*, p542.

145 M Aglietta, *A Theory of Capitalist Regulation* (London, 1979), pp77-8.

146 McPherson, *Battle Cry*, p859. See also E Foner, *Reconstruction* (New York, 1988), ch 1.

147 G Novack, 'Homage to John Brown', in *ARH*.

148 W E B Du Bois, *Black Reconstruction in America 1860-1880* (New York, 1969), chs IV and V.

149 *Speeches and Letters of Abraham Lincoln* (London, 1949), p203.

150 Foner, *Reconstruction*, p10.

151 McPherson, *Battle Cry*, p844.

152 Du Bois, *Black Reconstruction*, Foner, *Reconstruction*, and P Camejo, *Racism, Revolution, Reaction, 1861-1877* (New York, 1976).

153 See Kaoru Sugihara, 'Le Débat sur le capitalisme japonais (1927-1937)', *Actuel Marx* 2 (1987). Many have been dealt with in a most illuminating unpublished paper by Colin Barker, which I largely follow in the subsequent brief discussion.

154 C Barker, 'The Background and Significance of the Meiji Restoration of 1868';

copies are available from the author, c/o Department of Sociology, Manchester Polytechnic.

155 See in addition to ibid, 13ff, E K Trimberger, 'State Power and Modes of Production', *Insurgent Sociologist*, 7 (1977), and, on the tributary mode of production in general, C Wickham, 'The Uniqueness of the East', *Journal of Peasant Studies* 12 (1985).

It should be said that this view is controversial since, first, many Marxist students of Japan (Takahashi, Anderson et al) believe that Togukawa society was feudal, and secondly, many would doubt that the concept of a tributary mode of production is in fact preferable either to Marx's idea of an 'Asiatic Mode of Production' or to regarding pre-capitalist Asian societies as simply as feudal.

156 E K Trimberger, *Revolution from Above* (New Brunswick, 1978), p41; see generally chs 2 and 3. Trimberger regards Japan as the *only* full case of 'revolution from above' which she believes necessarily involves the intervention of 'autonomous military bureaucrats'. This seems much too restrictive. B Moore *The Social Origins of Dictatorship and Democracy*, (Harmondsworth, 1969) pp254-75, discusses why the Meiji Restoration was not accompanied—and challenged—by a 'peasant revolution'.

157 Takashi Toyoda, 'Révolution française et Révolution Meiji: étude critique des interprétations de Kosa et Rono', *AHRF*, 35 (1963), pp21-2.

158 Ibid, p18.

159 T Cliff, *Deflected Permanent Revolution* (London, 1983); see also my reflections in 'Trotsky's Theory of the Permanent Revolution and its Relevance to the Third World Today', *IS* 2:16 (1982).

160 C Hill, *God's Englishman* (Harmondsworth, 1972), *Milton and the English Revolution* (London, 1977), and *The Experience of Defeat* (London, 1984).

161 R Cobb, *The People's Armies* (New Haven, 1987), Bk II.

162 C Hill, *Change*, p279. See also Callinicos, *Making History*, ch 5.

163 *RFR*, pp4, 68, 133, 142, 155, 151.

164 R Brenner, 'Bourgeois Revolution'.

165 See G Therborn, *Science, Class, Society* (London, 1976), pp355-75, and G Labica, *Marxism and the Status of Philosophy* (Brighton, 1980), pp282-4.

166 A Callinicos, *Marxism and Philosophy* (Oxford, 1983), pp48, 51.

167 See especially E M Wood, 'The Separation of the Economic and Political in Capitalism', *NLR*, 127 (1981), which includes an acknowledgement to Comninel (p67n).

168 *RFR*, pp134, 170-3, 169: compare Marx, *Capital*, III (Moscow, 1971), p791.

169 *RFR*, p77. See the discussion of different versions of historical materialism and of a weaker 'materialist sociology' in A Levine, *The End of the State* (London, 1987), ch 5.

170 E O Wright, "Giddens's Critique of Marxism", *NLR*, 138 (1983), pp27-9. See also my *Making History*, ch 2.

171 *RFR*, p104.

The algebra of revolution

JOHN REES

The best of times, the worst of times

The name Hegel has often come to the lips of Marxists during great crises in history or at crucial turning points in the development of Marxism. When Marx and Engels first laid the foundations of historical materialism in the 1840s they did so by developing a critique of Hegel's thought. As Marx laboured on *Capital*, he said he found Hegel's *Logic* 'of great service to me'.[1]

When confronted with an unprecedented imperialist war and the collapse of the Second International Lenin looked to Hegel to help refurbish his understanding of Marxism. He concluded: 'It is impossible completely to understand Marx's *Capital*...without having thoroughly studied and understood the *whole* of Hegel's *Logic*. Consequently, half a century later none of the Marxists understood Marx!!'[2]

Again, in the great revolutionary crisis that shook Europe between 1919 and 1923, George Lukacs made his way to Marxism through a study of Hegel. The result, *History and Class Consciousness*, was the greatest work of Marxist philosophy since Marx himself. Between the invasion of Hungary in 1956 and the events of 1968 the Stalinist monolith began to crack and a new generation of activists looked for the authentic voice of revolutionary Marxism. They looked to the works in which the young Marx had engaged with Hegelianism and they looked to the work of George Lukacs.

By contrast, Hegel's name has been missing from those periods when the fortunes of a genuine revolutionary Marxism have been in decline. During the long night which stretched from the defeat of the 1848 revolutions to the Paris Commune, Marx himself noted how 'ill humoured, arrogant and mediocre epigones...began to take pleasure in treating Hegel...as a "dead dog".'[3] Similarly, as the Second International slid into bureaucratic reformist practice and a vulgar materialist theory, it had little time for Hegel. Even where it mentioned Hegel it focused on the dead formalism of his system, not the living dialectic at its core. Plekhanov was one of the best theoreticians of the Second International, yet Lenin noted, 'Dialectics *is* the theory of knowledge of [Hegel and] Marxism...to which Plekhanov, not to speak of other Marxists, paid no attention.'⁴ When the revolutionary storms of the 1920s had passed and Stalinism's dead hand lay over the movement, a similar deliberate neglect set in. Stalin's economic reductionism had no room for the notion of contradiction and constant change. It wanted to justify the status quo, not seek the internal contradictions that would spell its doom.

Today we face a crisis very different from both the bureaucratisation of the Second International and the rise of Stalinism. Nevertheless, socialist ideas which stress the active power of human beings to change society, and the inherent contradictions in the status quo which make such a project possible, are on the defensive once more. The retreat affects our theoretical tradition as well as our practical struggles.

The impulse given to the rebirth of genuine Marxism by the events of 1968 has all but died. Academic fashion has moved away from a concern with Hegel, the young Marx and Lukacs. Now post-structuralism and analytical Marxism hold sway over a much diminished territory. The latter rests on a notion, analogous to free market economics, of the individual as the fundamental building block of social theory, while the former decries any notion of understanding history. One of post-structuralism's leading lights has proclaimed his 'incredulity' at any 'grand narrative, such as the dialectics of Spirit...the emancipation of the rational or working subject, or the creation of wealth'.⁵ In other words, all previous attempts to understand history, from the Enlightenment to the present day, have been failures.

A return to one of the roots of Marxism, Hegelian philosophy, is an essential means to escape the shadow of such an irrational and all embracing pessimism. There can be no better opportunity to review Hegel's legacy than the bicentenary of the French Revolution. Hegel's philosophy has had such resonance in periods of crisis and revolution precisely because it was born of one such crisis. Hidden in its core is the last great attempt by a bourgeois philosopher to understand the dynamics of social change and social revolution. Hegel lived through the revolution and into the era of reaction that followed. He saw the death of the old society and looked fearfully at the shape of the new. This unique vantage point gave his philosophy the enduring value that Marx, Lenin and Trotsky all recognised. Marx and Engels founded historical materialism in opposition to Hegel's philosophy, but they never ceased to pay tribute to 'the colossal old chap'. Likewise, in renewing the Marxist critique of Hegel, we must also avow ourselves the pupils of that mighty thinker.⁶

The Enlightenment

Before we can understand Hegel we must understand his world. Hegel was deeply imbued with the values of the Enlightenment, the intellectual tradition of his times. He was both its last great inheritor and, until Marx, its greatest critic. The Enlightenment was a broad intellectual movement which championed religious toleration against the rule of superstition and tyranny, science and education against mysticism and ignorance, and favoured universal education and humane values. During the 18th century such ideas came to dominate the thinking of many Europeans—at least those who had the time, leisure and ability to read. If one project can summarise such a long and complex movement it must be the *Encyclopedia*. This was the great collaborative dictionary compiled under the eye of Diderot to which nearly every major French thinker, including Voltaire, Montesquieu and Rousseau, contributed. Charged with the belief that society should be organised along lines dictated by human reason, instead of the hierarchy of caste and privilege that marked aristocratic absolutism, the *Encyclopedia* set out to popularise the sum of human knowledge.

Such rationalist ideas invoked the authority not of God but of empirical science, even when the language in which they were expressed was designed to avoid the attention of the censor. Inevitably they were a challenge to authority. As Diderot wrote elsewhere, using the form of a dialogue between father and son,

> *'The point is, father, that in the last resort the wise man is subject to no law...'*
> *'Don't speak so loudly.'*
> *'Since all laws are subject to exceptions, the wise man must judge for himself when to submit and when to free himself from them.'*
> *'I should not be too worried if there were one or two people like you in town, but if they all thought that way I should go and live somewhere else.'*

As it happens, it is unlikely that more than one or two people in town did hold such ideas—at least not if they depended on the *Encyclopedia* to hear of them. Its 4,000 copies may have been widely disseminated throughout France but at £14 a subscription it reached only the very well off. Its 17 volumes of text and 11 of plates, produced between 1751 and 1772, mark a convenient summary of Enlightenment ideas. It is so convenient in fact that to leave an account of the Enlightenment with only a description of the *Encyclopedia* is to miss the important changes in attitudes that took place over the course of the century. Since these changes are vital to understanding Hegel's philosophy, we must briefly examine them.

The origins of the Enlightenment lie in the scientific revolution of the 17th century which in turn resulted from the growing strength of capitalist social relations, particularly in England. The growth of trade and craft manufacture was accelerated by technological improvements in surveying, navigation, metallurgy and dyestuffs. The increasing use of the compass in the West had already fostered exploration and trade. The development of the cannon promoted the study of ballistics and metallurgy. The earlier invention of printing allowed these new discoveries wider dissemination. This revolution in science both contributed to the intellectual environment which accompanied the English Revolution and received new impulse from the battles of the revolution and the settlement which followed. Such an atmosphere encouraged the empirical study of nature and the search for causal laws, rather than blind obedience to the dictates of the Church. The great scientists all maintained religious beliefs but saw the investigation of nature as the best way to worship its creator. Three figures, Francis Bacon (1561-1627), Isaac Newton (1642-1727) and John Locke (1632-1704), will serve to give an impression of the age.

The work of Francis Bacon, Lord Chancellor under James I, was largely ignored by his own generation, but it became important for the Puritan generation that followed him. His biography of Henry VII insisted on a causal explanation of history rather than a divine one. He claimed, 'Men have been kept back...from progress in the sciences by reverence for antiquity, by the authority of men accounted great in philosophy, and then by general consent.' His call for a new science was based on the belief that traditional learning, tied to Christian theology and the writings of the ancient Greeks, was 'a wicked effort to curtail human power over nature and to produce a deliberate artificial despair. This despair...confounds the promptings of hope, cuts the springs and sinews of industry, and makes men unwilling to put anything to the hazard of trial.'[8] This faith in human reason, scientific experiment and progress made Bacon a true precursor of the Enlightenment.

Isaac Newton's theory of gravity was the high point of the scientific revolution. It bound together all movement of matter in the heavens and on the earth in one single, mathematical law. It provided startling proof of Bacon's faith that human reason could, by careful observation and experiment, explain the workings of the natural world. Newton's own ideas, inevitably, were a mixture of the old world and the new. He believed in alchemy and insisted that although the universe operated according to mechanical laws, like the workings of a clock, God must still have set the clock running.[9] Newton's universe retained a role for God, but later Newtonians drew the logical conclusion and banished God to some distant first cause, while in the here and now science triumphed. Pope caught the impact graphically:

Nature and Nature's laws lay hid in night,
God said 'Let Newton be!' and all was light.

Newton's *Principia* was greeted by his colleague Halley with an ode which concluded:

In reason's light, the clouds of ignorance
Dispelled at last by science.[10]

These social, technical and intellectual developments resulted in one very important philosophical foundation of the Enlightenment—mechanical materialism. Thomas Hobbes (1588-1679) was the most radical of the materialists. He saw society as an unremitting 'war of all against all' in which self preservation was the only guiding thread, the basis of ethics. In this picture religion was entirely eliminated. This dark view found little echo in the first, more optimistic phase of the Enlightenment. It wasn't until this mood began to change in the latter half of the 18th century that Hobbes' influence began to grow.

In the meantime it was John Locke who made materialism the cornerstone of 18th century thought. Locke stands at the nexus of some key political and intellectual developments. He was involved in the Glorious Revolution of 1688 which, in overthrowing James II, finally ended claims to the Divine Right of Kings in England. His *Treatise on Civil Government* (1690) was the theoretical justification of the bourgeois settlement of 1688, arguing that the monarchy was simply a limited and revocable contract between ruler and ruled. Marx summarised the conditions that gave Hobbes and Locke such unparalleled intellectual sweep:

> *Hobbes and Locke had before their eyes both the earlier development of the Dutch bourgeoisie (both of them had lived for some time in Holland) and the first political actions by which the English bourgeoisie emerged from local and provincial limitations, as well as the comparatively highly developed stage of manufacture, overseas trade and colonisation. This particularly applies to Locke, who wrote during the first period of English economy, the Bank of England and England's mastery of the seas. In their case, and particularly in that of Locke, the theory of exploitation was still directly connected with economic content.*[11]

Locke's major philosophical work was the *Essay Concerning Human Understanding*, which extended the empirical method of the scientific revolution from the natural world into the realm of human affairs. Locke's huge leap forward was to reject the idea, advanced by Descartes, that ideas were innate. Locke argued that ideas were the direct result of sense impressions or, at the very least, the result of the deliberation of reason on the evidence gained from the senses. Moral values were also a result of evidence provided by the senses. What the senses found pleasurable, the mind dubbed good; what the senses found painful, the mind found immoral.

Locke, like Newton, kept within a Christian frame of reference, but the impact of his ideas led to secular and materialist social attitudes which underpinned much Enlightenment thought. Toleration of different beliefs was defended on the basis that they were the product of differing environments, not heresy or demonic possession. The equality of man was at least a possibility, since social inequality was the product of different environments, not heredity and lineage. Rationality, education and social reform were the key to progress. The stage was set for the spread of such ideas throughout Europe, for Diderot, Voltaire and Rousseau.

That such ideas could spread in Europe was proof that some of the same forces that had given them such a vigorous life in England were also at work in other countries. If we exclude England and certain Dutch cities, France was the most economically developed part of Europe. In the 40 years before the revolution the value of French trade quadrupled. Channel and Atlantic ports like Nantes and Bordeaux were transformed. France's cities were the largest on the continent. Factory based production had small but impressive footholds—one textile mill employed 12,000, the Anzin mining company 4,000, and in Paris there were 50 'manufactories' employing between 100 and 800. Some provinces, encouraged by entrepreneurial aristocrats, the new school of Physiocrats (or economists) and the government's own Department of Agriculture (established in 1761) were also beginning to employ new scientific agricultural techniques.[12] The materialist ideas that were part of the intellectual armour of the rising bourgeoisie in England, and received their fullest expression after the old order had been broken by the revolution of the 1640s, now took strongest root in France.

But it wasn't just emulation and common circumstances that encouraged the educated classes in France to adopt materialist ideas. England and France were not intellectual partners but commercial rivals. Where England led others must follow. 'Enlightened' monarchs throughout Europe were willing to promote mild reform, encourage their own bourgeoisies and give cautious backing to the new science so long as the process did not go beyond their control. The French, and other monarchies, balanced between the old order, on which their whole political prestige depended, and the rising bourgeoisie, on which they increasingly depended financially. Such harmony could only last so long as the bourgeoisie could tolerate being the dominant force economically while also being the junior partner politically. As it grew in strength the bourgeoisie became less tolerant and the monarchy, encouraged by the most unreformable nobles, tried to halt the processes it had long half encouraged.

George Rudé summarises this turning point:

> *The great question was: should the way to reform be sought by enlarging the authority of an 'enlightened' monarch at the expense of the estates; should aristocratic or other 'intermediate bodies' be strengthened as a check to the power of the Crown; or should the power of both be balanced, or eclipsed, by vesting greater responsibility in the hands of the people themselves? ...The answers given naturally varied from country to country and from class to class.*[13]

Such developments gave the latter half of the 18th century a quite different tone. The harmony of the Enlightenment began to turn to discord. A more active note began to sound. History might not inevitably be moving forward under the guidance of sweet reason—it might need a shove. One sign of the change was the dispute between Rousseau and Diderot. Rousseau had been one of the contributors to the *Encyclopedia*. In fact he wrote so much that he recorded 'I am worn out'. Nevertheless, he persisted because, 'I want to get at the throats of people who have treated me badly, and bile gives me strength, even intelligence and knowledge.'[14] One of the people who had treated Rousseau badly had been the Comte de Montaigu, Ambassador in Venice. Rousseau had been the ambassador's secretary, but his employer constantly referred to him as a 'servant'. Rousseau suffered the frustration of a whole generation who felt the old order blocked their rise to the positions and respect that their talents merited.

It was this situation, this social impasse, of which Rousseau's individual circumstances were just an example, that reflected itself in his work. He began to break with the cheerful Baconian optimism of the Encyclopedists. In the preface to the *Encyclopedia* Diderot had written that 'our aim is to gather all knowledge, so that our descendants, being better instructed, may become at the same time happier and more virtuous.'[15] Rousseau disagreed. Society was regressing, not advancing. 'Civilization' only 'cast garlands of flowers over the chains that men bore.'[16] Without war, conspiracy and tyranny there would be no history. Rousseau's attitude to society was unremittingly bitter:

> *The first man who fenced off a piece of land, took it upon himself to say 'This belongs to me' and found people simple-minded enough to believe him, was the true founder of civil society...*
>
> *Such was, or may have been, the origin of civil society and laws, which gave new fetters to the poor, and new powers to the rich...and to benefit a few ambitious persons, subjected the whole of the human race thenceforth to labour, servitude and wretchedness.*[17]

This note of class hatred and the notion of a decaying regressive social order was quite foreign to the *philosophes*. The notion that men had purposively made society, even if for the worse, began to break with mechanical determinism. Materialists like D'Holbach had argued that the world operated according to 'necessary and immutable laws' which 'distributed good and evil' among men.[18] Helvétius denied the existence of free will: 'All our thoughts and will must be the immediate effect or necessary consequence of impressions we have received.'[19] But Rousseau argued that human beings could arrest the slide into tyranny. His solution, the Social Contract, might not be democratic in the modern sense but it was certainly anti-feudal, and republican. It stressed that the will of the mass, the General Will, was free to make its own decisions and was not the puppet of material forces.

This new subjective strand became increasingly insistent in its opposition to mechanical materialism in the years before the French Revolution. But it received its most pronounced expression in Germany, not France. It was this tradition from which, and in opposition to which, Hegel's thought developed.

German conditions and German idealism

Since Marx it has been a truism that, because German society was so economically and socially backward, the German bourgeoisie achieved in thought what other nations achieved in deeds. If we are to understand Hegel's thought we need to spell out what this aphorism means.

The Germany into which Hegel was born was not a unified nation state. Throughout the 18th century it existed only as hundreds of small duchies, principalities, imperial free cities, petty kingdoms, bishoprics, margraviates and landgraviates loosely held together under the imperial crown of the Habsburg dynasty.[20] The economic and social structure of even the largest states, like Prussia, lagged far behind England and France. On the land the peasantry laboured much as they had done from time immemorial. Some Junkers, the Prussian aristocracy, wanted to make changes—but only to increase their hold over the peasants by replacing forced labour with wage labour. But 'in their deeply rooted class selfishness the mass of the Junkers did not even understand this.'[21] Only the defeats they suffered in the Napoleonic Wars clarified their thinking.

Some towns, like the trading towns of Hamburg and Hanover, were growing. The population of Berlin grew from 20,000 in 1688 to 70,000 by 1740. But even this was small compared with the Paris (approx 600,000) or London (nearer 800,000) of 1780.[22] In the towns production was mostly carried out within the confines of the old medieval craft guilds. The mass of urban dwellers were house-owning master craftsmen 'who grew up in the narrowest philistinism'.[23] The journeymen's associations, which had made attempts to break out of the guild system and create a free market, thus facilitating the rise of a bourgeoisie, had been crushed. The Prussian monarchy's Imperial Law of 1731 suppressed the last resistance and the Statute of Handcrafts of 1733 threatened imprisonment and, eventually, death for those who resisted. The result was that tiny craft enterprises survived. In 1800 there were still almost twice as many masters as journeymen.[24]

Despite these enormous obstacles there were some small signs of capitalist development. Saxony, where the beginnings of capitalism dated from before the Reformation, had long been a stronghold of the mining industry. The discovery of gold and silver in America began to threaten the mines, but Saxony's old trade and transport links, its wealth of minerals like lead, tin and coal and its advantageous geographical position protected its development. Leipzig fairs were the biggest trading markets in Eastern Europe and Chemnitz became a 'Saxon Manchester'. A calico mill employed 1,200 and a calico printing plant and cotton mill had over 3,000 workers. In Westphalia and the Rhineland, influenced by neighbouring France, industry was even more developed and more diverse. Cotton, wool and silk industries gave rise to bleaching, printing and dyeing enterprises. The iron founding, mechanical engineering, mining and arms industries employed a population of a density unheard of in other parts of Germany.[25]

These pinpoints of light in the black feudal night were important, but they were puny compared to England and France. For instance, English mills had 200 Arkwright water frames by 1790, while France had eight. Germany did not get her first until 1794.[26] The German bourgeoisie were marked by the backwardness from which they were emerging. Among the leading manufacturers of Berlin there were many who could scarcely write their own name, according to Prussian Privy Councillor Kunth. He thought the worst shortcoming of Prussian industry was the manufacturers' lack of education.[27] But if the commercial and industrial bourgeoisie were still weak, there was another sort of middle class which was more educated, more vociferous and growing in size.

The patchwork of quarrelsome German states vied with each other socially and politically as well as militarily and economically. In fact, since Prussia dominated the area militarily and the economy of other states hardly allowed them to keep up, the rivalry between them was often more political, cultural and social than anything else.

To compete in these terms meant to follow France. France was the cultural and social leader of 18th century Europe. The entire European aristocracy followed French fashion and spoke French as their first language. Even in Vienna, where German was spoken, it was peppered with imported French phrases. 'I am a great prince and have adopted the forms of government which befit a great prince, like others of my kind,' said Eberhard Louis, Duke of Württemberg, who ruled over a population no bigger than that of Paris.[28] In the tiny court of Weimar there were 200 officials, many of whom must have felt, like Rousseau, superior to those they served—especially since the German nobility were often no better off than British tenant farmers. Universities and court orchestras were important status symbols. Saxony maintained three universities, as many as England, despite having a total population of only 2 million. There were 37 universities in the Holy Roman Empire and another five in the German speaking areas beyond. In the Saxon court of 1716 the Elector boasted an orchestra of 65, a French choir of 20, a French ballet of 60 and a theatre company of 27. Some of the Elector's ministers had orchestras of their own. In Prussia the streamlined state structure, inherited from 'enlightened monarch' Frederick the Great, helped create a layer of educated officials.

With this mass of officials, clerks, lawyers, academics and artists came a boom in intellectual argument and debate. In the 1780s alone 1,225 periodicals were launched in Germany. Even though they were often quickly suppressed or censored, they outstripped the numbers in France. Such layers would often have felt deeply alienated from their aristocratic overlords. The universities produced 'highly qualified graduates for whom there was no work' and 'thousands of would-be writers [who] had no one to write for' since the aristocracy preferred French to German.[29] Contempt for German culture was little diminished from the time when Frederick the Great had refused a salary of 2,000 thalers to his librarian on the grounds that 'one thousand is enough for a German'.[30] This was 'a situation which left a whole class of young Germans thumb-twiddling and broody, staring out of windows, waiting.'[31]

It was from this combustible material of 'craftsmen and petty officials in church, school and state, and not from the big and medium bourgeoisie'[32] that successive waves of intellectual protest were to burst. While the *Sturm und Drang* (Storm and Stress) movement in art and Idealism in philosophy stood on the shoulders of the Enlightenment thinkers, the unreconstructed nature of German society made it impossible for them to accept the happy optimism of English, and to a lesser extent French, materialism. English materialism remained 'an esoteric doctrine, a secret of the top ten thousand'[33], since the English bourgeoisie had already gained a measure of political power and had no wish to use its science to dispel the mists of religion among the lower orders. English classical economy, typified by Adam Smith, was appropriate to a class that already wielded considerable economic power and was confident that its growing strength would deliver increased political power. German idealism was appropriate to a middle class which held ideas that it had neither the political nor economic power to realise. Consequently, it stressed the one thing left to it—the power of thought. Where Adam Smith saw the 'hidden hand' of the free market, Hegel was to see the 'cunning of Reason'. But before Hegel there was Kant.

Immanuel Kant (1724-1804), a philosophy professor in Koenigsberg, took up Rousseau's themes and insisted that intellect, mind, subjectivity and will were all essential to our picture of the world. It was said that the citizens of Koenigsberg set their watches by the professor's appearance for his daily afternoon walk. He only failed to appear on two occasions. The first was the publication of Rousseau's *Emile*. The second was the fall of the Bastille.[34] Rousseau's portrait was the only one in his study. But Kant's thought was more rigorous than Rousseau's ideas.

The *Critique of Pure Reason* (1781) broke more thoroughly than ever before with the whole tradition of French and English materialism. It insisted that our thoughts were not the automatic product of our environment as represented by our senses. Kant started by agreeing with the materialists that all knowledge *begins* with experience. But this only provides the *material* for thought. It does not provide the means and methods by which these materials, these raw sensations, are ordered, classified and related to one another. As Marcuse says, 'if it could be shown that these principles of organization were the genuine possession of the human mind and did not arise from experience, then the independence and freedom of reason would be saved.'[35]

But in rescuing an active role for the human mind Kant also cut himself off from continued interaction with the material world. He did so by arguing that the human mind has certain structures for interpreting experience and that these exist prior to any impulse that the mind receives from the external world. It necessarily followed that the human mind *produced* our experience of the world, rather than passively registering the world, as the materialists believed. Kant admitted that there was a 'real' world beyond that revealed by our mind but, since all that we knew was given to us by our mind, we could never know this world. Thus there was an unbridgeable gap between the 'thing in itself' and the thing as it appeared to us. The world had been cleaved in two. This is Kantian dualism.

Kant had won back an active role for human thought from the materialists, but at the cost of opening up a chasm between thought and the world to which it related. When there is no logical connection between human consciousness and the world it inhabits, philosophy often calls in morality to fill the void. Kant's system wanted to bridge the gap between what is and what ought to be, but all it could offer were moral strictures, a system of ethics. There might be contradictions in thought, argued Kant, but in reality 'everything that contains contradiction is impossible.' If there were no cracks in the facade of the real world then there was no place that the lever of active thought could be inserted in order to shift events.

This impasse in philosophy was only broken by the eruption of the

French Revolution. That unparalleled intervention of the masses into the course of history redefined the terms in which philosophers thought of the relationship between the active subject and the objective material world. Fichte, Kant's successor as Germany's leading philosopher, tried to solve the problem of dualism by making everything the emanation of thought. The real world was simply reduced to a projection of our minds. This was idealism with a vengeance, but it fitted the first enthusiasm with which many European intellectuals reacted to the French Revolution. Fichte's system, like the German middle class, thought actively and critically about the world, hoping that this would be sufficient to bring about real change in the real world.

Fichte's philosophy never survived the reverses and complexities of the revolution. It was Hegel who really expressed the experience of the French Revolution in a philosophical system, despite the fact that he was less politically radical than Fichte. Before we return to see how his theoretical revolution evolved in opposition to Kant and other idealist philosophers, we must first chart Hegel's attitude to the revolution in society.

The master theme of the epoch

For Hegel the French Revolution was indeed, in Shelley's phrase, the master theme of the epoch. His early republican ideas, his attitude to the Jacobins and the Terror, his joy at Napoleon's successes and his despair at his defeat, his hopes and fears about capitalist society, all marked key turning points in his philosophical theory.

In 1770 Georg Wilhelm Friedrich Hegel was born into precisely the class that we have seen to be the heart of the Enlightenment in Germany. His father was a civil servant in the government of the Duchy of Württemberg, and his brother became an army officer. He studied at the Stuttgart Gymnasium, or secondary school, graduating top of his class. Hegel's school studies imbued him with the ethos of the Enlightenment. In an essay on the religion of the Greeks and Romans he writes, 'Only when a nation reaches a certain stage of education, can men of clear reason appear amongst it, and reach and communicate better concepts of divinity to others.'[36]

In 1788, the year before the French Revolution, he graduated to the *Tübinger Stift*, a theology seminary attached to the State University of Tübingen, which prepared students for service in the government, teaching or the Church. Hegel studied philosophy and religion.

He shared rooms with, and became the close friend of, the poet Friedrich Hölderlin and fellow philosopher Friedrich Schelling. Together they planted a 'liberty tree' to celebrate the French Revolution and danced around it singing the *Marseillaise* and other revolutionary songs. They are also said to have been involved in a secret club which read the writings of the revolution and which came under investigation by the authorities.[37] When Hegel left Tübingen in 1793 to take up a post as a private teacher with a patrician family in Berne the friends parted with the words *'Reich Gottes!'* ('To the coming of God's kingdom'). Soon, they hoped, French events would be repeated in Germany. In the same year Hölderlin wrote,

> *I love the race of the coming centuries... For this is my blessed hope, the faith which keeps me strong and active—our descendants will be better than ourselves, freedom must come at last, and virtue will thrive better in the holy warming light of freedom than under the ice-cold sky of despotism. We live in a period where everything is working for the better.*[38]

Hegel undoubtedly shared his friend's Enlightenment sentiments, including the religious colouration added by German circumstances. Hegel saw the revolution implementing the rational order long predicted by Enlightenment thought. Now the rational mind could renovate an irrational world. Even in later life, when the first enthusiasm for the revolution had long faded, Hegel would maintain,

> *As long as the sun has stood in the heavens and the planets circled around it, we have never yet witnessed man placing himself on his head, that is, on thought, and building reality according to it...but now man has come for the first time to recognise that thought should rule spiritual reality. This was a magnificent dawn. All thinking beings joined in celebrating this epoch. A sublime feeling ruled that time, an enthusiasm of spirit thrilled through the world, as if we had now come to the real reconciliation of the divine with the world.*[39]

At the time, life in Berne and a study of Kant and English political economy helped focus Hegel's mind on the concrete application of his thought, rather than the simple celebrations of the revolution that occupied him in Tübingen. Hegel said of Berne, 'In no country that I know is there so much hanging, racking, beheading and burning as there is in the Canton of Berne.'[40] He was appalled by the political corruption involved in the selection of the ruling council. In a letter to Schelling he complains that:

> *All the intrigues in the princely courts...are nothing compared with the combinations that go on here. The father nominates the son or the groom that will bring in the heaviest dowry, and so on. In order to understand an aristocratic constitution, one has to spend one such winter here.*[41]

During this period Hegel saw himself as working within the Kantian framework. He tells Schelling, 'From the Kantian system and its ultimate consummation I expect a revolution in Germany.'[42] But the impact of

events in France was already equipping Hegel with an understanding
of historical change that reached beyond Kant's abstract categories. In
the same letter to Schelling, Hegel celebrated 'the fact that mankind...is
being treated with so much reverence' because it proves 'that the halo
which has surrounded the heads of the oppressors and the gods of the
earth has disappeared.' He then went on to explain how the revolution
in philosophy and the revolution in society are related:

> *The philosophers demonstrate this dignity* [of man]; *the people will learn to
> feel it and will not merely demand their rights, which have been trampled
> in the dust, but will themselves take and appropriate them. Religion and politics
> have played the same game. The former has taught what despotism wanted
> to teach: contempt for humanity and its incapacity to reach goodness and
> achieve something through man's own efforts. With the spreading of the ideas
> about how things should be, there will disappear the indolence of those who
> always sit tight and take everything as it is. The vitalising power of ideas—
> even if they still have some limitation, like those of one's country, its
> constitution etc—will raise the spirits.*[43]

This is an early example of the great themes of Hegel's philosophy.
The leading role of philosophy, the 'vitalising power of ideas', the
keystone of idealism is here. Notice how it is not the limitations of one's
country that shape thought, but thought that transforms the limitations
of the society. But in this letter there is also a revolutionary conception
of historical change, of the way that social movements and ideas interact
to produce historical change. This is the enduring conquest which Hegel's
philosophy won from the experience of the French Revolution and which
Marx inherited.

During Hegel's stay in Berne events in France were taking a decisive
turn. Under internal and external threat the revolution put Robespierre
in power. To overcome this dual threat of counter-revolution Robespierre
and the Jacobins unleashed the Terror. This was the point at which many
of the revolution's erstwhile intellectual admirers throughout Europe,
like Tom Paine and Wordsworth, began to recoil from their early
enthusiasm. In one sense Hegel was no exception. He had little sympathy
with the Jacobins and the *sans-culottes* and even less with the Terror.

In 1794 he wrote to Schelling complaining of the Terror. In the
Phenomenology of Mind (1806) he reiterated his criticisms, referring
to the Terror as 'absolute fear'. The Terror was the demand for absolute
freedom uncontrolled by any institutional limit. The Terror was 'merely
the *fury* of destruction'. But once this fury has 'completed the destruction
of the actual organisation of the world' it has no plan about how the
world should be reconstructed, what a new, better society should be.
Therefore the Terror 'exists now just for itself...an object which no longer
has any content.' For this reason 'the sole work and deed of universal

freedom is therefore *death*, a death which has no inner significance or filling...it is thus the coldest and meanest of all deaths, with no more significance than cutting off the head of a cabbage or swallowing a mouthful of water.'[44]

Hegel's hostility was based on a clear class appraisal of the situation. The Jacobins' decrees and the Maximum on prices were surely what Hegel had in mind when he attacked the 'supreme public authority' whose 'pedantic craving to determine every little detail' means that 'the appointment of every village schoolmaster, the expenditure of every penny for a pane of glass...the appointment of every toll-clerk...is the immediate emanation and effect of the highest authority.'[45] The Jacobins were endangering the principle that 'in the states of the modern period...all legislation hinges upon security of property.'[46] But for all his abhorrence of the Jacobins it is important to be clear that Hegel did not reject the gains of the revolution, or even the necessity of the Terror. He wrote that the tyranny (by which he meant Robespierre) 'is *necessary* and *just* to the extent to which it *constitutes and maintains the state as a real individual entity.*' Once the tyrant ceases to be necessary he is overthrown,

> *Tyranny is overthrown by the people because it is abhorrent and base, etc.: but in reality only because it is superfluous. **The memory of the tyrant is execrated;** but...he has acted as a god only in and for himself and expects the ingratitude of his people. If he were wise he would divest himself of his powers as they became superfluous; but as things are his divinity is only the divinity of the animal: blind necessity which deserves to be abominated as sheer evil. This was the case with **Robespierre**. His power abandoned him, because **necessity had abandoned him** and so he was violently overthrown. That which is necessary comes to pass, but each portion of necessity is normally assigned to individuals. One is counsel for the prosecution and one for the defence, another is judge, a fourth executioner; but all are necessary.* [47]

Here Hegel mirrored the attitude of the mainstream of the French bourgeoisie: Robespierre was a god so long as he was necessary. While he was necessary even the threat to private property was preferable to the success of the counter-revolution. But once the counter-revolution was beaten back, Robespierre was no longer tolerated. The impact of the Jacobin dictatorship also had far more wide ranging consequences for Hegel's thought. It reinforced not only his commitment to democracy and his distrust of the 'perfidious Robespierrists', but also his belief that the state was indispensable. This change did not take place immediately. As late as 1796, at the end of his time in Berne when his republican sentiments were at their height, Hegel could write, 'We must...transcend the state. For every state is bound to treat free men as cogs in a machine...hence the state must perish.'[48] But two years later Hegel had become convinced that, on the basis of the Terror, 'Anarchy has become distinguished from freedom; the notion that a firm government is indispensable for freedom has become deeply engraved on men's minds.' Order which guaranteed property was vital, albeit allied to 'the notion that people must have a share in the making of laws.'⁴⁹ Such a framework would enable Hegel to welcome the rise of Napoleon as the inheritor of the revolution, the guarantor of bourgeois stability and the liberator of Germany from the feudal yoke.

There was a second change in Hegel's thought as a result of events in France. He began to think more critically about the legacy of the Enlightenment. The Jacobins generally and Robespierre in particular were the self confessed followers of the Enlightenment thinkers. After all, was it not the Enlightenment belief that by altering men's environment we could improve their natures which stood behind Saint-Just's epigram, 'It is for the legislator to make men into what he wants them to be'?⁵⁰ Wasn't Robespierre Rousseau's ardent pupil? Hegel now began to question whether the stark project of the Enlightenment—to confront a recalcitrant world with the rational schemes of man—doesn't lead to the guillotine.

Initially this may seem like a collapse into a straightforward conservative opposition to change, but it is not. It is the beginnings of overcoming the duality of thought and reality that we saw in Kant's philosophy. Hegel is beginning to see that human reason cannot simply oppose itself to the structure of reality, it must search out those elements in the real world which are tending towards change and ally itself with them. Freedom is not the attempt to frustrate the necessary structure of the world, but the appreciation of that neccessity. Freedom is to act in accordance with necessity. It was a point that Marx would bend to his own purposes in the debate with the utopian socialists, the last impoverished descendants of the Enlightenment line.

Another major theme also began to surface during Hegel's time in Berne. The changes in his thought are only discernible in some important but esoteric studies of ancient Greece and of the origins of Christianity. Hegel puzzled over how the beautiful unity of Greek civilisation, where each individual felt at one with the society in which he lived, degenerated to the modern situation with individuals pitted one against each other and all against the state. He also examined how it was that Christianity developed from the heartfelt belief it once was to the formalistic, externally imposed code that he saw around him. The historical inaccuracy of these observations is not the point. Their importance lies in the fact that Hegel had begun to raise the question of alienation. How was it that the institutions and ideologies that human beings created came to dominate their lives, how did they lose their vitality and become dry husks waiting to be blown away by the wind of historical change? While in Berne these ideas were only present in dim outline, but they were to become central to the development of Hegel's thought.

Hegel felt isolated in Berne so, in 1797, he gladly accepted a teaching post that Hölderlin had found for him in Frankfurt. Once back in Germany Hegel began to think about how the gains of the French Revolution might help to sweep away the unreconstructed feudal states that surrounded him. Hegel was only in Frankfurt until 1801 when Schelling found him a job as a lecturer at the University of Jena. Nevertheless there are some fragmentary writings from the Frankfurt period which show us that Hegel was still thinking through how changes in history could leave old institutions stranded as anachronisms. They also show that, despite the Terror, Hegel was clear that a bourgeois revolution was still a necessity in Germany.

In *The German Constitution* Hegel again wrestled to produce a historical understanding of the problems that confront society: we must understand that it is not 'arbitrariness and chance that make it [society] what it is' and that we should see 'that it is as it ought to be'.[51] This is a plea for understanding how things emerge in the course of history, not a recipe for political quietism. This is made clear in *On the Recent Domestic Affairs of Württemberg* (originally called *That Magistrates Should be Elected by the Citizens*) where Hegel says,

> *How blind they are that hope that institutions, constitutions, laws which no longer correspond to human manners, needs and opinions, from which the spirit has flown, can subsist any longer.*

And he saw that:

> *Calm satisfaction with the present, hopelessness, patient acquiescence...have changed into hope, expectation, and a resolution for something different. The picture of better and juster times...has moved all hearts and set them at variance with the actuality of the present.*[52]

Hegel came even closer to the heart of things when he moved to Jena. Although its bloom was fading by 1801, Jena had been the centre of the Enlightenment and the *Sturm und Drang* movement. Not only was Schelling there, but so, until recently, was Fichte, Germany's leading philosopher. Schiller and the Schlegal brothers were also at Jena. Hegel published some minor works and, after he became an associate professor in 1805, he began work on the first major statement of his system, the *Phenomenology of Mind*. His work was rudely interrupted by the Battle of Jena. After their victory Napoleon's troops seized the city, burning down Hegel's lodgings in the process. He escaped, clutching the second half of the manuscript of the *Phenomenology* in his arms. The experience didn't undermine Hegel's full hearted support for Napoleon which lasted until the Emperor's defeat at Waterloo.

On the night before the Battle of Jena Hegel wrote, 'This morning I saw the Emperor—this world soul—ride through the town...it is a marvellous feeling to see such a personality, concentrated in one point, dominating the entire world from horseback... It is impossible not to admire him.'[53] In a letter to a friend he said, 'All wish the French army luck.' Hegel's mood reflected that of many bourgeois republicans throughout Europe—the hope that Napoleon would free them from the old order, avoiding recourse to the methods of the revolution itself.

A new decisive shift took place in Hegel's thought at about this time. Althouth he saw the battles of Napoleon's armies as world shattering events, it was not the bayonets and cannon that were the real the cause of social change. It was the changing spirit of the age, the collective consciousness, which determined that things must change. This was the real motivating force. This spirit, often identified with philosophy, was the real first cause of events, simply using commanders and their cannon as means to its end. Napoleon, like Robespierre before him, had become necessary, but he acted blindly. Only philosophy saw the pattern of events unfolding behind cannon smoke. Only philosophy had made the battles possible:

> *Philosophy is something lonely; it does not belong in the streets and the market place, yet it is not alien to man's actions...spirit intervenes in the way the world is ruled. This is the infinite tool—then there are bayonets, cannon, bodies. But...neither bayonets, nor money, nor this trick nor that, are the ruler. They are necessary like the cogs and the wheels of a clock, but their soul is time and spirit that subordinates matter to its laws.*[54]

The role of philosophy in this 'time of ferment, when spirit moves forward in a leap' is to 'welcome its appearance and acknowledge it while others, who oppose it impotently, cling to the past', as Hegel announced in his end of term lecture of 1806.[55]

Hegel expected great things of Napoleon and, in some senses, he was not disappointed. Even before the period of French occupation the revolution had already forced sweeping changes in Germany's ramshackle structure. The supposedly mighty Prussian state had been forced to sue for peace in 1795, after which 'it withdrew from great world affairs to carry on a semblance of life under the shield of cowardly neutrality, hated and scorned by all...it was utterly finished, intellectually and morally, financially and militarily.'[56] Then in 1801 Napoleon forced the German Emperor to sign a treaty which relinquished his Rhine territories, just as the Prussians had done. Some 1,150 square miles with a population of four million were lost to Germany. Even then the German Princes proved incapable of reordering their society, so, in 1803 and in agreement with Russia, Napoleon forced the abolition of more than a third of the 300 German states.

In 1805 England enticed Austria and Russia into war with France. The Prussians promised the Tsar aid but their emissary had not even arrived with the news before Napoleon beat Austria and Russia at Austerlitz. Prussia rushed back into Napoleon's arms. Austria was forced to cede 1,140 square miles and 800,000 inhabitants. These lands went primarily to German states. Napoleon kept his army in southern Germany and swept away countless more petty states. A population of one and a quarter million occupying 550 square miles were divided between 16 states who declared themselves independent of the German Emperor. This was the Confederation of the Rhine and it recognised Napoleon as its protector. The Prussians considered revolt, but the Battle of Jena put an end to that. Some form of bourgeois reconstruction, often based on the Napoleonic legal code, followed in many of these states. But, to the extent that French occupation led to bourgeois rule, it began to forfeit the support of those who had been happy to see it deal blows to the old order. The bourgeoisie, always fearful of thoroughgoing transformation, would now be happy to take their deliverance from Napoleon's hands and bid him farewell. They got their chance in 1812 when war broke out between France and Russia. The wars of liberation now meant that a united Europe opposed Napoleon. He was deposed for the first time in 1814 and for a second and final time in 1815.

Waterloo was a victory for old Europe, but too much had been changed for the old order ever to be the same again. There was no better proof than the fact that the Prussian aristocrats had driven their troops to war by promising a free and independent Germany. The King of Prussia even promised a constitution if his subjects would save his throne. Thus the old order could only get their citizens to fight the inheritor of the bourgeois revolution it they promised them the fruits of bourgeois rule. Nevertheless, reaction followed. As Mehring says,

If the people had overthrown a foreign despot, the princes had overthrown the heir of the bourgeois revolution, and if what followed was not the reconstruction of old Europe, it was indeed a stale and desolate reaction.[57]

We left Hegel celebrating Napoleon's victory at Jena and forecasting the opening of a new epoch. How did he react to the course of French occupation and its ultimate demise? How did these dramatic events affect his philosophy? Throughout his time in Jena and later as a newspaper editor in Bamberg (1807-1808) and as Rector of the Gymnasium in Nuremberg (1808-1816) Hegel was an unstinting supporter of Napoleon. He hoped 'the great constitutional lawyer in Paris' would teach the German Princes the lessons of the French Revolution. He was, however, worried that the state structure would be modernised and reformed without necessarily introducing the 'most noble' aspect of the French experience, 'the liberty of the people, its participation in elections and decisions'. It was a well founded fear. During this period Hegel became even more firmly convinced that 'theoretical work achieves more in the world than practical. Once the realm of ideas is revolutionised, actuality does not hold out.'[58] With Napoleon's armies achieving the work that the indigenous bourgeoisie were too afraid to contemplate, the revolution in thought was increasingly the only option.

This period of dramatic social change is the most productive period of Hegel's life. He wrote the great mature statement of his philosophy, the *Science of Logic*, and published it between 1808 and 1816. In 1816 he wrote the *Encyclopedia of the Philosophical Sciences*. What Hegel achieved in these works was to condense the experience of the great social contradictions of his age, filtered through a debate with their previous philosophical expressions, into a theoretical system. Hegel had seen the massive conflicts of his age at first hand. He had seen great ideas come to power only to achieve the opposite of what their authors intended, seemingly impregnable states blown away, great classes humbled, the religion of centuries discarded and a new world emerging from the ruins. Hegel, as we have seen, believed that philosophy played a pivotal role in all this. His mature system sought to fuse logical categories of analysis with the real course of historical change. The contradictions of thought *are* the contradictions of reality. The power of thought *is* the power to change reality. What is true of the methods of thought is simultaneously true of the history of the world. The history of the world is the rationality of the human mind working itself out in time. This is self evidently an idealist method but, equally self evidently, it is also an historical method which seeks to explain the totality of social change by examining the conflicts and contradictions at its heart. It is, therefore, the real birth of the dialectic in its modern form.

Hegel felt this great conquest of the rational mind to be under threat as anti-French sentiment grew, threatening the gains made by Napoleon. All through this period Hegel opposed the growth of the anti-French liberation movement which he saw as consisting of 'Cossacks, Bashkirs, Prussian patriots'. In a letter he said, 'I am willing to fall down on my knees if I see one liberated person.'[59] Napoleon's defeat and first exile struck him low: 'It is an immense spectacle to see an enormous genius destroy himself. This is the most tragic thing that exists. The whole mass of mediocrities presses incessantly with all the absolute iron of its gravity.' In his Rectorial address of 1815 he said,

We must oppose this mood which uselessly misses the past and yearns for it. That which is old is not to be deemed excellent just because it is old, and from the fact that it was useful and meaningful under different circumstances, it does not follow that its preservation is commendable under changed conditions—quite the contrary... The world has given birth to a great epoch.[60]

Hegel held out no hope when Napoleon returned from exile, but if there were any hope of victory Hegel says he would have put a rifle on his shoulder and joined the battle. After Waterloo a note of resignation became the leitmotif of Hegel's thought. Hegel never reconciled himself to a return of the old order. 'The dead', he said, 'cannot be revived.' But he did reconcile himself to the partly reformed and modernised Prussian state of the 1820s and 1830s. In 1818 he took the chair in philosophy at Berlin, now the capital of one of the two superpowers of the German Confederation. From here Hegel dominated German intellectual life for two decades until his death in 1831.

Perhaps the most well known words that he ever wrote, beautiful as they are, contain his most profound pessimism:

> *When philosophy paints its grey in grey, then has a shape of life grown old.*
> *By philosophy's grey in grey it cannot be rejuvenated but only understood.*
> *The owl of Minerva spreads its wings only with the coming of the dusk.*[61]

Philosophy can no longer imbue the age with the urge for change, as Hegel once maintained. It can only understand a world that has already grown old. The owl of Minerva, the symbol of knowledge, takes flight only when the great events of the day are over. All that philosophy can teach us now is to find 'the rose', the symbol of joy, 'in the cross of the present'. History has reached its culmination in the present state and the current philosophy. Hegel was wrong of course, but Avineri shows why it is wrong to be too dismissive,

> *The point...is that...the socio-political order has been completely transformed.*
> *The order Hegel is now beginning to defend is not the old order he so radically*
> *attacked in 1801. It is not Hegel's views which have changed in the crucial*
> *decade between 1805 and 1815, but the whole fabric of German social and*
> *political life which has been transformed by the tremendous jolt it had received*
> *from the Napoleonic wars.*[62]

Even in its most conservative form Hegel's system continued to shock. Hegel was afraid that his *Philosophy of Right* might be banned and when the king heard that it contained a view of constitutional monarchy which reduced the monarch's role to formally agreeing legislation he asked suspiciously, 'What if I don't agree to dot the i's and cross the t's ?'[63] But for all this, Hegel *had* become more conservative. Throughout the 1820s and 1830s he preached that history had reached its end and, for 20 years, the stability of reaction seemed to bear him out. But in 1830 new revolutions swept Europe and Hegel railed against them. He even found the English Reform Bill too much to stomach. Mehring claims his students deserted him in favour of his pupil, Eduard Gans, who emphasised the revolutionary side of the master's teaching. 'At the time it was said in Berlin that the great thinker died of this painful experience, not of the cholera.'[64]

Having looked at the intellectual and social circumstances into which Hegel was born and traced the outline of his thought as it changed in reaction to the events of the French revolution, it is now time to examine some of his major theories more closely.

Labour and alienation

So far we have stressed the Enlightenment tradition and the French Revolution as the forces which shaped Hegel's thought. But Hegel's ideas were also shaped by the Industrial Revolution. In fact much of the power of his thought is a product of the fact that 'Hegel does know bourgeois society, but his estimation of it is very low'.[65] Of course only a little of this knowledge could come from direct experience given the underdeveloped nature of German society. Hegel depended on his reading about the most advanced industrial society of his day, England. He had read the English classical economists, including Adam Smith, as early as his stay in Frankfurt. In strictly economic terms Hegel never progresses beyond the ground marked out by the English economists and his treatment lacks the kind of concrete analysis which they provide. This is a product both of Hegel's idealism and of backward conditions in Germany. But Hegel does integrate political economy into his wider understanding of history and this requires him to attempt to penetrate the appearance of economic relations and to spell out the contradictions at their heart.

Marx pointed out that 'when Hegel adopts the standpoint of modern political economy' he sees '*labour* as the *essence*, the self-confirming essence, of man.'[66] Hegel understood alienation as lack of control over the work process, as forced, unfree labour. Partly this was a reflection of the way he saw the lifeless institutions of the old order counterposed to the living vitality of the new classes that made the French Revolution. But there can be little doubt that Hegel also drew the abstract picture of alienation from the living reality of capitalism, as these passages from his 1805-6 lectures show:

> The abstraction of labour makes man more mechanical and dulls his mind
> and his senses. Mental vitality, a fully aware, fulfilled life degenerates into
> empty activity... He can hand over some work to the machine; but his own
> life becomes correspondingly more formal. His dull labour limits him to a
> single point and work becomes more and more perfect as it becomes more
> and more one sided... The individual...is subject to a web of chance which
> enmeshes the whole. Thus a vast number of people are condemned to utterly
> brutalising, unhealthy and unreliable labour in workshops, factories and
> mines, labour which narrows and reduces their skill. Whole branches of

industry which maintain a large class of people can suddenly wither away at the dictates of fashion, or a fall in prices following a new invention in other countries, etc. And this entire class is thrown into the depths of poverty where it can no longer help itself. We see the emergence of great wealth and great poverty, poverty which finds itself unable to produce anything for itself.[67]

In the same lectures Hegel defined his concept of objectification: '(a) In the course of work I make myself into a thing, to a form which *exists*. (b) I thus externalise this my existence, make it into *something alien* and *maintain* myself in it.'[68] Here we have the root of Hegel's weakness. Alienation is not seen, as in Marx, as a social relationship whereby a class controlling the means of production alienates the worker's product from him, where the laws of the market operate beyond control, producing an alien environment. In Hegel, to produce any real object in the real world is an act of objectification. To work is to externalise yourself. Alienation is the inevitable outcome of all labour, not just of labour under capitalism.

The only answer to such a condition is mentally to reconcile yourself to the world, to see that you have created the object, even if you no longer control it. This is possible for Hegel because all labour is ultimately *mental labour*. Nevertheless, he saw that man created his own world through his own efforts. He also saw that man lost control over his own creation. As Marx says,

*The importance of Hegel's Phenomenology...lies in the fact that Hegel conceives the self creation of man as a process, objectification as loss of object, as alienation and suppression of this alienation; that he therefore grasps the nature of **labour** and conceives objective man—true, because real man—as a result of his own labour.*[69]

Such an active conception of man's self creation could only come after Kant's break with the determinism of the Enlightenment materialists. But in developing the idea of alienation (or, more properly, objectification) Hegel had stepped beyond Kant. Firstly, as Marx notes, Hegel saw labour as 'a process', something which takes place over time. This is to see labour as subject to change and develops the historical sense that Hegel gained from the events of his era. Secondly, there is division, loss, alienation and, therefore, conflict at the heart of this process of 'self creation'. We can see this if we examine a famous passage from the *Phenomenology* called the master-slave dialectic, sometimes referred to as the dialectic of lordship and bondage.

Even conservative commentators, like Charles Taylor, recognise that this passage is 'one of the most important in the *Phenomenology*, for the themes are not only essential to Hegel's philosophy but...the underlying idea, that servitude prepares the ultimate liberation of the slaves, and indeed general liberation, is recognisably preserved in Marxism. But the Marxist notion of the role of work is also foreshadowed here.'[70] Hegel's theme is the way in which the primitive 'war of all against all' emerges into a relationship of lordship and bondage. We should not imagine, however, that Hegel is trying to describe an actual historical event. Like Rousseau's state of nature, or the 'Robinsonades' of the classical economists, this is intended as a parable about the nature of class society. Its content is incomparably richer than either Rousseau's or Adam Smith's visions of the emergence of 'civilisation'.

We are first introduced to the lord and the bondsman as two 'unequal and opposed...shapes of consciousness'. The lord is 'the independent consciousness whose essential nature is to be for itself'. The bondsman is 'the dependent consciousness whose essential nature is to live...for another'. The lord has power over 'the object of desire' and the bondsman only exists to fulfil that desire. The lord lives only to consume, but he can only gain his desires through the labour of the bondsman.

But it is the bondsman who actually prepares the products for the lord, so he is the one who affirms his independence from the world of things. The lord merely consumes, 'the sheer negation of the thing'. But through his work the bondsman achieves something more.

At first it seems as if the bondsman simply lives in 'fear of the lord'. Indeed Hegel believed this fear to be 'the beginning of wisdom', since society must start with rulers and ruled in order to overcome primitive chaos. But whereas the lord's consumption of the fruit of someone else's labour is only a 'fleeting' satisfaction, 'work, on the other hand, is desire held in check, fleetingness staved off; in other words, work forms and shapes the thing.' In his work the bondsman comes to see his own power and consciousness:

> ...in fashioning the thing, he becomes aware that...he himself exists essentially and actually in his own right...
>
> It is in this way, therefore, that consciousness, **qua worker**, comes to see in the independent being of the object its **own** independence...Through this rediscovery of himself by himself, the bondsman realizes that it is precisely in his work wherein he seemed to have only an alienated existence that he acquires a mind of his own.[71]

Thus the tables have been turned. The lord now exists only through another, the bondsman. The lord only enjoys the world through another's labour and even then only 'fleetingly'. But the bondsman, who previously suffered an 'alienated existence' in his work, has now escaped from the mental world of servitude by discovering a 'mind of his own' through the work he performs, work that 'acquires an element of permanence.'

Three things should be noted here. Firstly, this analysis allows Hegel to see that 'the high road to human development, the humanization of man, the socialisation of nature can only be traversed through work' and that 'the advance of consciousness goes through the mind of the servant not that of the master.'[72]

Secondly, the terms of this relationship form the characteristic Hegelian triad of thesis, antithesis and synthesis. The lord's dominance is the first term, the bondsman's labour on the object is the mediation between them and the conflict between the two terms results in the emergence of a new consciousness in the bondsman. Hegel believes all three terms are necessary for society to progress. The bondsman's fear of the lord remains 'inward and mute' unless he is set to work in the lord's service. This service forms and disciplines the bondsman's fear so that it achieves work in the 'real world of existence'. From this process emerges the new consciousness which overcomes the bondsman's alienation. The negation has been negated.

Thirdly, the dialectic of lordship and bondage confirms the idealist nature of Hegel's analysis. Only the bondsman's *consciousness* has been transformed, not his real relation to the lord. There has been a revolution in thought, but no revolution in social relations. The Hegelian dialectic starts with the dominant consciousness of the lord and the subservient consciousness of the bondsman and ends with the transformed consciousness of the bondsman. The 'real world of existence' and work only features as the mediating middle term. By contrast, Marx would insist that the first term in the dialectic is material reality and the final term the human activity by which it is transformed. The dialectic is thereby transformed from a closed process into an open ended one.

Hegel's inability to override his idealism is the great tragedy of his philosophy. It means that whenever he does have an insight into the nature of real capitalist contradictions it appears either as a useless empirical adjunct to his philosophy, the proverbial fifth wheel, or as a conflict that must be resolved in thought. This is precisely the fate of his great analysis of alienation.

It is this reconciliation with alienation which led Hegel to the belief that ownership of private property is the way to overcome objectification. We repossess our lost selves in bourgeois ownership. Not seeing the historically transitory nature of capitalism's war of all against all, Hegel reveres the state as the guardian who stands above the fray ensuring fair play. His idealism has hobbled his revolutionary dialectic and led it back into bourgeois respectability.

World History—truth formed in the womb of time

Hegel's *Philosophy of History* spells out the key concepts of his dialectic more clearly than any of his other writings. Hegel began by explaining why non-philosophical methods of looking at history are inadequate. Since Hegel's views not only help define his own approach but also deliver a blow to some still fashionable methods of studying history, we will take a brief look at this discussion.

Least acceptable is the view held by the ancient Greeks Herodotus and Thucydides. This is 'for the most part limited to deeds, events, and states of society, which they had before their eyes... They simply transferred what was passing in the world around them, to the realm of representative intellect.'[73] Modern times have transformed this parochial history because 'our culture is essentially comprehensive, and immediately changes all events into historical representations.'[74] Even so, such histories still contain much that is 'anecdotal, narrow and trivial'. Hegel had contempt for the kind of history that concentrates on the personal details of historical figures, an approach he disparagingly described as 'the psychology of the valet'.

Only a few writers manage to 'take an extensive view—to see everything'. To see the totality is out of the question for those who 'from below merely get a glimpse of the great world through a miserable cranny.'[75] Hegel aimed for a total history, history which has a pattern and a meaning. One only has to think of various empiricist historians, local specialists or even, despite their achievements, the 'history from below' school to see that Hegel's views are more than historical curios.

Hegel was also dismissive of 'didactic history', the sort that 'Rulers, Statesmen, Nations, are wont to be emphatically commended to.'[76] Hegel was not against understanding 'the lessons of history' but he was against the kind of writer who simply 'arranges and manipulates' history so that he can 'insist upon his own spirit as that of the age in question.'[77] What we now call historiography, what Hegel called the 'History of History', suffers from a similar defect. Writers who just pick other historians' work apart are 'putting subjective fancies in the place of historical data'.

Finally, Hegel was against the kind of approach that has become so entrenched in contemporary higher education and which has been given a fashionable gloss by post-structuralists. This divides history into history of art, history of law, history of religion, history of madness, history of sexuality, or, to quote the title of the thesis of one post-graduate with whom I was at college, the history of the post-war bungalow. This approach is useless if it simply studies these issues in isolation from the totality of historical development, in their 'external relations'. These studies can only overcome their 'superficiality' if the 'connection of the whole is exhibited'.[78]

Thus Hegel broke from many of the ahistorical traditions of study which marked the Enlightenment and which still persist today. He even said, 'We must proceed historically—empirically. Among other precautions we must take care not to be misled by professed historians who...are chargeable with the very procedure of which they accuse the philosopher—in introducing *a priori* inventions of their own into the records of the past.'⁷⁹ This, as we shall see, was a promise that Hegel could not keep. Nevertheless, it is a testimony to the strong historical sense that he was given by the revolution.

Hegel, as we have seen, also rejected the empiricist notion that history is just a succession of dates and events. Neither was he happy with a simple causal explanation, the billiard ball theory of history, where one event causes the next and so on in an infinite regression. Hegel found, on one level at least, that societies are totalities and that change occurred because they developed internal contradictions, not simply because they were the last link in a chain which stretched back in history to 'who knows where?' To God? Again Hegel was ultimately unable to solve this dilemma, but he grappled with it for so long that his analysis provided crucial material for those who came after him.

The reason that Hegel was unable to solve this contradiction lies in his view of historical change. For Hegel the world worked according to a rational process, which could be understood by scientific laws. This, as in much Enlightenment thought, was true of both nature and of society. But for Hegel, as for Anaxagoras whom he cited favourably, there was also a difference:

*The movement of the solar system takes place according to unchangeable laws. These are Reason, implicit in the phenomena in question. But neither the sun nor the planets, which revolve around it according to these laws, can be said to have any consciousness of them.*⁸⁰

But human beings can become conscious of the rational principles which govern social development. In fact, for Hegel, the whole of human history is about the way in which the rational structure of society is revealed to the consciousness of men. At the dawn of human history the rational structure of the world is hidden from consciousness but, through the successive phases of historical development, this rationality becomes clear to men. At the start of the process men are *implicitly* rational—they are rational but they are not aware of the fact. At the end of the process they are self-consciously rational—they know and understand that reason governs the world.

The historical process is therefore identical with the rational method of scientific investigation. History is a gigantic scientific investigation strung out in time. This conception is already a massive advance on most Enlightenment thought. Kant, it will be remembered, had left human knowledge hopelessly knocking at the door of material reality. Hegel had already surpassed this viewpoint in the *Phenomenology of Mind*. The very title tells us why. Mind, human rationality, is not confined to its own world, cut off from the thing in itself. It is connected to phenomena, to things as they appear in the real world. Indeed, the whole structure of the *Phenomenology* is designed to lead thought from its everyday methods of perception to the heights of philosophical reason. This process, Hegel argued, was both possible and necessary because everyday commonsense thought was a mass of contradictions that could only be resolved by moving to progressively greater abstractions. The contradictions at each level powered the progress to the next level. Hegel now proposes to show that history has the same sort of structure as mind.

For Hegel history was reason coming to self consciousness. He had a unique term for reason which we must pause to explain because the German word, *Geist*, has no English equivalent. The normal English translation, Spirit, is so misleading as to require elaboration. *Geist* is the sum of the content of human consciousness as it has developed throughout history. Today, when we talk about a common culture or ideology, or the world view of a certain epoch it captures something of what Hegel meant by *Geist*. Nevertheless, there is a problem even with seeing *Geist* even in these terms. Since no one human being, class or nation can ever rise above their own particular 'spirit of the age' they can never embody the whole of *Geist*. This has led some to a religious interpretation that identifies *Geist* with God. In some passages Hegel himself was not above this mysticism. Following the master's death division broke out among his followers. Right Hegelians tended to translate *Geist* as Spirit, in order to give Hegel a religious colouring, while Left Hegelians translated *Geist* as Mind, insisting on a secular interpretation.[81]

I have continued to translate *Geist* as Spirit for two reasons. Firstly, it is the most common translation. Secondly, a Marxist understanding of Hegel does not primarily depend on rescuing him from religious interpretations as it does for liberal scholars. In any case Hegel's thought did have a genuinely mystical dimension which stems from his idealism.

Spirit developed through history because it never wasted the gains of previous epochs. These were preserved, albeit in a different form, in the subsequent age. At the end of the process the entire achievements of the development of human thought were summarised in Spirit. In a similar way the entire content of the *Phenomenology* was preserved in its last category, Absolute Knowledge, and the entire content of the *Science of Logic* is preserved in its last category, the Absolute Idea. It would not be good enough, however, simply to look at the last stage of development and believe that you have comprehended the whole. The truth is contained in the *process* of change, not in any one of its concepts, even the last, which summarises this process.

These are pathbreaking notions. The idea that everything is an interrelated whole and that this totality is in a constant process of change; the view that static concepts are useless and that what is needed is to see things as a process, not as stable entities; to recognise that all this change is not the result of external impact but of internal contradiction, all this is completely to revolutionise the modes of thought that dominated the Enlightenment. Let us now examine the use to which Hegel put these ideas.

As we have seen, Hegel began with the assertion that the world was rationally structured—'Reason is sovereign of the world.'[82] But in a blow against Kant and Fichte, Hegel insisted,

> *Reason is not so powerless as to be incapable of producing anything but a mere ideal, a mere intention, having its place outside reality, nobody knows where; something separate and abstract, in the heads of certain human beings.*[83]

Kant had split the totality of human experience into mind and 'outside reality'. Hegel insisted on their unity, a unity of opposites. For most of history reality was only implicitly rational and men did not recognise this. Nevertheless, Reason or Spirit was at work in both the dumb rationality of the objective reality and the subjective reason of men. History shows how these two rationalities merge into one self conscious rationality. Against Kant, Hegel insisted on the unity of subject and object.

This may become clearer if we can recognise here an echo of the master-slave dialectic in the *Phenomenology*. There too the slave only came to consciousness when he saw that the objective process of work was not the alienated existence he first thought, but the route to liberation. In history generally men overcame their alienation from the objective world when they recognised it as another aspect of the rationality that inhabits their own subjective mind. For Hegel, as for Marx, human history presented long stretches in which man was faced with a hostile environment over which he exercised little control—he is alienated. For both thinkers, in very different ways, human beings could only alter this situation through a series of revolutions in society, revolutions that stemmed from the internal contradictions of those societies. It was because progress could only come through conflict that Hegel said,

> *The history of the world is not the theatre of happiness. Periods of happiness are blank pages in it, for they are periods of harmony—periods when the antithesis is in abeyance.*[84]

The contradiction (or antithesis) that Hegel referred to is very different from that between the forces and relations of production. Hegel's contradiction, as we might expect, was between two forms of consciousness, as it was in the master-slave dialectic. In any given society the institutions, laws, morals and beliefs embody a certain stage in the development of reason. Hegel called this the 'spirit of the age'. The greater the appreciation of rationality, the more free a people had become. Thus in Oriental society only one man, the emperor, was free, and even he was not really free since he was a despot. In Greek society only some men were free, since the localised nature of the Greek city states and the slavery on which they were based prevented the knowledge of freedom becoming general. Only with the rise of individuality, the product of Christianity, and the modern representative state was an era of general freedom and rationality possible. The transition from one form of society to another was a result of a contradiction that emerges in the spirit of the age.

When nations or historical epochs are born they are free of contradiction. The contradiction between the total potential rationality and freedom of mankind (Spirit) and the particular social structure is not in evidence. Spirit and the spirit of the age are at one. The people 'are moral, virtuous and vigorous' while they pursue Spirit's 'grand objects' and 'defend its works.'[85]

But when the 'objective world, that exists and persists in a particular form of worship, customs, constitution and political laws' hardens and grows old it ceases to represent the full potential for reason that has been developing among its citizens. Spirit leaves the people. Within the society some people begin to look at their own laws and institutions and question what is really rational about them and what is merely accidental, contingent and irrational. Those who look beyond the age are now the true bearers of Spirit. Theirs is the 'universal thought', reason reaching beyond its age:

> *Universal thought...shows up the limitations with which it is fettered—partly suggesting reasons for renouncing old duties, partly itself **demanding reasons** and the connection of such requirements with universal thought, and not finding that connection seeking to impeach the authority of duty generally as destitute of sound foundations.*[86]

At the same time as some are looking for a new rationality on which to build society, others are simply renting and tearing a social structure which no longer fits the needs of the age. The 'isolation of individuals from each other and from the whole [ie society] makes its appearance.' This process of decay means that 'aggressive selfishness and vanity, personal advantage, corruption, unbounded passion, egoistic interests' all advance 'at the expense of the state'. This is an example of the 'cunning of reason' which not only uses the positive search for a new rationality as its tool to destroy the old order but also makes use of the more base materials that lie to hand. Thus it is that the old order, created by reason, is swallowed up by reason once it has served its turn—'Zeus and his race are swallowed up, and by the very power that produced them.'[87]

Yet as society moves on to a more self consciously rational form it does not leave its past behind. It takes with it all that was genuinely advantageous about the old order, preserving it in its new form. 'Spirit annuls the reality' but 'it gains the essence of that which *it only was.*'[88] A new social reality has emerged, but the real revolution was a revolution in thought:

> *We must remark how perception—the comprehension of being by thought— is the source and birthplace of the new and in fact higher form... The particular form of Spirit not merely passes away in the world by natural causes in time, it is annulled in the automatic self-mirroring activity of consciousness.*[89]

In a more general form we must repeat the comments made at the close of the section on labour and alienation. Hegel mirrored the fantastic revolutionary changes of his own time in the categories of thought, surpassing all previous philosophies in the process. The picture of an old order grown sclerotic and crisis ridden, the emerging contradictions and the view of progress through a revolutionary change that preserved the gains of the old order are dramatic precursors of Marx. But again Hegel's idealism, inevitable given his class position and the development of the intellectual traditions of which he was a part, brought the revolutionary insights back into the quiet harbour of bourgeois thought. Once again the formal mechanism which achieved this was the negation of the negation in its idealist form.

Just as labour was reduced to a middle term in the dialectic of lordship and bondage, so here 'the realising *activity*...is the middle term.' The two poles which it united were 'the complex of external things—objective matter' and 'the *Idea*, which reposes in the penetralia of Spirit.'[90] The really revolutionary activity of changing society was only allowed out for a brief walk before it was dragged back into the lecture hall to receive some more instruction at the hands of philosophy. The movement began with rationality in its dumb objective form and ended with rationality in its conscious, articulate form. This is a dialectic that has assumed its end before it begins, a dialectic in which the contradiction is never really allowed to fight it out in social form.

Hegel's dialectic—the rational kernel and the mystical shell

'The quickest way of getting a headache', wrote Lenin when he studied Hegel's *Science of Logic*, where the dialectic appears in its fullest form.[91] Partly this is because of the legendary complexity of Hegel's language. This is ultimately a function of conditions in Germany. Hegel may have wished to 'teach philosophy to speak German',[92] but Germany was not willing to listen. Philosophy had ceased to speak German, Marx said, because German had ceased to be the language of thought when, following Napoleon's defeat, reaction set in. The Spirit spoke in mysterious words because the words that could be understood were no longer permitted.[93] Partly also Hegel's idealism ensured that his thought was genuinely mysterious. The Spirit was a mystical substitute for a class that was incapable of making its own revolution. This mystical substitute was then projected back into history. It is only one step from here to religion.

But Hegel is difficult partly for reasons that are not caused by character and circumstance. His theories use terms and concepts that are unfamiliar because they go beyond the understanding of which everyday thought (or even most bourgeois theory) is capable. That is why Marx based his own thought on a critique of the Hegelian dialectic. If we are to understand Marx then we must have a little patience with some of the key ideas in the dialectic. The next few paragraphs, where we explore what Marx called 'this harsh, grotesque melody',[94] will not be easy. But their full meaning should become clearer in the passages that follow where Marx makes use of these ideas.

In the *Philosophy of History* Hegel described how Spirit, the accumulated totality of human knowledge, unfolded over time as a result of contradictions in the various societies in which it was inadequately embodied. In the *Phenomenolgy*, as we have noted, Spirit emerged from the contradictions in the inadequate forms of everyday thought. The *Science of Logic* is this same process looked at in terms of scientific method, the process of 'thinking about thinking'. Spirit now stands before us without historical dress or the garb of everyday thought.

The *Science of Logic* was Hegel's attempt to bring together all the different ways that we look at the world—empirical thought, art, religion, natural science—and to show how they are connected. The *Science of Logic* was itself, therefore, an example of one of Hegel's key concepts—totality. From the very elementary concepts at the start of the book, Hegel showed how each concept is connected to every other concept. This process continues until the final concept (the Absolute Idea) is shown to be the summation of all the previous ideas in the book. One concept gives birth to the next by a process of contradiction. Science, like history, is dialectical.

How this process works is shown in the famous first contradiction in the *Logic*. Trotsky, when he examined this passage, said that it 'seemed at first glance a subtle but fruitless play of ideas. In fact, this "game" brilliantly exposes the failure of static thinking.'[95]

The *Logic* begins with the most abstract of all human ideas, Being. This is the bare notion of existence shorn of any colour, size, shape, taste or smell. This first concept is also, in its way, a totality. Although Being reveals no characteristics or distinguishing marks, it does nevertheless include everything. After all, everything must *exist* before it can take on any particular characteristics. Being is therefore a quality that is shared by everything that exists; it is the most common of human ideas. Every time we say, 'This is...', even before we say what it is, we acknowledge the idea of pure Being. But Being also contains its opposite, Nothing. The reason is that Being has no qualities and no features which define it. If we try to think about pure Being it simply disappears into thin air. So if we try to say what Being is we are forced to the opposite conclusion, Being equals Nothing.

But even Nothing is more than it seems. If we are asked to define Nothing we are forced to admit that it has at least one property—the lack or absence of any qualities. This may be only a negative definition, nevertheless it is a definition. This presents us with a strange dilemma: Being is Nothing, and yet Nothing is something. Hegel, however, is not so stupid as to think that there is no difference between Being and Nothing, even though this is what our logical enquiry seems to suggest. All that this contradiction means is that we must search for a new term which can explain how Being and Nothing can be both equal and separate (or a 'unity of opposites', in Hegel's jargon). Hegel's solution is the concept of Becoming.

In German Becoming means both 'coming to be' and 'ceasing to be'. By replacing two static concepts with one dynamic concept, by seeing a process of change instead of stable definitions, Hegel superseded the ideas of Being and Nothing with a third term which contained both these ideas and at the same time surpassed them.

This is the decisive advance that is contained in Hegel's dialectic. It not only sees the world as a totality in which each part is connected to all the other parts, it also sees that the relationships between the parts are contradictory. It is the search to resolve these contradictions that pushes thought past commonsense definitions which see only separate, stable entities. Lenin seized the key point in his notes on the *Logic*: 'Shrewd and clever! Hegel analyses concepts that usually appear dead and shows there *is* movement in them.'[96]

But normal, empirical concepts were not abandoned. In fact Hegel thought that the standard empirical procedure of breaking things down into their constituent parts, classifying them and recording their properties was a vital part of the dialectic. This is the first stage of the process (where we tried to define Being). It is only through this process of trying to capture things with 'static' terms that we can see the need to define something by its relations with the totality, rather than simply by its inherent properties. To show their transitory nature Hegel called these stable points in the process of change 'moments'. Hegel said that the whole was 'mediated' by its parts. So empirical definitions were not irrelevant. But they were an inadequate way of looking at the world and so in need of a dialectical logic which could account for change.

Finally, this process reveals the characteristic stages in the Hegelian dialectic. First the 'immediate totality' (Being), is broken down into its contradictory definitions or parts (Being as Nothing, and vice versa). This is the 'first negation'. Then these 'moments' are shown to require that they be united in a new 'concrete totality' (Becoming). This new totality negates the parts. It is, therefore, the famous 'negation of the negation.' This new 'concrete' totality is much richer and more varied because it contains within it the parts by which it was 'mediated'. Lenin was quick to recognise the heart of the dialectic at work in this process, 'the splitting of a single whole and the cognition of its contradictory parts...is the *essence*...of dialectics.'[97]

Let us now turn to Marx's famous passage where he makes use of these ideas. Marx says that in political economy it 'seems correct' to begin analysing society by looking at 'the population which is the basis...of the whole act of production'. But then Marx goes on:

> *Nevertheless, this is shown on closer examination to be wrong. Population is an abstraction, if I omit the classes, for example, of which it consists. Those classes are an empty word if I do not know the elements on which they are based. For example, wage labour, capital etc.*[98]

Here Marx is breaking down an immediate totality (population) into its mediating parts, or moments (classes, wage labour etc). That he is quite deliberately using Hegel's terms is shown by the passage which comes next:

> *Therefore, if I begin with population, then that would be a chaotic conception of the whole, and through closer determination I would come analytically to increasingly simpler concepts; from the conceptualised concrete to more and more tenuous abstractions, until I arrived at the simplest determinations.*

This is the process we described as the first negation. Marx goes on to show how a new totality emerges from the negation of this negation:

> *...the journey would [now] be taken up in reverse until I finally arrived at population, this time however, not as a chaotic conception of the whole but as a rich totality of many determinations and relationships...the concrete is concrete because it is the sum of many determinations.*

Here Marx makes devastating use of Hegel's method, but he has transformed it in two vital ways. Firstly, for Marx this is a *method of analysis*, not an account of the structure of society itself (although it may reveal the structure of society). For Hegel the two are identical. Marx *did* think that society was dialectically structured but he did not think that the method of analysis and the real structure of the world were identical.[99] Hegel, being an idealist, developed a dialectic which dealt with patterns of thought, with the way in which concepts and ideas changed. Marx therefore found this dialectic was most easily assimilated at the level of method and that it had to be transformed most radically when applied to reality. This is why there is such a striking similarity of language in the above, comparatively rare, passage where Marx discusses his method.

Secondly, even at the level of method Marx insisted that the real world is both the starting point and the conclusion of dialectical analysis. For Marx the 'tenuous abstractions' from the real social world are only a clarifying middle term. Marx says that 'the real subject, after as before, remains outside the head in autonomous existence...society must always be borne in mind as the presupposition of any conception.'[100] For Hegel the opposite is true—tenuous abstractions are the start and the end of the dialectic. The point of the dialectical method in Marx is to reveal social contradictions to thought and to show how they can be overcome in practice. As Lenin put it, 'From living perception to abstract thought, *and from this to practice*—such is the dialectical path of the cognition of truth.'[101] But in Hegel the point of dialectic is to reveal the contradictions in reality so that they can be 'overcome' in thought. To see this more clearly we need to look at Marx's critique of Hegel's idealism.

Not better than the age, but the age at its best

Hegel's dialectic surpassed all previous and, so far, all further developments in bourgeois philosophy because it summarised the experience of the international bourgeoisie at the high point of its development as a revolutionary class. He was, as he aspired to be in a youthful poem, 'not better than the age, but the age at its best'.[102] Only a theoretical position based on a new revolutionary class was capable of incorporating and further developing his insights. It is not a coincidence that some of Marx's most penetrating critiques of Hegel were written at the same time as he recognised the working class as the agent of social change.

Marx's criticism of Hegel starts with his conception of man. For Hegel what separated man from the natural world was his consciousness. In fact, 'for Hegel *human nature, man*, is equivalent to *self-consciousness*.' This was the root of Hegel's idealism—he thought that the mind is the man. Any activity or labour that man performs was the activity of mind. Marx saw things differently. Man is distinguished from the natural world by conscious *labour*. Man is an animal, part of the natural world, but he distinguishes himself from it by being able to consciously direct his work. Marx and Engels say,

> *Men can be distinguished from animals by consciousness, by religion or anything else you like. They themselves begin to distinguish themselves from animals as soon as they begin to **produce** their means of subsistence, a step which is conditioned by their physical organisation.*[103]

So man's 'physical organisation', his material needs, make him part of nature. But, unlike the spider and the bee, who make their webs and hives from instinct, man consciously plans his labour.

This vital difference between Marx and Hegel results in completely opposed views on two key questions: the nature of alienation and the relationship between subject and object. For Hegel any labour in the real world, the creation of any real object, is a form of alienation. If man is defined by, is only happy in, the world of thought then any real activity must be a form of alienation. In Hegel alienation and objectification are the same thing. Alienation is the 'human condition'. In Marx, on the contrary, man *must* affirm himself in labour—his 'physical organisation' demands it. Moreover, since labour is the natural way in which man makes the world in his own image, it is only under certain socially produced circumstances that he can experience this natural capacity as 'alien'. These are the conditions of class society where a ruling class owns the means of production and controls the products of labour, ie the ruling class has alienated the means and products of labour.

These different attitudes to alienation necessarily demand very different solutions. For Hegel the alienation of thought can only be overcome when thought comes to terms with, recognises itself in, the objective world. Once thought has seen that it created the world it will be content that the world must be rational. In this view, simply understanding the root of alienation is the same as overcoming it, as we saw in the master-slave dialectic. For Marx alienation is not an inevitable aspect of the human mind but a social structure which can only be abolished by a social movement. In a beautifully succinct aphorism Marx and Engels say,

> *In order to supercede the **idea** of private property, the **idea** of communism is enough. In order to supercede private property as it actually exists, **real** communist activity is necessary.*

On the question of subject and object: Hegel believes that thought is the really active element (the subject) and that material reality is the object. Even this is a sham opposition in Hegel because material reality has no life independent of thought—it is only an aspect of thought. This is why Hegel talks about the *identity* of subject and object (of thinking and being). But for Marx, as we have seen, human labour is the really existing unity of subject and object. Man is a natural being (ie an objective being) who has conscious powers. This is the basis on which it is possible to understand Lukacs's claim that the working class is both the subject and the object of history. Theory reproduces this objective dialectic in thought. To do so it must adopt different methods to those involved in Hegel. Trotsky made this distinction brilliantly in his *Philosophical Notebooks*:

> *The dialectic of consciousness (cognition) is not thereby a **reflection** of the dialectic of nature, but it is a **result** of the lively interaction between*

consciousness and nature and—in addition—a method of cognition issuing from this interaction... [104]

The identity of being and thinking according to H[egel] signifies the identity of objective and subjective logic, their ultimate congruence. Materialism accepts the correspondence of the subjective and the objective, their unity, but not their identity, in other words it does not liberate matter from materiality, in order to keep only the logical framework of regularity, of which scientific thought (consciousness) is the expression. [105]

Hegel's method does 'liberate matter from materiality' because it makes it simply an aspect, a moment, in the dialectic of thought. It then presents this 'logical framework' drained of content as science. This is precisely the function of the *Science of Logic*. Marx is absolutely clear that he cannot accept the dialectic, or the conception of the negation of the negation, in its Hegelian form. This is because the negation of the negation is the mechanism by which Hegel reabsorbs the contradictions of the material world into thought (as we saw in all three sections on alienation, history and dialectic). Marx says, 'The supersession in thought, which leaves its object in existence in reality, thinks it has actually overcome it.' [106]

Marx argues that it is a 'great achievement...to have opposed the negation of the negation'. [107] And because Hegel's dialectic begins and ends in thought, Marx says it is correct to see 'the negation of the negation *only* as a contradiction in philosophy itself'. [108]

This is the root of the conservatism of Hegel's system. It not only leaves reality untouched, but preaches reconciliation with a reality which appears as the product of rational thought. This is why Marx taxes Hegel not only with being an 'uncritical idealist' but also with being an 'uncritical positivist'. Hegel expels reality from thought, only to let great uncriticised chunks of it in through the back door. Hegel is simply looking for a political body in which he can house his logic, says Marx. He is not interested in empirically examining the 'logic of the body politic'. The result is that Hegel finds it 'very easy to fasten on what lies nearest at hand and prove that it is an *actual* movement of the Idea.' This is the theoretical root of Hegel's support for the reactionary Prussian state, and indeed for all the institutions of bourgeois society—the family, law, the monarchy and so on. Hegel not only preaches reconciliation, he attempts to show that this reconciliation is the *inevitable* outcome of human thought. Hegel is therefore both conservative *and* fatalistic.

For all these reasons, Marx's dialectic must have a quite different structure. Firstly, as we have shown, it must make a greater distinction between the dialectic in theory and the dialectic in society. Hegel's history was pre-ordained. It simply lived out the progress of reason. But real history cannot be squashed down into the neat intellectual categories of logic. Real struggles contain all sorts of leaps and diversions, institutions carried over from other eras and peculiarities of development. This is why Marxists have had to develop all sorts of concepts—like Trotsky's theory of combined and uneven development and Lenin's idea of the key link in the historical chain—which are unique to a materialist dialectic.[109]

Secondly, Marxism must insist that the dialectic in society is not primarily a dialectic of subject and object, but more importantly a dialectic rooted in man's attempt to transform nature and the class contradictions that this attempt engenders. Human beings *are* the subject and object of history. Theory is an expression of this fact, not one of its two constituting poles. This is why crude materialism and idealism are seen by Marx as two abstractions which emphasise, each in its one-sided manner, a common essence. Only by seeing things in this way can we fully understand Marx when he says, 'The coincidence of the changing of circumstances and of human activity or self-changing can be conceived and rationally understood only as *revolutionary practice*.'[110]

Thirdly, this social dialectic does not have a closed, fatalistic character. Social contradictions are never automatically resolved. They have to be resolved by a struggle. Class contradictions may be 'mediated' by the totality of the social structure, but they cannot be resolved by this process as in Hegel. The resolution can only come via the struggle for a higher form of society. Consequently, whether, or in what way, the negation is negated is a question of political activity. The dialectic is not, however, totally open ended. The possibilities of resolution are limited—Rosa Luxemburg's socialism or barbarism, Marx's social revolution or the 'common ruin of the contending classes'—but neither are they pre-determined.

Last judgement on Hegel?[111]

Marx and Engels, having 'settled accounts with our former philosophical consciences',[112] turned their backs on philosophy in order to study the real economic contradictions of capitalist society. But philosophy has not turned its back on Marxism. While capitalism exists, philosophy, like its supernatural relation, religion, will always be with us. The pull of bourgeois ideas, be they materialist or idealist, and the emergence of new problems constantly demand that we return to the fundamentals of our theory in order to clarify, extend and defend Marxism.

Of course, no theory alone can prevent error, but the better founded our theory the greater our capacity to see our way in the struggles with which the working class is confronted. For instance, when we talk of the way in which one phase of the class struggle is both a break from the previous phase and at the same time a continuation of it, we are using dialectical terms. When we talk of fighting for reforms by revolutionary means, dialectics stand behind the formulation. The better we understand the method, the better our chances of understanding the struggle.

Hegel's philosophy stands in the same relation to that task as the lessons of the Great French Revolution do to our politics as a whole. We cannot repeat the experience uncritically—it was the revolution of a very different class—but we can learn from it. Hegel marked a high point from which all subsequent bourgeois philosophy has either fallen back into dualism or else contented itself with elaborations of ideas that can be found, in microcosm, in his thought. Although Hegel could not ultimately solve the problem of Kantian dualism, his attempt contained some key revolutionary developments.

Marx inherited these developments and transformed them into the basis of a materialist dialectic. 'I should very much like to make intelligible to the ordinary human intelligence—in two or three printer's sheets—what is *rational* in the method which Hegel discovered,'[113] said Marx. He never did have the time and, although we have Lenin and Trotsky's notebooks on Hegel and Lukacs's *History and Class Consciousness*, we still have much to learn from Hegel. Despite all his mysticism, Hegel remains the great founder of the algebra of revolution.[114]

Notes

My thanks to Alex Callinicos, Sue Clegg, Lindsey German, Chris Harman, Paul McGarr, John Molyneux and Ann Rogers for their comments on the first draft and to my comrades on the editorial board of *Socialist Worker* for their patience.

1   Marx, Engels, *Selected Correspondence* (Moscow, 1955), p93.

2   Lenin, *Collected Works* Vol 38 (Lawrence and Wishart, 1961) p180.

3   Marx, *Capital* Vol I (Penguin, 1976), p102.

4   Lenin, op cit, p362.

5   J F Lyotard, *The Post Modern Condition* (Manchester University Press, 1984), p xxiii, quoted by A Callinicos in 'Postmodernism, Post-Structuralism, Post-Marxism?', in *Theory, Culture and Society*, vol 2, number 3, 1985.

6   The full phrase, 'I am of course no longer a Hegelian, but I still have a great feeling of piety and devotion towards the colossal old chap', is Engels', see *Selected Correspondence*, p162. The expression, 'I therefore openly avowed myself the pupil of that mighty thinker' is from *Capital* Vol I, p 102-103.

7   *Entretien d'un père avec ses enfants* (1770), quoted by N Hampson, *The Enlightenment, an evaluation of its assumptions and values* (Pelican,1968), p190.

8   Quoted in N Hampson, ibid, pp36-37.

9   See, for instance, P M Harman, *The Scientific Revolution* (Methuen, 1983), pp30-32.

10   Pope and Halley's verse is quoted in N Hampson, op cit, p38.

11   Marx and Engels, *The German Ideology* (Lawrence and Wishart, 1970), p111.

12   See G Rudé, *Revolutionary Europe 1783-1815* (Fontana, 1964), pp11-12.

13   Ibid, pp34-35.

14   Quoted in M Cranston, Introduction to Rousseau, *The Social Contract* (Penguin, 1968), p14.

15   Quoted ibid, p16.

16   Quoted ibid, p16.

17   Ibid, p21.

18   Quoted in N Hampson, op cit, p94.

19   Ibid, p126.

20   A Landgrave is 'a count having jurisdiction over a territory, and having under him several inferior counts' according to the Shorter OED.

21   F Mehring, *Absolutism and Revolution in Germany 1525-1848* (New Park, 1975), p151.

22   N Hampson, op cit, pp45 and 63.

23   F Mehring, op cit, p154.

24   Ibid.

25   For economic conditions in Germany, see Mehring, ibid, pp149-169.

26   N Hampson, op cit, p169.

27   Ibid, p169.

28   Ibid, p60.

29   R Christiansen, *Romantic Affinities, Portraits From An Age 1780-1830* (London, 1989), pp74-75.

30   See N Hampson, op cit, p61.

31   R Christiansen, op cit, p75.

32   F Mehring, op cit, p169. The parallels with the social origin of the most determined sections of the French revolutionary leadership and with the leadership of 'deflected permanent revolutions' in the 20th century are interesting.

33   F Mehring, op cit, p173.

34   See E J Hobsbawm, *The Age of Revolution 1789-1848* (Abacus, 1977), pp82 and 304.

35   H Marcuse, *Reason and Revolution* (London, 1977), p21.

36   See S Avineri, *Hegel's Theory of the Modern State* (CUP, 1972), p2.

37   See ibid, p3, and G Lukacs, *The Young Hegel* (Merlin, 1975), p10.

38   R Christiansen, op cit, p84.

39   Quoted in C Taylor, *Hegel* (CUP, 1975), p424.
40   See Avineri, op cit, p6.
41   Ibid, p3.
42   Ibid.
43   Ibid, p4.
44   G W F Hegel, *Phenomenology of Spirit* (OUP, 1977), pp359-360.
45   Quoted in Avineri, op cit, p48.
46   Ibid, p9.
47   Hegel, *Realphilosophie*, quoted in Lukacs, op cit, pp310-311.
48   Hegel, *Erstes Systemprogramm des Deutschen Idealismus*, quoted in Marcuse, op cit, p12.
49   Quoted in Lukacs, op cit, p308.
50   See N Hampson, op cit, p281.
51   See Avineri, op cit, p39.
52   Ibid, p37.
53   Ibid, p63.
54   Ibid, p64.
55   Ibid.
56   Mehring, op cit, p137.
57   Ibid, p148.
58   Quoted in Avineri, op cit, p68.
59   Ibid, p70.
60   Ibid, p71
61   Hegel, *Philosophy of Right* (OUP, 1952), p13.
62   Ibid, p70.
63   Mehring, op cit, p183.
64   Ibid, p184.
65   Ibid, p182.
66   Marx, *Economic and Philosophical Manuscripts*, in *Early Writings* (Pelican, 1975), p386.
67   Quoted in Lukacs, op cit, p331.
68   Ibid, p334.
69   Ibid, pp385-386.
70   Taylor, op cit, pp154-155.
71   *Phenomenology*, op cit, p118-119.
72   Lukacs, op cit, p327.
73   *Philosophy of History* (New York, 1956), p1.
74   Ibid, p3.
75   Ibid, p3.
76   Ibid, p6.
77   Ibid, p7.
78   Ibid, p8.
79   Ibid, p10.
80   Ibid, p11.
81   See M George and A Vincent's admirably clear introduction to G W F Hegel, *The Philosophical Propaedeutic* (Blackwell, 1986), pxxiii.
82   *Philosophy of History*, op cit, p9.
83   Ibid.
84   Ibid, pp26-27.
85   Ibid, p74.
86   Ibid, p76.
87   Ibid, p77.
88   Ibid.
89   Ibid, p77.
90   Ibid, p27.

91   Marx suffered from a worse affliction on his first encounter with Hegel, complaining
      of 'sleepless nights, isolation, illness'. see M Rubel, *Marx, Life and Works*
      (Macmillan, 1965), p2.
92   See Avineri, op cit, p63.
93   See Mehring, op cit, p172.
94   Quoted in M Rubel, op cit, p2.
95   L Trotsky, *Notebooks 1933-35: Writings on Dialectics and Evolution* (New York,
      1986), p103.
96   Lenin, *Collected Works Vol 38*, p110.
97   Ibid, p359.
98   Marx quoted in T Carver, *Texts on Method* (Blackwell, 1975), pp72-73.
99   This is one good reason why Lenin is right to say that it is more correct to talk
      of the unity, rather than the identity, of opposites. See *Collected Works* Vol 38, p359.
100   Marx, Introduction to the *Grundrisse*, quoted in T Carver, op cit, pp73-74.
101   *Collected Works*, op cit, p171.
102   Quoted in Lukacs, op cit, p105.
103   *The German Ideology*, op cit, p42.
104   *Notebooks*, pp101-102. By 'nature' Trotsky means material reality (as opposed to
      consciousness), not just the animal and inorganic world. As he makes clear (p102),
      Trotsky believes that any dialectic of nature would, again, have a different structure.
      He rightly points out that in eliding the two forms of dialectic 'the danger lies in
      transference—under the guise of objectivism'—of the birth pangs, the spasm of
      consciousness, to objective nature.' This is of course Hegel's sin, but we might
      also add that the sin of the Second International and Stalinism was transference—
      under the guise of the 'laws of history'—of a 'naturalised' dialectic into the realm
      of social development.
105   L Trotsky, *Notebooks*, op cit, p77.
106   *Economic and Philosophical Manuscripts*, in *Early Writings* op cit, p394.
107   The great achievement of which Marx speaks is Feuerbach's, see the *Economic
      and Philosophical Manuscripts* in *Early Writings*, (Pelican, 1975), p381.
108   Ibid, p382. See also the passages on the negation of the negation on p393.
109   Thus Trotsky, unlike most Marxist accounts of the dialectic, argues that the
      transformation of quantity into quality, not the negation of the negation, is the key
      concept in the dialectic. Since it is the slow accumulation of change which then
      results both in unevenness and great leaps in history it is not hard to see Trotsky's
      reasoning here. He even argues that the triad, usually treated as almost synonymous
      with the negation of the negation, 'is the "mechanism" for the transformation of
      quantity into quality'. See *Notebooks*, p99. I am not arguing that the negation of
      the negation is a useless concept, merely that it is the part of the Hegelian dialectic
      that needs to be most extensively purged of fatalistic traces.
110   Third Thesis on Feuerbach in *Early Writings*, op cit, p422.
111   *The Trumpet of the Last Judgement on Hegel, the Atheist and Anti Christ* was an
      anonymously published in 1841 by Bruno Bauer after his suspension from a teaching
      post at Bonn University for proposing a left Hegelian toast. It is possible that some
      sections of the pamphlet were written by Marx. See M Rubel, op cit, p4.
112   *Preface to a Contribution to The Critique of Political Economy*, in *Early Writings*,
      op cit, p427.
113   *Selected Correspondence*, op cit, p93.
114   The phrase was coined by Alexander Herzen (1812-1870), a leading Russian
      democratic revolutionary.